Other Books by Leo Rosten

THE EDUCATION OF H*Y*M*A*N K*A*P*L*A*N
THE WASHINGTON CORRESPONDENTS
THE STRANGEST PLACES
DATELINE: EUROPE
HOLLYWOOD: THE MOVIE COLONY, THE MOVIE MAKERS
112 GRIPES ABOUT THE FRENCH (WAR DEPARTMENT)
SLEEP, MY LOVE
THE DARK CORNER
A GUIDE TO THE RELIGIONS OF AMERICA (ed.)
THE RETURN OF H*Y*M*A*N K*A*P*L*A*N
THE STORY BEHIND THE PAINTING
RELIGIONS IN AMERICA (ed.)
CAPTAIN NEWMAN, M.D.
THE MANY WORLDS OF LEO ROSTEN
A MOST PRIVATE INTRIGUE
THE JOYS OF YIDDISH
A TRUMPET FOR REASON
PEOPLE I HAVE LOVED, KNOWN, OR ADMIRED
ROME WASN'T BURNED IN A DAY: THE MISCHIEF OF LANGUAGE
LEO ROSTEN'S TREASURY OF JEWISH QUOTATIONS
DEAR "HERM"
A NEW GUIDE AND ALMANAC TO THE RELIGIONS OF AMERICA (ed.)
THE LOOK BOOK (ed.)
THE 3:10 TO ANYWHERE
O K*A*P*L*A*N, MY K*A*P*L*A*N!
THE POWER OF POSITIVE NONSENSE
PASSIONS AND PREJUDICES
INFINITE RICHES: GEMS FROM A LIFETIME OF READING
SILKY!
KING SILKY!
HOORAY FOR YIDDISH: A BOOK ABOUT ENGLISH
LEO ROSTEN'S GIANT BOOK OF LAUGHTER
THE JOYS OF YINGLISH

Leo Rosten's

Carnival of Wit

*and wisdom; plus wisecracks, ad-libs, malaprops, puns,
one-liners, quips, epigrams, boo-boos, dazzling ironies, and
wizardries of wording, plus surprising tidbits from politics,
philosophy, biography, and (yes!) gossip—*
from Aristotle to Groucho Marx

COMPILED AND MANICURED BY

LEO ROSTEN

A DUTTON BOOK

DUTTON
Published by the Penguin Group
Penguin Books USA Inc., 375 Hudson Street,
New York, New York 10014, U.S.A.
Penguin Books Ltd, 27 Wrights Lane, London W8 5TZ, England
Penguin Books Australia Ltd, Ringwood, Victoria, Australia
Penguin Books Canada Ltd, 10 Alcorn Avenue,
Toronto, Ontario, Canada M4V 3B2
Penguin Books (N.Z.) Ltd, 182–190 Wairau Road,
Auckland 10, New Zealand

Penguin Books Ltd, Registered Offices:
Harmondsworth, Middlesex, England

First published by Dutton, an imprint of Dutton Signet,
a division of Penguin Books USA Inc.
Distributed in Canada by McClelland & Stewart Inc.

First Printing, November, 1994
10 9 8 7 6 5 4 3 2 1

REGISTERED TRADEMARK—MARCA REGISTRADA

LIBRARY OF CONGRESS CATALOGING IN PUBLICATION DATA
Leo Rosten's carnival of wit : and wisdom, plus wisecracks, ad-libs,
malaprops, puns, one-liners, quips, epigrams, boo-boos, dazzling
ironies . . . from Aristotle to Groucho Marx / compiled and manicured
by Leo Rosten.
p.   cm.
ISBN 0-525-93716-1
1. Wit and humor—History and criticism. 2. Wit and humor.
I. Rosten, Leo Calvin.   II. Title: Carnival of wit.
PN6147.L46   1994
808.88'2—dc20   94-15392
                                                                            CIP

Printed in the United States of America
Set in Century Expanded and Novarese
Designed by Eve L. Kirch

To
the memory of my sister
HELEN
(born Hinda)
who
so loved laughter, and
brought merriment
wherever she went.

ACKNOWLEDGMENTS

I thank (with fervor), Hugh Rawson, a superlative editor and morale-booster; Erna Helwig, my indispensable secretary and organizer; Charles Brunie, for countless acts of friendship; and Zimi, my wife, for her indestructible humor and sanity during those stretches of doubt and frustration that accompany any writer's work.

—LEO ROSTEN

READER, PLEASE NOTE:
SPECIAL WARRANTY

If you are not completely delighted with this book, just return it to me, with the receipt showing exactly how much you paid.

I promise to return your receipt within five days.

—LEO ROSTEN

CONTENTS

PART III: CAFÉ SOCIETY AND *THE NEW YORKER*

PART IV: CAVEATS

LIST OF CATEGORIES

Man is the missing link between apes and human beings. —Konrad Lorenz

There is always an easy solution to every human problem—simple, plausible, and wrong. —H. L. Mencken

Man is the only animal that blushes—or ought to. —Mark Twain

PREFACE

Part I: The Anatomy of Wit

Wit is a scintillating (and rare) form of humor. And one of its most exasperating aspects is defining it, giving it an identity as sharp and precise as a razor to distinguish it from its funny, seductive, but lesser cousins: wisecracks, quips, repartee, one-liners, boo-boos, lucky verb inversions, ludicrous incongruities, and so on.

Wit must be precise and pitiless. It must be as emphatic as the crack of a whip. Wit lampoons conformity. It is the enemy of the trite, the conventional, and the conformist. It offers no latitude to platitude. Wit is the champagne of levity.

WIT VS. WISECRACKS

A huge psychological chasm separates a wisecrack from a witticism. The difference between them is the difference between a dart and a firecracker. A wisecrack conveys scorn and is usually soon forgotten. A witticism explodes—radiates and endures; it remains quotable because, unlike a wisecrack, time does not enfeeble its relevance or blunt its humor.

1

It was Coleridge who said:

> What is an epigram?
> A dwarfish whole.
> Its body brevity
> And wit its soul.

And Dorothy Parker topped this, centuries later, with her taunting

> Brevity is the soul of lingerie.

Miss Parker, whose reputation for wit (*and* wisecracks) has flourished, once made this notable distinction: "Wit has truth in it; wisecracking is simply calisthenics with words."

Words convey, relate, contend; wit *dances*. It endows data with delight. It bubbles with a sense of mischief. It is always impudent, irreverent, corrosive—and somewhat arrogant.

ASTUTE MOCKERY

We sent missionaries to China so the Chinese could get to heaven, but we wouldn't let them into our country.   —PEARL S. BUCK

American women expect to find in their husbands a perfection that English women only hope to find in their butlers.
                                        —W. SOMERSET MAUGHAM

When I was eleven, I thought that women were solid from the neck down.   —C.E.M. JOAD

The dipsomaniac and the abstainer both make the same mistake: They regard wine as a drug and not as a drink.
                                        —G. K. CHESTERTON

Because philosophy arises from awe, a philosopher is bound to be a lover of myths and poetic fables. Poets and philosophers are alike in being big with wonder.   —THOMAS AQUINAS

The swiftest way to give you my differentiation between wit and wisecracks is by example:

WIT	WISECRACK
Martyrdom is the only way in which a man can become famous without any ability. —GEORGE BERNARD SHAW	I'm a very good housekeeper; whenever I leave a man, I keep his house. —ZSA ZSA GABOR
Tradition does not mean that the living are dead, but that the dead are living. —G. K. CHESTERTON	Never slap a man in the face if he's chewing tobacco. —ABE MARTIN
When a man brings his wife a gift for no reason, there's a reason. —MOLLY MCGEE	Men aren't attracted to me by my mind, but what I don't mind. — GYPSY ROSE LEE
It's not what we know that hurts; it's what we know that just ain't so. —KIN HUBBARD (also attributed to Will Rogers)	Poets have been mysteriously silent on the subject of cheese. —G. K. CHESTERTON
	I can't remember your name, but don't tell me. —ALEXANDER WOOLLCOTT

The most effective wit casts a sudden and surprising (and usually cynical) light on familiar subjects. Consider the following gem:

Fashions are induced epidemics. —GEORGE BERNARD SHAW

I cannot think of a more decisive use of two words; they totally redefine a subject ("fashion") long immured in cant—and now explained in operational terms. . . .

Shaw's triumphant epigram is reinforced by Anatole France's acute Gaelic revelation:

"Only men who are not interested in women are interested in women's clothes; men who like women never mention what they wear."

The only jocosity I know that matches this is Lin Yutang's cunning:

"All women's dresses are merely variations on the external struggle between the admitted desire to dress and the unadmitted desire to undress."

Or take the refreshing:

A yawn is a silent shout.—G. K. CHESTERTON

After reading that, a yawn may never again be accepted as a soporific reflex. Chesterton was a genius at such historic redefinitions: "Silence," he ruled, "is the unbearable repartee." He could also tantalize the reader by wondering why poets have been "mysteriously silent on the subject of cheese."

THE RARITY OF WIT

Thoreau said that most men "lead lives of quiet desperation." I think that more lead lives of prolonged tedium. Has it ever occurred to you how very, very few people, during their entire lives, rarely say anything worth repeating? How very, very few men or women ever say anything that even remotely borders on wit?

Aristotle called wit "educated insolence." He actually held it presumptuous for youth to *try* to be witty. We have come a very long way from that. Today's young comics are bumptious, verbally clumsy, tasteless, vulgar; they seem more driven to shock than to amuse. Indeed, they seem to think that merely shocking is itself funny. "Black humor" may be defined as calculated vulgarity, or outright obscenity designed to disgust anyone over forty.

WIT AND LAUGHTER

Laughter, it may be noted, is a human activity (perhaps the only one) without *any* biological purpose: It only provides relief from a pleasant, induced tension.

Laughter, technically speaking, is a motor reflex produced by the coordinated interplay of fifteen muscles, in a contraction of fifteen different facial muscles, accompanied by significantly changed breathing! (I thought you might like to set all this to music.)

A survey of American children aged eight to fifteen, concluded (in 1968) that the mortifications, discomfort, or hoaxing of others readily caused laughter; but witty remarks passed unnoticed. *You will never find wit in a kindergarten.* You will find pranks, mud pies, jokes, and visual play (pratfalls) that elicit guffaws. But *never*, in a kindergarten, will you find wit.

For wit is an adult creation. It lies in the province of intelligence and acuity in manipulating language. Children, absorbed in the acquisition of a vocabulary, command few words that offer the *opportunity* to play on, or with. Nor are they swift enough or deft enough to put language through the hoops of verbal deception.

PASSAGES THAT MADE ME SMILE

How saintly people look when seasick.   —SAMUEL BUTLER

Idealist: One who upon observing that a rose smells better than a cabbage concludes that it will also make better soup.
        —H. L. MENCKEN

No man is lonely while eating spaghetti; it takes too much attention.
        —CHRISTOPHER MORLEY

Her face was her chaperone.   —RUPERT HUGHES

"Shut up," he explained.   —RING LARDNER

I'm not afraid of death. I just don't want to be there when it happens.
        —WOODY ALLEN

The great question that has never been answered, and which I have not yet been able to answer despite my thirty years of research into the feminine soul, is: "What does a woman want?"
        —SIGMUND FREUD
        —Answer (by unknown maven): "Shoes!"

HOW I DISCOVERED EPIGRAMS

I have all my life been an insatiable reader. And because I was an immigrant (at age three I was brought to America from Poland) and raised in a world and neighborhood (in Chicago) where Yiddish was a first tongue to many, I was mesmerized by the sounds and cadence of English. I think that I came to English words and speech with a sharper appetite (and responsiveness) than most of my contemporaries.

The first wisecrack I ever heard was this: "A man chases a woman until she catches him." It is a perfect example of the humorous insight that may crown a simple reversal of conventional wording. Hundreds of such witticisms have been born out of playful contrariness, or from the fortunate and fortuitous transposition of words:

I must decline your invitation owing to a subsequent invitation.
—OSCAR WILDE

Of all the sexual aberrations, the most peculiar is chastity.
—RÉMY DE GOURMONT

Injustice is relatively easy to bear; what stings is justice.
—H. L. MENCKEN

I shall never forget the chill that ran down my spine when I first read Anatole France's incomparably satiric, "The Law, in its awesome impartiality, gives both the rich and the poor the right to steal bread or sleep under bridges."

Words must surely be the most powerful drug the human species ever invented. In my adolescence I became an absolute nut about epigrams. I collected them the way some boys collect stamps. For years, obsessed with a fear of forgetting anything, I wrote down every bon mot I read or heard. My pockets became filing cases for tersities of wisdom (scribbled on scraps of paper, backs of envelopes, margins torn from newspapers), a hodgepodge of verbal wonders—from Ring Lardner to "Kin" Hubbard to Will Rogers, and the peerless masters: Mark Twain, G. K. Chesterton, Oscar Wilde, Bernard Shaw, H. L. Mencken (the most neglected and effective iconoclast in American letters).

I reveled in admiration over the genius that could marshal words with so much originality to achieve such deft insight. In a way I honed my mind on the whetstones of epigrams. And so I came to suspect, long before I encountered Sigmund Freud, that witticisms are stratagems to evade the censors of power, that comedy is a complex masquerade, [and] that murder oft peeps through the masks of our wit; that humor is the messenger of truths that churn behind the camouflage of levity, that mockery is the most impish and agile of stratagems devised to puncture the platitudes that stifle all our minds and strangle all our precious mischief.

UNFORGETTABLE IMAGES

I would rather go to bed with Lillian Russell stark naked than with Ulysses S. Grant in full military regalia.   —MARK TWAIN

She was a large woman who seemed not so much dressed as upholstered.   —JAMES MATTHEW BARRIE

He gave her a look you could have poured on a waffle.
          —RING LARDNER

(After Stephen Douglas pilloried him in a debate): If I were two-faced [as Douglas charged], would I be wearing this one?
          —ABRAHAM LINCOLN

Year after year my bubbling booty grew. I invested in a ream of three-by-five cards and began to file my golden horde in shoeboxes wheedled from friendly merchants.

Endlessly shuffling and rearranging these cards, I began to discover distinguishing characteristics. Epigrams, clearly, are blazing flashes of illumination—sometimes more clever than true, prized by intellectuals much more than by the masses. Proverbs, on the other hand, are packages of human experience. They are a people's primer of living—and folk sayings are their homely brothers; both are distilled common sense. They are the primers we inherit from the past. They are portable wisdom, the school of the untutored.

I think I should tell you that I became so hypnotized by my hobby that (as I have written elsewhere) I began to *visualize* my obsession: I began to see aphorisms as dressed in silk, proverbs as wrapped in fur, and epigrams as bedecked with sequins. As for folk sayings, it soon seemed obvious that they ran around in honest homespun.

ASTRINGENT OBSERVATIONS

He used statistics the way a drunkard uses lampposts—for support, not illumination.   —ANDREW LANG

Opera in English is about as sensible as baseball in Italian.
                                                        —H. L. MENCKEN

Screens: The wire mesh that keeps flies from getting out of the house.
                                                        —ABE MARTIN

Out of snow, you can't make cheesecake.   —JEWISH FOLK SAYING

The difference between truth and fiction is that fiction has to make sense.   —MARK TWAIN

We are descended not only from monkeys, but from monks.
                                                        —ELBERT HUBBARD

My private treasure of quotations became an unexpected introduction into new kingdoms of reason, psychology, philosophy, ethics. They taught me much about logic by inverting it. I recognized an author's satire and sarcasm as a celebration of "right thinking."

My growing library of perceptions sharpened my own thinking; it flashed light into places where reason falters for lack of light; it stripped argument of padding; it clarified puzzling complexities by the antiseptic application of scoffery.

As my experience and confidence grew, I exercised the license to rephrase a translated quotation. Translators are often not themselves writers, or persons with an attunement to the special structure of humor. I felt I had a sharper ear, a more sensitive sense of diction. If you think me presumptuous, please tell me which of the following examples pleases you: In each case, the first line, in quotation marks, is the quotation I found; the second line, in italics, is my alteration:

"Who does not please his parents will have disobedient sons."
The son who does not obey his father will have sons who do not obey him.

"What is plain talk to your face is a falsehood behind your back."
What is candor to your face is slander behind your back.

"What a deaf man does not hear, he figures out for himself."
The deaf imagine what they cannot hear.

I felt no hesitation in performing similar surgery on quotations from other languages.

Part II: The Varieties of Wit

The realm of humor can be very wide, broad, spacious, and silly. It ranges from the elegance of, say, Rochefoucauld to the wry drollery of Will Rogers and "Abe Martin," from the fastidious insolence of Oscar Wilde to the thigh-slapping, "chaw tobacco" expectorations of "Kin" Hubbard.

Consider, then, the categories into which I have divided the sprawling, mocking, mischievous, and endlessly illuminating body of mirth we think funny.

GAGS

A gag is any broad visual device or action meant to trigger laughter. The word "gag" seems to have come from the world of circus clowns, vaudeville, and silent movies, notably as the product of specialists who worked for such pioneers of visual comedy as Hal Roach, Buster Keaton, and the Keystone Kops. Their gagmen worked right on the movie sets, suggesting bits of "business" or action (pratfalls, silly haberdashery, brattish children, pompous Englishmen slipping on banana peels—any practical joke or trick).

As the profession of comedians grew, the demand for gagmen soared. In vaudeville, nightclubs, radio, and movies, gagmen attained the status of "writers." Among the names of these experts in lampoonery must be included some of the most skillful laughmakers of their times. Their names are hidden in the credits for such classics of radio and television as the shows starring Johnny Carson, Jack Benny, Milton Berle, Bob Hope, and Burns and Allen, as well as *I Love Lucy*, *M*A*S*H*, *All in the Family*, *The Mary Tyler Moore Show*, and *The Golden Girls*.

ONE-LINERS

The one-liner as a comedy form is exactly that: a funny line with its own beginning, middle, and end. One-liners became a modern staple of stand-up comics in nightclubs, bars, beer joints, "tryout" gin mills, etc. The masters of this peculiar genre were Bob Hope and Milton Berle; in recent years they have given way to Henny Youngman and Rodney Dangerfield. Here are three sublime examples, all from Rodney Dangerfield:

Children! How times have changed! Remember thirty years ago when a juvenile delinquent was a kid with an overdue library book?

I haven't spoken to my wife in years—I didn't want to interrupt her.

I said to my mother-in-law last year, "My house is your house." The next day she sold it.

I, for one, feel grateful to Henny Youngman for the candor with which he answered a television interviewer on April 11, 1993. "How do you go about writing your one-liners?" asked the reporter. Mr. Youngman replied: "I don't write them, I *buy* them. . . . I never wrote a joke in my life."

Mr. Youngman was too modest: His deadpan, dyspeptic delivery adds a distinct style to his comedic effectiveness.

SPARKLING DESCRIPTIONS

[W. H.] Auden's face looks like a wedding cake left out in the rain.
—STEPHEN SPENDER

Fully dressed, Heywood Broun looks like an unmade bed.
—DOROTHY PARKER

Young man, take a haircut; you look like a chrysanthemum.
—P. G. WODEHOUSE

To my embarrassment I was born in bed with a lady.
—WILSON MIZNER

Henry James writes as if it is a painful duty.   —OSCAR WILDE

Put three grains of sand inside a vast cathedral, and the cathedral will be more closely packed with sand than space is with stars.
—SIR JAMES JEANS

Dorothy Parker is a cross between Little Nell and Lady Macbeth.
—ALEXANDER WOOLLCOTT

A highbrow is a man who has found something more interesting than women.   —EDGAR WALLACE

PUNS

Puns are, no doubt, the most frequently attempted form of wit via wordplay—and, all in all, are the least successful: They are usually banal. Most puns are ersatz wit, but some turn out surprisingly well. I give you a handful I think undeniably apt—and funny.

Diplomacy is lying in state.   —OLIVER HERFORD

Every crowd has a silver lining.   —P. T. BARNUM

None but the brave desert the fair.   —WILSON MIZNER

Occasionally he takes an alcoholic day.   —OSCAR WILDE

My grandmother is over eighty and still doesn't need glasses. Drinks right out of the bottle.   —HENNY YOUNGMAN

The saintly Dr. Albert Schweitzer did not hesitate to resort to inspired punnery when he told a reporter: "In case my life should end with the cannibals, I hope they will write on my tombstone: 'We have eaten Dr. Schweitzer. He was good to the end.'"

MALAPROPISMS

People who are witty *know* when they are being witty (or trying to be). But people who garner laughter through a boo-boo, malapropism, or other fracture of English are usually surprised by the laughter that some word or phrase or idiom elicits. I mean luminaries such as Yogi Berra, Samuel Goldwyn, Dizzy Dean, and a platoon of less famous souls (bumblers). Of this group, Goldwyn is probably the most famous—and Yogi Berra the unintentionally funniest. In the collection of cameos sprinkled through the main body of my text, I celebrate the bravado (I know no more appropriate word) with which a Mae West, a Yogi Berra, or a Groucho Marx has embroidered the language of Shakespeare, Mark Twain, and E. B. White.

I don't care about that; it rolls off my back like a duck.
          —SAMUEL GOLDWYN

I don't pay any attention to him. I don't even ignore him.
          —SAMUEL GOLDWYN

What do you mean, the story is too caustic? Who cares about expense?
          —ATTRIBUTED TO SAMUEL GOLDWYN

Sculpture: My wife's hands are so beautiful. I'm having a bust made of them.   —SAMUEL GOLDWYN

When you come to a fork in the road, take it. —YOGI BERRA

SATIRE

The aristocrat of wit is satire—the most intricate, elegant, and exacting of literary forms. Satire is judgmental, usually a derisive commentary—on manner, decorum, taste, customs—or on the social order as a whole. It is an acidulous mixture of scorn doused with derision and drenched in mockery. It uses ridicule to clothe its criticism; it aims arrows instead of wielding hatchets; it aims to deflate and make ludicrous.

Satire is a form of sarcasm that proceeds from unconcealed snobbery, and certainly about what is proper or vulgar, in good taste or outré. Satire exposes pretension; it exalts breeding over boasting. Here are some eminent satirists: George Orwell, Voltaire, Oscar Wilde, Mark Twain. . . .

SATIRICAL DEFINITIONS

Applause: The echo of a platitude. —AMBROSE BIERCE

Abortion: The Jewish position is that a fetus is a fetus until it gets out of medical school. —ANONYMOUS

Antidote: The medicine that kills dotes. —A CHILD

Bore: A person who talks when you want him to listen.
—AMBROSE BIERCE

Diplomat: A man who remembers a woman's birthday but never her age. —ROBERT FROST

Glamor: The undefinable something about a girl with a big bosom.
—ABE BURROWS

Middle age: When you begin to exchange your emotions for symptoms. —IRVIN S. COBB

Murderer: One presumed to be innocent until declared insane.
—OSCAR WILDE

Mathematics: The subject in which we never know what we are talking about, nor whether what we are saying is true.

　　　　　　　　　　　　　　　　　—BERTRAND RUSSELL

Someone once said that in the entire animal kingdom only three species cannot abide being laughed at: mortals, monkeys, and dogs. I have never forgotten that—and I have not the faintest notion whether it is true.

TYPOS

Nothing makes me yok faster than a typographical error in a newspaper, magazine, advertisement, or house organ. The best of these boo-boos are Freudian slips that cry out for preservation.

I give you a handful from my collection. To list the sources of these gems—*Elgin* (Ill.) *Courier, Chicago Tribune, Los Angeles Times*—would simply encumber my text without increasing your pleasure.

All the following are true—absolutely exact and uncorrected. Trust me.

They were married and lived happily even after.

Mr. Baker sent this telegram to his wife: *"HAVING WONDER-FUL TIME. WISH YOU WERE HER."*　　　　　　　—JOHNNY

Upon arriving at the Honolulu Airport, two men were given coveted lays by Hawaiian maidens.

Mrs. and Mrs. Oliver Strong request the pleasure of your presents at the marriage of their daughter. . . . [If only Freud were alive. . . .]

On hotel restaurant menu: Dreaded Veal Cutlet . . . $4.50

Miss O'Hayer has been raising birds for many years and is credited with having the largest parateets in the state.

Sergeant Alfred Blaine is a twenty-year veteran defective on the police force.

(Correction printed the next day): Sergeant Blaine is a twenty-year veteran detective on the police farce.

HUMOR VIA SIMPLE TRANSPOSITION

"Work is the curse of the drinking classes." That is, of course, simply a rearrangement of the hoary admonition "Drink is the curse of the working classes." What makes the transposition interesting is that it is the creation (if that's not too exalted a word) of Oscar Wilde.

The greatest and most prolific generator of aphorisms in the English language (or in any language, if you count the number of entries Wilde is given in any collection of quotations in any language) was not above coining a banality just so it got a laugh.

Every student of English style, the English theater, or English humor must contend with the gigantic figure of Oscar Wilde. He is without doubt the most widely quoted aphorist in the world. Any collection of epigrams, translated from English into virtually any language, will contain more entries from Wilde than from, say, even Voltaire, or George Bernard Shaw, or Mark Twain.

I use the word "contend" to make clear my own ambivalence about Wilde. He is clearly (with La Rochefoucauld) the Grand Master of Wit. For sheer elegance and gaiety Wilde is unsurpassed. But he will say or write *any*thing that shocks, startles, or offends. He totally lacks empathy. He was a slave to Fame, even if it meant shabby Notoriety.

It is these aspects of Wilde that make him a lesser thinker in *my* mind than George Bernard Shaw, H. L. Mencken, G. K. Chesterton, and—always—that fountain of humor springing from good sense, acute observation, and the clear antic eye of the self-educated genius, Mark Twain.

My admiration for Oscar Wilde's epigrams is diminished by his readiness to say absurd, foolish things simply to be amusing:

> As long as war is regarded as wicked, it will always have its fascination. When war is looked upon as vulgar, it will cease to be popular.

I do not regard this as witty; I think it ridiculous.

Sometimes Wilde coined wit simply by changing the critical word in a cliché to its opposite.

> Never buy anything simply because it is expensive.

This turned out to be astute and funny, even if, as I think, it was inadvertent.

Wilde often tossed off similar mechanical inversions of clichés:

I am not young enough to know anything [after Chesterfield].

He had the kind of face which, once seen, is never remembered.

Only an outrageous poseur could have written:

One half of the world does not believe in God, and the other half doesn't believe in me.

To Wilde, cleverness was all, even if the cleverness was achieved at the expense of plausibility or ordinary sense: for example, "If one tells the truth, one is sure, sooner or later, to be found out"; or, "Time is a waste of money"; or, "He hasn't a single redeeming vice." As Dorian Gray, one of Wilde's most celebrated creations, put it, "He would sacrifice anybody for the sake of an epigram."

And yet, when Oscar Wilde arrived at Ellis Island to begin a nationwide lecture tour of the then much smaller, much less powerful, influential, or *formidable* United States, he struck a publicity bull's-eye with his reply to a custom agent's usual question about bringing items of value into the United States.

Wilde, astonishingly dressed in velvet breeches, carrying a huge flower, ad-libbed (apparently) one of the boldest and most original responses on record: "Sir," said Wilde, "I have nothing to declare except my genius."

The same indifferent improvisation as Wilde's occasionally seduced G. K. Chesterton, a most brilliant writer, an erudite and independent critic, and a dazzling logician. Chesterton once tossed off this "epigram":

If a thing is worth doing, it is worth doing badly.

The line is simply nonsense.

Much funnier and much more meaningful is strip-teaser Gypsy Rose Lee's delicious:

If a thing is worth doing, it is worth doing slowly . . . very slowly.

G. K. Chesterton, matchless when at his best, once rumbled, "It is a pity that people travel in foreign countries; it narrows their minds so much." (Does it?)

Anyone can play this game of mechanical inversion: Just take a proverb or saying and change the critical word. It took me ten minutes to concoct the following:

Always look a gift horse in the mouth.

Never judge a cover by its book.

Penny-wise, pound smart.

He'd gladly give you the shirt off your back.

There is a destiny that ends our shapes.

Part III: Café Society and The New Yorker

During the 1930s and 1940s, New York nurtured a new constellation of social groupings that came to be known, most aptly, as "Café Society." Café Society blended Broadway and Park Avenue and Hollywood; or Times Square and Wall Street and Washington. For the first time, in New York, regular meeting grounds blossomed for actresses and financiers, scions of society (Jock Whitney) and financiers (Bernard Baruch), powers in the theater (Billy Rose) and visiting caliphs from "the Coast" (David Selznick, Darryl Zanuck, Howard Hughes, movie directors galore), stars from London (Laurence Olivier, Bea Lillie, Gertrude Lawrence, Noël Coward), and socialites from Palm Beach and the Riviera.

This was the Golden Age of Wit. It was the age of celebrity—and personalities. In Daniel Boorstin's excellent phrase, certain persons became celebrated simply for being well known. They crowded such fast-growing nightspots as El Morocco, the Twenty-one Club (perhaps the most exclusive restaurant in the world), the Copacabana, Sardi's, and the Stork Club.

Here old society (the Harrimans, Rockefellers, Astors, Biddles, Whitneys) met for talk, gossip, dancing, and liaisons of a more carnal nature. Here starlets and tycoons and ambitious politicos paraded their paramours.

The very air throbbed with "inside" stories of scandals, fitful marriages, fresh amours, and incipient divorces. In Café Society, wit and repartee were at a premium; names were not dropped, they were paraded; put-downs won wide approval; and this whole circus of talent and ultrasophistication, drenched with ambition and glamor, night after night was feverishly reported in newspaper columns and on radio programs by a vast corps of gossip columnists and syndicated newspaper reporters of "entertainment."

WIT AND THE PRESS

Night after night, talented and celebrated reporters reported sparkling wisecracks in a manner unparalleled in the history of journalism. The very efforts to debunk celebrities, remarks Professor Daniel Boorstin wittily, are self-defeating, for they increase our interest in the fabrication. The corps of gossip columnists was unmatched for size, energy, and a sharp, merciless eye for "items." These journalists were syndicated: Walter Winchell, Damon Runyon, Bugs Baer, Ed Sullivan, Dorothy Kilgallen, scholarly Franklin Pierce Adams, Irvin S. Cobb, Leonard Lyons, Lou Sobol, Sidney Skolsky, Irving Hoffman. Rare indeed was the newspaper or radio program that did not run the syndicated lucubrations of smarmy Louella Parsons or stylish Hedda Hopper.

This was the very heyday of Gossip and the Golden Age of Wit— and Gossip carried with it a ripe, rich cargo of wisecracks, retorts, malaprops, triple entendres. The pages (and columns) of *Variety* and *The Hollywood Reporter*, as well as the newspaper and gossip columns of Broadway, rang and sparkled with "items" and broadcast them around the world.

THE NEW YORKER

During the early 1930s, a group of writers for *The New Yorker* and several famous newspaper columnists, playwrights, and theater directors fell into the habit of lunching, more or less frequently, at a large round table in the green dining room of the Algonquin Hotel, a block from the editorial offices of *The New Yorker*.

The contributions of *The New Yorker* remain distinctive to this very day. Those who went to Hollywood, lured by very large salaries, made movies infinitely more elegant, urbane, sophisticated—and funny. Their wit lent irony, irreverence, and a new dimension to the screen and in the many columns that lived off Hollywood's wit and sent Hollywood's humor to the farthest corners of the globe.

The cachet of *The New Yorker* in the thirties, forties, and fifties became something with which to conjure. Read by anyone interested in fiction, the theater, the arts, movies, or creative journalism, *The New Yorker* established an identity as unique as it was acute, urbane, sophisticated—and very funny. The names of authors appeared only at the end of their articles. Special departments, such as Profiles (brief, brilliant pen-portraits of people as diverse as deposed monarchs, philosophical lobstermen, professional pugilists, chess champions, political muck-a-mucks, tennis players, financial wizards, actors and actresses, and "society personalities" of every persuasion) gave the magazine an identity, flavor, insight, and irreverence found in no other journal in the world. Whether you were in Paris or Hong Kong, Washington or Hollywood, it was inevitable to see *The New Yorker* on a coffee table or hear it mentioned at a dinner party. Its wit pervaded American culture and saturated American humor.

This extraordinary journal was conceived and brilliantly edited by a tall, ungainly hick from the West named Harold Ross. He was no fashion plate: He fancied a short "brush" haircut, and he looked less like the editor of *The New Yorker* than a space salesman for a plumbing journal. He was aptly described (by Wolcott Gibbs) as a "dishonest Abe Lincoln."

Ross's extraordinary unfamiliarity with books, belles lettres, the theater, and the movies was forever astonishing to those who worked with or for him: The man sometimes seemed to be pretending to be a yokel.

Once he asked James Thurber, "Is Moby Dick the man or the whale?" Another time he said earnestly, "Don't think I'm not trying to be incoherent." These gaffes make all the more remarkable Ross's taste, honesty, and sense of humor. He was a genius as an editor or as a judge of material. No one could explain him. So far, no one has.

JOKEMAKERS

The heyday of radio, nightclubs, and vaudeville produced a truly astonishing array of comedians. Need I mention more than Fred Allen, Bob Hope, George Burns and Gracie Allen, Jack Benny, Milton Berle, Martha Raye, Eddie Cantor, Red Skelton, Georgie Jessel, Danny Kaye, Danny Thomas, the Four (originally Five) Marx Brothers, and the Ritz Brothers? Since few (very few) comedians write all of their own material, the market for comedy/skit/joke/"story line"/gagmen and writers grew with phenomenal speed.

Some comedians (Benny, Hope, Berle) employed as many as four to six writers—so that teams of writers worked on shows that would air (on radio network series) on alternate weekends.

These writers were rarely known to an audience. In fact, it was not until the movies came along that the names of the "ghostwriters" were even mentioned at all, and names such as Carl Reiner, Milton Josefsberg, Mel Brooks, and two dozen others were formally credited.

It was the ghostwriters who poured a rich stream of laughter—jokes, wisecracks, anecdotes, one-liners, puns, all the coruscating varieties of humor—into the entertainment fare for the nightclubs and vaudeville circuits, the radio networks and movie stages in Astoria.

In time, many of the comics were lured to Hollywood, and their ghostwriters went along. And in more time, the comedy writers produced radio shows and movies on their own: notably Carl Reiner, Mel Brooks, and Woody Allen (né Konigsberg).

As for television, the medium that devoured skits/series on a scale never before seen, I think it not an exaggeration to say that television became a catchall for every form of quip, one-liner, gab, "grabber," joke, or characterization (the weirder the better).

CAMEOS

I have given the carnival of wit that follows a certain variety and, I trust, attractiveness, by including, in their alphabetical place, brief vignettes of some of the most distinctive wits I quote; and I have ended each cameo with a dozen or so of my favorite examples of their humor.

Do these examples sometimes repeat witticisms already printed under their categorical designation (Love, Truth, Conscience, Politics)? I hope so. I believe that occasional repetitions of outstanding quotations are salubrious. Repeating eminently respectable ideas never harmed a reader.

My cameos include Yogi Berra, G. K. Chesterton, Noël Coward, Dizzy Dean, Samuel Goldwyn, Groucho Marx, H. L. Mencken, Dorothy Parker, Bertrand Russell, George Bernard Shaw, Casey Stengel, and Mae West. Each vignette will, I think, give you a compact rendition of the subject's personality—and distinctive style of jocosity.

Several cameos contain information you will not find anywhere else—by which I mean information drawn from my personal acquaintanceship (casual or prolonged) with the subject.

The cameos try to convey the personal "flavor," the distinctive slant, of each person and the light it cast on the body of his or her special brand of humor, an especially valuable ingredient for those readers under, say, fifty, who have not the faintest notion of who some of these talented, unique wits (or malapropists) actually were. I thought it would be a pity to let some of my personal observations go unrecorded.

Part IV: Caveats

It was not until my long labors on this long book had been completed that I began to wonder why some of my (and, no doubt, your) favorite wits were either totally absent or astonishingly few in number. Many a writer or performer, playwright or screenwriter simply did not produce a body of wit/wisecracks large enough to register an impact on its own.

Examples: S. J. Perelman. Or Preston Sturges. Or Noël Coward. Or George S. Kaufman. Widely admired (and feared) as the deadliest wit of his time, Kaufman was sour, saturnine, gloomy, and vaguely demonic. He had a genius for collaborating on comedies (with Marc Connelly, Edna Ferber, and Moss Hart), impregnating them with vitriolic repartee, and directing them with matchless pace. Yet the only independent Kaufman witticism that has come down to us seems to be "Satire is what closes on Saturday night."

I met Mr. Kaufman several times in Hollywood. And when I expressed my admiration for his work, his response was curt, perfunctory, and, I thought, rude. Then I learned from others not to take offense: "George is just the least congenial, snooty, snotty guy you'll ever run across."

Or take Oscar Levant, a man whose wit was profuse—and much admired in Broadway's restaurants and the homes of Beverly Hills. Levant was a jokester with one fatal flaw: He never stopped trying. He was exhausting to be with. He was a severely depressed man, spent years in psychoanalysis (then in hospitals: "They made me leave because I was depressing all the other inmates"). He considered any conversation an endless clothesline on which to hang endless wisecracks. Some were good: "An epigram is a wisecrack that has played Carnegie Hall" (whatever *that* means). To me he once confessed, "I'm so goddamn miserable I smoke forty cigarettes and drink twenty cups of coffee a day." The funniest, bitterest thing I ever heard him say was, "First thing I do after I get up in the morning is sharpen my teeth."

Levant was, of course, an accomplished pianist, perhaps the best living performer of George Gershwin, and a popular movie comedian (many of his movie wisecracks, which he uttered with a loose-lipped

scowl, were probably his own). He popped more pills than anyone I
ever met, and he died young, disappointed, sick, and, I think, baffled.

I am *not* surprised by the rarity with which such matchless humorists as P. G. Wodehouse or E. B. White or James Thurber get into
anthologies such as this one, for theirs is an art steeped in humor, of
which wit is one subdivision. Humor is much broader, more benevolent, more spacious, less acidulous (or nasty) than wit.

We smile—fondly—at humor, which is enduring; but we laugh—
often with malice—at wit.

NO BIBLE? NO SHAKESPEARE?

I must also warn you that I have included only a few lines from
the Bible—and a few from Shakespeare. There are, after all, *dozens*
of collections or concordances of quotations from both of these hallowed wonders. But of *wit*, or humor of any kind, the Holy Book is
woefully impoverished, whereas Shakespeare is the supreme writer-
dramatist-epigramitist of our noble tongue. Any who want to plumb
the Bible or Shakespeare for their treasures need only consult a con-
cordance or dictionary of quotations. I see no reason to relieve you of
so simple and rewarding an expedition. It robs you of the incalculable
rewards of serendipity.

THE PROBLEM OF ATTRIBUTIONS

So many witticisms come from sources unknown, and the original
authors of so many sources will forever remain unknown, that, to relieve the tedium of crediting Anonymous or Anon. over and over, or
Author Unknown, I have occasionally invented attributions—using
names it amuses me to create anew and to add a sparkle of surprise
to the endless listing of unadorned "Anon." Such brazen fabrications
as "Moishe Pisher," "Shmulke Potofsky," or "Yussele Bulbenick" are
merely stand-ins for those unknown soldiers whose headstones are
bare in the unnoted and uncelebrated cemeteries of the frivolous. I
thank them just the same.

Over and over, one hears (or asks), "Is that really true? Did Hum-
perdinck Poltzkin really say, 'Life is just a bowl of caries'?" The most
meticulous scholars have failed to find valid evidence to link any number of famous quotations to their eminent (but alleged) authors.

Take Nathan Hale's glorious "I only regret that I have but one life
to lose for my country." It turns out that this revered declaration first

appeared in print in the 1848(?) memoirs of one William Hull, a friend—and Hull confessed that the British officer who told him that those hallowed words were actually Nathan Hale's last on earth was probably using Hale's remembered phrase from Joseph Addison's famous play *Cato* (1730):

What pity is it
That we die, but once to serve our country.

I, for one, admit that although Harry Truman is credited with saying "If you can't stand the heat, stay out of the kitchen," it sounds more like Mrs. Truman than the president, and I suspect that's where Harry first heard it—and liked it—and used it to drive a point home. It is a most effective reprimand.

Or take "the iron curtain." Surely that immortal image was Winston Churchill's, in 1946, at his speech in Westminster College, Fulton, Missouri. True. But "the iron curtain" had been used a year earlier (by the unspeakable Josef Goebbels). And the Talmud says (*Pesachim* 85:2), "Nor can an iron wall [or curtain] separate Israel from God." In 1914 the queen of Belgium (born in Bavaria) said, "Between me and the Germans there is now a bloody iron curtain." In 1915 journalist George Crile called France "a nation with an iron curtain at its frontier." In 1920 Lady Ethel Snowden wrote (in a book called *Through Bolshevik Russia*), "We were behind the iron curtain at last!" In 1921 a P. Mohr wrote, in a journal called *Information About Eastern Questions*, "Russia lay concealed behind an iron curtain." And six months before Churchill's speech—whoa! Enough, enough.

I *hate* to tell you this, but Abraham Lincoln, as revered and quoted an American as ever lived, almost surely did not say "You can fool all of the people some of the time, and some of the people all of the time, but you can't fool all of the people all of the time." *No* credible historian credits the quote to Abe. Indeed, the first mention of the immortal litany attributing it to Lincoln did not appear in a book published until forty *years* after Lincoln's assassination.

A current flapdoodle is flapping around a sublime quip that recently surfaced in book circles: "Wagner's music isn't as bad as it sounds." Arguments rage (without persuasive evidence), most insisting that the quote is from one of Mark Twain's delicious travel pieces. I love the quote. It smells and sounds and resonates like the real Mark. In structure, rhythm, and that explosively innocent climax, nothing seems more typical of the Master.

But no one has found it in any of Twain's voluminous writings (eighty-four volumes, when collected)! No one. Still, I continue to believe he said it, because it is so truly Twainian.

MULTIPLE ATTRIBUTIONS

Many witticisms and phrases are so catchy that they are credited to more than one wit ("Don't fence me in"; "Read my lips"; "Go ahead, make my day!"). Others are so nonforgettable as to give birth to a dozen alleged authors; I never doubted that Howard Dietz of MGM said of the hyperthyroid actress Tallulah Bankhead, "A day away from Tallulah is like a month in the country"—but soon after he said it, the quip had been credited to Moss Hart, Oscar Levant, Ilka Chase, Goodman Ace, George S. Kaufman, Alexander Woollcott, Robert Benchley, Irving Hoffman (columnist for *The Hollywood Reporter*), and, for all I know, a dozen others.

"A man will fight harder for his interests than for his rights" was independently said or written by Napoleon, Aristotle, Machiavelli, H. L. Mencken, and perhaps a dozen more. I have indicated such multiple attributions by using a slash:

The aphorism above is credited:

Napoleon/Aristotle/Machiavelli/Mencken

Life is too short to spend one's time in prolonged, tiresome searches for so academic a matter as the verifications of the ancestry (or bastardry) of a phrase.

Besides, some ideas become so obvious that it is not surprising that they are uttered, in the purest of formulations, at different times, in different places, by different persons. I'm rather sure that Sigmund Freud's electrifying conclusion, after decades of analyzing patients (". . . most men are trash"), has been the same conclusion reached by dozens of less celebrated observers of the follies, deceits, cruelties, and treacheries of the human species.

Television, with its abundant monologists, interviews, roundtables, and endless talk-talk-talk shows, has become an instant disseminator of clever (whether original or plagiarized) wisecracks. How many are original, and how many were created by a star's press agent or scriptwriter may never be known.

I once went to an early dinner with a famous comedian who presided over a popular game show on television. We went from the restaurant to the backstage set for his program. At the door to his dressing room he said, "I'll see you later . . . but now I have to review my spontaneous ad-libs. . . ."

In the fullness of time, of course, it does not matter (nor will it matter) whether it was George Burns or Bob Hope or Fred Allen or Johnny Carson or one of their *writers* who said, "Isn't it a shame that all the people who can solve our country's problems are busy cutting hair and shining shoes?"

I ask you to consider this comment by Hesketh Pearson, a true English maven, in his introduction to *Common Misquotations* (1934):

> Misquotation is, in fact, the pride and privilege of the learned. A widely read man never quotes accurately, for the obvious reason that he has read too widely.

I would like to stress this point in the most positive way I know:

> Misquotation is, in fact, the pride and privilege of the learned. A widely read man never quotes accurately, for the obvious reason that he has read too widely.   —LEO ROSTEN
>   New York, N.Y.

Actors/Acting

Long experience has taught me that in England nobody goes to the theatre unless he or she has bronchitis.   —JAMES AGATE

Actors are the only honest hypocrites. . . . They wear the livery of other men's fortunes: Their very thoughts are not their own.
—WILLIAM HAZLITT

The actor is not quite a human being—but then, who is?
—GEORGE SANDERS

I got all the schooling any actress needs—that is, I learned to write well enough to sign contracts.   —HERMIONE GINGOLD

The art of acting consists in keeping people from coughing.
—RALPH RICHARDSON

Greek tragedy: The type of drama where the hero says to his sister, if you don't kill Pa, I will.   —SPYROS SKOURAS

Opening night: The night before the play is ready to open.
—George Jean Nathan

Acting is like roller skating. Once you know how to do it, it is neither stimulating nor exciting.   —George Sanders

With the exception of a few Europeans and a very few Americans, actors are basically an uncultured, uncivilized, pretentious lot.
—John Simon

An actor's face and physique are his assets, and he is compelled to devote as much attention to them as a glassblower to his respiration.
—Leo Rosten

Some of the greatest love affairs I've known have involved one actor, unassisted.   —Wilson Mizner

Why are overactors called "hams"? Because minstrel-show performers used heavy makeup to appear in "blackface"—and used ham fat to remove it. Called "ham fat men," the "fat" in time vanished.
—Leo Rosten

The world is a stage, but the play is badly cast.   —Oscar Wilde

---

"Method acting"? Mine involves a lot of talent, a glass, and some cracked ice.   —John Barrymore

If you ask me to play myself, I will not know what to do. I do not know who or what I am.   —Peter Sellers

Acting is an outlet for neurotic impulses.   —Marlon Brando

Acting is a masochistic form of exhibitionism. It is not quite the occupation of an adult.   —Laurence Olivier

You can pick out actors by the glazed look that comes into their eyes when the conversation wanders away from themselves.

—MICHAEL WILDING

The public *sees* actors at their trade; it *sees* how they earn their living. The public never sees a Morgan making money or a Ford making cars; but it does see a Robert Taylor making faces.   —LEO ROSTEN

Who in his right mind wants to hear actors *talk*?

—HARRY WARNER

Miss Hepburn runs the gamut of human emotions from A to B.

—DOROTHY PARKER

He can't act. He can't sing. He's bald. He can dance a little.

—MOVIE EXECUTIVE
ABOUT FRED ASTAIRE'S SCREEN TEST, 1929

I shall never understand the weird process by which a body with a voice suddenly fancies itself as a mind. It's about time the piano realized it has not written the concerto.   —JOSEPH MANKIEWICZ

England produces the best fat actors.   —JIMMY CANNON

Modesty in an actor is as fake as passion in a call girl.

—JACKIE GLEASON

Acting is a form of deception, and actors can mesmerize themselves almost as easily as an audience.   —LEO ROSTEN

The real secret of acting is—sincerity. Once you learn to fake that, you're in.   —JEAN GIRARDOUX/GEORGE BURNS/GROUCHO MARX

No one can really *like* an actor.   —ALFRED HITCHCOCK

Adolescence/Youth

Since adolescents are too old to do the things kids do and not old enough to do things adults do, they do things nobody else does.

—ANONYMOUS

Adolescent: A teenager who acts like a baby when you don't treat him like an adult.   —VAYR VAIST

Adolescence: A stage between infancy and adultery.   —ANONYMOUS

Don't laugh at a youth for his affectations; he is only trying on one face after another to find his own.   —LOGAN PEARSALL SMITH

You don't have to suffer to be a poet. Adolescence is enough suffering for anyone.   —JOHN CIARDI

Adolescence is a kind of emotional seasickness. Both are funny, but only in retrospect.   —ARTHUR KOESTLER

An adolescent in his round of joyless promiscuity is no more a revolutionary than a pickpocket is a socialist; he is merely taking adult prerogatives without taking adult responsibility, taking without earning.   —DONALD BARR

Adolescence: I went to my son's school to see his guidance counselor. He told me my boy was out: He'd be back in one to three years.

—RODNEY DANGERFIELD

Advertisements

Exactly as printed in the press:

AUTOMATIC BLANKET
Ensure sound sleep with one of our
authorized dealers.

Rev. Jarvis has spoken in the largest Baptist churches in America. To miss hearing him will be the chance of a lifetime!

GIVE US YOUR DIRTY CLOTHES
Ladies! If you drive by our new launderette and drop off your clothes, you will receive very swift attention!

URGENTLY WANTED,
BY MACHINE TOOL FACTORY
Male parts handlers.
Box 132

ROOM WANTED
Young, sentimental, loving male. Loves to play. Wants Room and Board with loving female. Cannot pay rent, but offers true love, constant company, and 24-hour protection. Will serve as escort to and from classes if desired. Will keep you warm all night long. Allows you complete freedom to date others. Call EG 4-6627.

DO NOT CALL unless you are truly interested in giving a home to this adorable puppy.

WHITLEY ACADEMY
In beautiful Vermont. Coeducational.
Special openings for boys.

WANTED: Tamer lion, by lion tamer.—AD IN *VARIETY*

BED FOR SALE
Four-poster, over 100 years old.
Perfect for antique lover.

Notice on church bulletin board:
Sunday: Rev. M. Farnsworth will talk on ETERNITY AND YOU.
Come early—If you want to be sure of getting a seat in the back.

You can tell the ideals of a nation by its advertisements.
—NORMAN DOUGLAS

The advertisement is one of the most interesting and difficult of modern literary forms. —ALDOUS HUXLEY

Advertisements contain the only truths to be relied on in a newspaper. —THOMAS JEFFERSON

Advice

Never play leapfrog with a unicorn.
—ORIENTAL SAYING

* * *

When a man comes to me for advice, I find out the kind of advice he wants, and I give it to him. —JOSH BILLINGS

When you go to a restaurant, choose a table near a waiter.
—JEWISH SAYING

*When a woman tells you her age, it's all right
to look surprised, but don't scowl.*
                    —ATTRIBUTED TO WILSON MIZNER

                    *   *   *

If you want to get rid of somebody, just tell 'em something for their
own good.   —FRANK MCKINNEY ("KIN") HUBBARD

I hate quotations. Tell me what you know.
                              —RALPH WALDO EMERSON

The man afraid of leaves should not enter a forest.
                        —JEWISH/NATIVE AMERICAN SAYING

Don't tell your friends about your indigestion. "How are you?" is a
greeting, not a question.
                    —ARTHUR GUITERMAN/ROBERT BENCHLEY

Illusions are comforting; just don't act upon them.
                                   —JEWISH SAYING

You can get more with a kind word and a gun than you can with a
kind word alone.
              —JOHNNY CARSON (ALSO ATTRIBUTED TO AL CAPONE)

In baiting a mousetrap with cheese, be sure to leave room for the
mouse.   —H. H. MUNRO ("SAKI")

Whoever fights monsters should see to it that in the process he does
not become a monster. When you look into an abyss, the abyss also
looks into you.   —FRIEDRICH WILHELM NIETZSCHE

When you press a stone, the stone presses back.   —ISAAC NEWTON

Sleep faster; we need the pillows.   —MY FATHER

If you want to know how old a woman is, ask her sister-in-law.
—EDGAR WATSON ("ED") HOWE

Better measure ten times and cut once, instead of measuring once and cutting ten times.   —COMMON SAYING

Never consult a woman about her rival, a coward about a war, or a merchant about a bargain.   —MANNY SCHLOTT

One of my old formulas is to be an enthusiast in the front part of your heart and ironical in the back.   —OLIVER WENDELL HOLMES, JR.

When a man seeks your advice he generally wants your praise.
—LORD CHESTERFIELD

"Easy come, easy go" does not apply to houseguests.
—LEO ROSTEN

When a crook kisses you, count your teeth.   —COMMON SAYING

Be wiser than other people if you can, but do not tell them so.
—LORD CHESTERFIELD

Never eat at a place called Mom's.
Never play cards with a man named Doc.
And never lie down with a woman who's got more troubles than your own.   —NELSON ALGREN

Never ascribe to an opponent motives meaner than your own.
—JAMES MATTHEW BARRIE

Let thy maid servant be faithful, strong, and homely.
—BENJAMIN FRANKLIN

It is better to be embarrassed than ashamed.   —TALMUD

Lend before witnesses, but give without them.   —ANONYMOUS

Never try to pacify a man at the height of his anger.
—ADAPTED FROM TALMUD

Entrances are wide; exits are narrow.   —JEWISH SAYING

For that tired, run-down feeling, try jaywalking.
—*FARMERS' ALMANAC*

If you protest long enough that you're right, you're wrong.
—JEWISH SAYING

Never run after your own hat—others will be delighted to do it; why spoil their fun?   —MARK TWAIN

Ransom a captive before you feed the poor; no act of charity is greater.   —JOSEPH CARO

When you get to the end of your rope, tie a knot and hang on.
—FRANKLIN D. ROOSEVELT

Your health comes first—you can always hang yourself later.
—MY UNCLE

The best of animals needs a whip, the purest of women a husband, the cleverest of men advice.   —IBN GABIROL

Love thy neighbor, yet don't pull down your hedge.
—BENJAMIN FRANKLIN

Do not unto others as you would they should do unto you; their taste may not be the same.   —GEORGE BERNARD SHAW

The only thing to do with good advice is to pass it on; it is never of any use to oneself.   —OSCAR WILDE

Don't ask the doctor; ask the patient.   —MY MOTHER

It is not worthwhile to go 'round the world to count the cats in Zanzibar.   —HENRY DAVID THOREAU

If you want people to think you wise, just agree with them.
                                        —LEO ROSTEN

When you're hungry, sing; when you're hurt, laugh.
                                        —JEWISH FOLK SAYING

Never complain, never explain.
                          —BENJAMIN DISRAELI/HENRY FORD II

Look out for yourself—or they'll pee on your grave.
                                        —LOUIS B. MAYER

There's one way to find out if a man is honest: Ask him. If he says yes, you know he is crooked.   —MARK TWAIN/GROUCHO MARX

There is only one rule for being a good talker: Learn to listen.
                                        —CHRISTOPHER MORLEY

Men give away nothing so liberally as their advice.
                          —FRANÇOIS DE LA ROCHEFOUCAULD

Don't talk about yourself; it will be done when you leave.
                                        —ADDISON MIZNER

When you have got an elephant by the hind legs and he is trying to run away, it's best to let him run.   —ABRAHAM LINCOLN

Never put off until tomorrow what you can do the day after tomorrow.
                                        —MARK TWAIN

Start every day off with a smile—and get it over with.
                                        —W. C. FIELDS

Put all your eggs in one basket, and watch the basket.
—MARK TWAIN

Always help those who are being persecuted.
—NACHMAN OF BRATSLAV

Never wrestle with a chimney sweep.   —H. H. ASQUITH

Instead of loving your enemies, treat your friends a little better.
—EDGAR WATSON ("ED") HOWE

When you are weaponless, at least act brave.
—ADAPTED FROM TALMUD

Never give in! Never give in! Never, never, never, never—in nothing great or small, large or petty—never give in except to convictions of honor and good sense.   —WINSTON CHURCHILL

How is it possible to expect mankind to take advice when they will not so much as take warning?   —JONATHAN SWIFT

It was a high counsel that I once heard given to a young person, "Always do what you are afraid to do."
—RALPH WALDO EMERSON

Don't jump on a man unless he's down.
—FINLEY PETER DUNNE ("MR. DOOLEY")

What is lofty can be said in any language, and what is mean should be said in none.   —MAIMONIDES

The race is not always to the swift, nor the battle to the strong, but that's the way to bet.   —DAMON RUNYON

In a house of the hanged, ask no one to hang up your coat.
—MANY CULTURES

Be nice to people on your way up because you'll meet them on your
way down.   —WILSON MIZNER/W. C. FIELDS

Let us not be too particular; it is better to have old secondhand diamonds than none at all.   —MARK TWAIN

Avoid fried meats which angry up the blood. If your stomach disputes
you, lie down and pacify it with cool thoughts. Keep the juices flowing
by jangling around gently as you move. Go very light on the vices,
such as carrying on in society. The social ramble ain't restful. Avoid
running at all times. Don't look back: Someone might be gaining on
you.   —LEROY ("SATCHEL") PAIGE

Never speak ill of yourself; your friends will always say enough on
that subject.   —CHARLES-MAURICE DE TALLEYRAND

When in trouble, mumble.   —LEO ROSTEN

Buy Old Masters; they fetch a much higher price than old mistresses.
                              —LORD BEAVERBROOK

It is easier to stay out than get out.   —MARK TWAIN

Always do right; this will gratify some people and astonish the rest.
                              —MARK TWAIN

Trust everybody, but cut the cards.
                              —FINLEY PETER DUNNE ("MR. DOOLEY")

In Maine we have a saying that there's no point in speaking unless
you can improve on silence.   —EDMUND MUSKIE

Habit is . . . not to be flung out of the window, but coaxed downstairs
a step at a time.   —MARK TWAIN

If everyone sweeps in front of his door, the whole city will be clean.
                              —URBAN SAYING

If at first you don't succeed, before you try again, stop to figure out what you did wrong. —LEO ROSTEN

You don't save a [baseball] pitcher for tomorrow. Tomorrow it may rain. —LEO DUROCHER

If you can't be funny, be interesting. —HAROLD ROSS

If you have nothing to say, say nothing. —MARK TWAIN

As long as words are in your mouth, you are their lord; once you utter them, you are their slave. —IBN GABIROL

A tongue can be a dangerous enemy, so can yours—to yourself no less than to others. —ANONYMOUS

Do not take life too seriously; you will never get out of it alive. —ELBERT HUBBARD

Never anger a heathen, a snake, or a pupil. —TALMUD

African Americans

I am probably the only living American, black or white, who just doesn't give a damn. —ADAM CLAYTON POWELL

I never believed in Santa Claus because I knew no white dude would come into my neighborhood after dark. —DICK GREGORY

Just being a Negro doesn't qualify you to understand the race situation any more than being sick makes you an expert on medicine. —DICK GREGORY

It is not healthy when a nation lives within a nation, as colored Americans are living inside America. A nation cannot live confident of its tomorrow, if its refugees are among its own citizens.

—PEARL S. BUCK

To be a Negro in this country and to be relatively conscious is to be in rage almost all the time.   —JAMES BALDWIN

I want to be the white man's brother, not his brother-in-law.

—MARTIN LUTHER KING, JR.

Freedom is never voluntarily given by the oppressor; it must be demanded by the oppressed.   —MARTIN LUTHER KING, JR.

Age/Aging

Forty is the old age of youth; fifty is the youth of old age.

—VICTOR HUGO/FRENCH PROVERB

Dying while you are young is a great boon in your old age.

—SEBASTIAN TRABISH

I've never known a person who lives to 110 who is remarkable for anything else.   —JOSH BILLINGS

When you hit seventy, you eat better, you sleep sounder, you feel more alive than when you were thirty. Obviously, it's healthier to have women on your mind than on your knees.   —MAURICE CHEVALIER

Age is not a particularly interesting subject. Anyone can get old. All you have to do is live long enough.   —GROUCHO MARX

Nature abhors the old.   —RALPH WALDO EMERSON

He whom the gods favor dies young.   —PLAUTUS

Middle age is when your age starts to show around your middle.
—ANONYMOUS

The old believe everything, the middle-aged suspect everything, the young know everything. —OSCAR WILDE

All sorts of allowances are made for the illusions of youth; and none . . . for the disenchantments of age.
—ROBERT LOUIS STEVENSON

I am in the prime of senility. —BENJAMIN FRANKLIN

When a man fell into his anecdotage, it was a sign for him to retire from the world. —BENJAMIN DISRAELI

Every man desires to live long, but no man would be old.
—JONATHAN SWIFT

No one is so old as not to think he can live one more year.
—CICERO

Few people know how to be old.
——FRANÇOIS DE LA ROCHEFOUCAULD

Old men have more regard for expediency than for honor.
—ARISTOTLE

Tho good die young—because they see it's no use living if you've got to be good. —JOHN BARRYMORE

Spring makes everything young again—except man.
—JEAN-PAUL RICHTER

What a man does in youth darkens his face in old age.
—MY AUNT RIVKE

That point in life where, when your wife tells you to pull in your stomach, you already have.   —ANONYMOUS

He is old enough to know worse.   —OSCAR WILDE

One of the delights known to age, and beyond the grasp of youth, is that of Not Going.   —J. B. PRIESTLEY

Young men want to be faithful and are not; old men want to be faithless and cannot.   —OSCAR WILDE

When you win, you're an old pro. When you lose, you're an old man.   —CHARLEY CONERLY

You're never too old to grow younger.   —MAE WEST

When people tell you how young you look, they are also telling you how old you are.   —CARY GRANT

The three ages of man: youth, middle age, and "You're looking wonderful!"   —FRANCIS CARDINAL SPELLMAN/DORE SCHARY

You know you're getting old when the candles cost more than the cake.   —BOB HOPE

Middle age: The time when the thing you grow most in your garden is tired.   —ANONYMOUS

For the ignorant, old age is winter; for the learned, it is the harvest.   —HASIDIC SAYING

Middle age: When you're home on Saturday night, the telephone rings, and you hope it's the wrong number.   —RING LARDNER

> The prosperity of a country can be seen simply in how it treats its old people. —NACHMAN OF BRATSLAV
>
> After fifty, a man begins to deteriorate, but in the forties he is at the maximum of his villainy. —H. L. MENCKEN

Agnostics/Atheists

I do not consider it an insult, but rather a compliment to be called an agnostic. I do not pretend to know what many ignorant men are sure of—that is all that agnosticism means. —CLARENCE DARROW

Compulsion in religion is distinguished peculiarly from compulsion in every other thing. I may grow rich by an art I am compelled to follow; I may recover health by medicines I am compelled to take against my own judgment; but I cannot be saved by a worship I disbelieve and abhor. —THOMAS JEFFERSON

Few sailors are atheists, for they are in daily peril. —ANONYMOUS

Agnosticism simply means that a man shall not say he knows or believes that for which he has no grounds for professing to believe. —THOMAS HUXLEY

Alcohol

Alcohol is a very necessary article . . . it enables Parliament to do things at eleven at night that no sane person would do at eleven in the morning. —GEORGE BERNARD SHAW

Altruists

Men are the only animals that devote themselves, day in and day out, to making one another unhappy. It is an art like any other. Its virtuosi are called altruists.   —H. L. MENCKEN

I think there is only one quality worse than hardness of heart and that is softness of head.   —THEODORE ROOSEVELT

America

The mission of the United States is one of benevolent assimilation.
—WILLIAM McKINLEY

Ancestry

Nothing is more disgraceful than for a man who is nothing to hold himself honored on account of his forefathers; and yet hereditary honors are a noble and splendid treasure to descendants.   —PLATO

I don't know who my grandfather was; I am much more concerned with what his grandson will be.   —ABRAHAM LINCOLN

Every king springs from a race of slaves, and every slave has had kings among his ancestors.   —PLATO

Send your noble blood to market and see what it will buy.
—ANONYMOUS

Snobs talk as if they had begotten their ancestors.
—HERBERT AGAR/ALFRED ADLER

Consider whether we ought not to be more in the habit of seeking honor from our descendants than from our ancestors; thinking it better to be nobly remembered than nobly born; and striving so to live, that our sons, and our sons' sons, for ages to come, might still lead their children reverently to the doors out of which we had been carried to the grave, saying, "Look, this was his house, this was his chamber." —JOHN RUSKIN

Angels

The virtue of angels is that they cannot deteriorate; their flaw is that they cannot improve. Man's flaw is that he can deteriorate; and his virtue is that he can improve. —TALMUD

Smells are the fallen angels of the senses. —HELEN KELLER

He who has fed a stranger may have fed an angel. —TALMUD

Anger

Anger makes dull men witty, but keeps them poor.
—FRANCIS BACON

When angry, count four; when very angry, swear. —MARK TWAIN

Anger begins with madness and ends in regret. —HASDAI

Applications

One of the least-known gold mines for humor, sagacity, despair, or hope is that huge body of Applications (for jobs, mates, accomplices, employers, servants, et al.) that fills many a column in our press. Down the years I have collected a few gems: I know you will not believe some of them, but take my word for it: All are true. (I have changed some names to protect the guilty.)

Insurance policy application:
> Beneficiary: Alice P. Moody
> Relationship to you: Miserable

Marital status: Eligible

Name: Rinaldo Piaccelli
Address: 166 Mulberry St.
Length of residence: 29 feet

Name: Violet Andrews
Address: 832 Eustace Way
Date of birth: Feb. 7, 1959
Weight: 6 pounds, 10 ounces
Color hair: None

Name: Hortense Naomi Dressler
Sex: Not yet

Architecture

Architecture is frozen music.   —GOETHE

A doctor can bury his mistakes but an architect can only advise his client to plant vines.   —FRANK LLOYD WRIGHT

Arguments

The most savage controversies are those about matters as to which
there is no good evidence either way.   —BERTRAND RUSSELL

Arguments are to be avoided; they are always vulgar and often con-
vincing.   —OSCAR WILDE

I have found you an argument; but I am not obliged to find you an
understanding.   —SAMUEL JOHNSON/BENJAMIN DISRAELI

The best way of answering a bad argument is to let it go on.
                                          —SYDNEY SMITH

Behind every argument is someone's ignorance.
                                          —LOUIS D. BRANDEIS

"For instance" is not proof.   —HEBREW SAYING

It's better to debate a question without settling it than to settle a
question without debating it.   —JOSEPH JOUBERT

Controversy: A battle in which spittle or ink replaces the injurious
cannonball and the inconsiderate bayonet.   —AMBROSE BIERCE

The worst-tempered people I've ever met were people who knew they
were wrong.   WILSON MIZNER

In debate, rather pull to pieces the argument of thine antagonist, than
offer him any of thine own, for thus thou will fight him in his own
country.   —HENRY FIELDING

Those who [today] demand a "meaningful dialogue" are demanding a
discussion that promises in advance to end up agreeing with them.
                                          —LEO ROSTEN

You raise your voice when you should reinforce your argument.
—SAMUEL JOHNSON

My wife was too beautiful for words, but not for arguments.
—JOHN BARRYMORE

He is more apt to contribute heat than light to a discussion.
—WOODROW WILSON

In our home, we have a rule: You can disagree with a man's position as much as you want—*after* you have been able to state it to his satisfaction.   —J. IRWIN MILLER

Sometimes a scream is better than a thesis.
—RALPH WALDO EMERSON

No man can think clearly when his fists are clenched.
—GEORGE JEAN NATHAN

We must not [today] mistake noise for weight, anger for argument, militance for virtue, or gripes for principles.   —LEO ROSTEN

No one is as deaf as the man who will not listen.   —JEWISH SAYING

Of all eloquence a nickname is the most concise; of all arguments the most unanswerable.   —WILLIAM HAZLITT

Much of the force as well as grace of arguments, as well as of instructions, depends on their conciseness.   —ALEXANDER POPE

Treating your adversary with respect is giving him an advantage to which he is not always entitled.   —SAMUEL JOHNSON

Argument is the worst sort of conversation.   —JONATHAN SWIFT

Vilify! Vilify! Some of it will always stick.   —BEAUMARCHAIS

We think very few people sensible except those who agree with us.
—FRANÇOIS DE LA ROCHEFOUCAULD

The only argument available with an east wind is to put on your overcoat. —JAMES RUSSELL LOWELL

I am bound to furnish my antagonists with arguments, but not with
comprehension. —BENJAMIN DISRAELI

Art/Artists

The function of art is to make that *understood* which in the form of
an argument would be incomprehensible. —LEO TOLSTOY

Painting: The art of protecting flat surfaces from the weather and
exposing them to the critic. —AMBROSE BIERCE

I do not paint a portrait to look like the subject, rather does the person
grow to look like his portrait. —SALVADOR DALI

Art for art's sake makes no more sense than gin for gin's sake.
—W. SOMERSET MAUGHAM

Art is a higher type of knowledge than experience. —ARISTOTLE

People say, "I have no ear for music." They never say, "I have no eye
for painting." —PICASSO

Art happens—no hovel is safe from it, no prince may depend upon it,
the vastest intelligence cannot bring it about.
—JAMES MCNEILL WHISTLER

Art is a jealous mistress. —RALPH WALDO EMERSON

As the influence of religion declines, the social importance of art increases; we must beware of exchanging good religion for bad art.
—ALDOUS HUXLEY

The perfection of art is to conceal art.   —QUINTILIAN

Art, like morality, consists in drawing the line somewhere.
—G. K. CHESTERTON

The more horrifying this world becomes, the more art becomes abstract.   —PAUL KLEE

What is the most difficult part of a picture? The part that is to be left out.   —A JAPANESE PAINTER

Scratch an artist and you surprise a child.
—JAMES HUNEKER

What garlic is to salad, insanity is to art.
—AUGUSTUS SAINT-GAUDENS

Nothing so resembles a daub as a masterpiece.   —PAUL GAUGUIN

Painting is silent poetry, and poetry is painting with the gift of speech.
—SIMONIDES

The English public takes no interest in a work of art until it is told that the work is immoral.   —OSCAR WILDE

Everyone wants to "understand" art. Why not try to understand the song of a bird?   —PABLO PICASSO

The revolutionary role of the artist is to liberate us from the prisons of the familiar.   —LEO ROSTEN

All art is autobiographical; the pearl is the oyster's autobiography.
—FEDERICO FELLINI

Very modern painting: Things *can't* be as bad as they're painted.
—LEO ROSTEN

The most immoral and disgraceful and dangerous thing that anybody can do in the arts is knowingly to feed back to the public its own ignorance and cheap taste.
—EDMUND WILSON

✳   ✳   ✳

There are moments when art almost attains the dignity of manual labor. —OSCAR WILDE

If that's art, then I am a Hottentot. —HARRY S TRUMAN

It's clever, but is it art? —RUDYARD KIPLING

All art is a kind of subconscious madness expressed in terms of sanity.
—GEORGE JEAN NATHAN

Modern art is what happens when painters stop looking at girls and persuade themselves that they have a better idea. —JOHN CIARDI

If the painter wishes to see beauties to fall in love with, it is in his power to bring them forth, and if he wants to see monstrous things that frighten or are foolish or laughable, he is their Lord and God.
—LEONARDO DA VINCI

[of Leonardo da Vinci]: He bores me. Should have stuck to his flying machines. —PIERRE AUGUSTE RENOIR

The artistic temperament is a disease that affects amateurs.
—G. K. CHESTERTON

We feel a pleasure in Botticelli that few if any other artists can give us. . . . He got music out of design.   —BERNARD BERENSON

French nudes look as if they had just taken off their clothes; Greek nudes as if they had never put them on.   —S. C. HALL

Every time I paint a portrait I lose a friend.
                                   —JOHN SINGER SARGENT

Abstract art: A product of the untalented, sold by the unprincipled to the utterly bewildered.   —AL CAPP

The true artist will let his wife starve, his children go barefoot, his mother drudge for his living at seventy, sooner than work at anything but his art.   —GEORGE BERNARD SHAW

Art does not render what is visible; art *makes* visible.
                                          —PAUL KLEE

Beyond a certain point great art is best accepted, like miracles, without explanation.   —JOHN CANADAY

Art is life seen through a temperament.   —EMILE ZOLA

The nature of artistic attainment is psychologically inaccessible to us.
                                   —SIGMUND FREUD

Less is more.   —MIES VAN DER ROHE

Pictures must not be too picturesque.   —RALPH WALDO EMERSON

Painting is the music of God, the inner reflection of his luminous perfection.   —MICHELANGELO

All art is a revolt against man's fate.   —ANDRÉ MALRAUX

To reveal art and conceal the artist is art's aim.   —OSCAR WILDE

An art theater: That's a place where the theater is clean—the pictures are filthy.   —HENNY YOUNGMAN

I have no desire to prove anything by dancing. I have never used it as an outlet or as a means of expressing myself. I just dance.
                                               —FRED ASTAIRE

Once you admit Jackson Pollock to the ranks of great painters, anybody can paint; once junk can be sculpture, anybody can be a sculptor. The difficulty is being taken out of everything, and as a result the riffraff takes over.   —JOHN SIMON

Generally speaking, the . . . theatre is the aspirin of the middle classes.
                                            —WOLCOTT GIBBS

Visitor: M'sieur Matisse, you have made the arm on that girl much too *long.*
Matisse: That is not a girl, madame; it is a painting.

Seeing is an art; it must be learned.   —JOHN CONSTABLE

I shut my eyes in order to see.   —PAUL GAUGUIN

One beautiful morning, El Greco sat in a room with the curtains tightly drawn. Invited to go out for a walk, El Greco said, "No. The sunlight would disturb the light that is shining within me."

So-called modern art is merely the vaporing of half-baked, lazy people. There is no art at all in connection with the modernists.
                                            —HARRY S TRUMAN

A work of art always surprises us; it has worked its effect before we have become conscious of its presence.   —HERBERT READ

The great tragedy of the artistic temperament is that it cannot produce any art.   —G. K. CHESTERTON

The more minimal the art, the more maximum the explanation.
          —HILTON KRAMER

Art is a lie that enables us to realize the truth.   —PABLO PICASSO

There are only two styles of portrait painting, the serious and the smirk.   —CHARLES DICKENS

Good painting is like good cooking; it can be tasted, but not explained.
          —MAURICE VLAMINCK

The world today doesn't make sense, so why should I paint pictures that do?   —PABLO PICASSO

I am glad the old masters are all dead, and I only wish they had died sooner.   —MARK TWAIN

The object of art is to give life a shape.   —JEAN ANOUILH

Only an auctioneer can equally and impartially admire all schools of art.   —OSCAR WILDE

Atheism

Not only is there no God, but try getting a plumber on weekends.
          —WOODY ALLEN

The spread of atheism among the young is something awful; I give no credit, however, to the report that some of them do not believe in Mammon. —LOGAN PEARSALL SMITH

Thanks to God, I am still an atheist. —LUIS BUÑUEL

Atheism . . . is too theological. —G. K. CHESTERTON

The best reply to an atheist is to give him a good dinner and ask him if he believes there is a cook. —LOUIS NIZER

An atheist is a man who watches a Notre Dame-Southern Methodist University game and doesn't care who wins.
—DWIGHT D. EISENHOWER

Wanting to be an atheist does not make you one.
—NAPOLEON BONAPARTE

I don't believe in God because I don't believe in Mother Goose.
—CLARENCE DARROW

An atheist is a man who has no invisible means of support.
—JOHN BUCHAN/FULTON J. SHEEN, ET AL.

I was a freethinker before I knew how to think.
—GEORGE BERNARD SHAW

Nobody talks so constantly about God as those who insist that there is no God.
—HEYWOOD BROUN

* * *

Bachelors

Marriage has many pains, but celibacy has no pleasures.
—SAMUEL JOHNSON

Bachelor: A man who can take women or leave them—and prefers to do both. —*PLAYBOY*

"Home Sweet Home" must surely have been written by a bachelor.
—SAMUEL BUTLER

A bachelor never quite gets over the idea that he is a thing of beauty and a boy forever. —HELEN ROWLAND

Bachelor: A man who comes to work each morning from a different direction. —SHOLEM ALEICHEM ET. AL.

Beauty

Beauty is only sin deep.   —H. H. MUNRO ("SAKI")

If truth is beauty, how come no one has their hair done in the library?
                                   —LILY TOMLIN

Let us face it: Beauty is a bit of a bore.   —W. SOMERSET MAUGHAM

In no civilized country has the artist ever chosen to give an erect organ to his representations of ideal masculine beauty.
                                   —HAVELOCK ELLIS

Any girl can be glamorous; all you have to do is stand still and look stupid.   —HEDY LAMARR/MARLENE DIETRICH/ELIZABETH TAYLOR

> *To a toad, what is beauty? A female with two pop eyes, a wide mouth, yellow belly, and spotted back.*
>
>   —VOLTAIRE

                *   *   *

When a girl has no other virtues, a freckle can be considered one.
                          —YITZCHOK MACTAVISH II

All brides are beautiful—and all corpses look pious.
                         —ADAPTED FROM TALMUD

She got her good looks from her father. He's a plastic surgeon.
                          —GROUCHO MARX

A beautiful woman should break her mirror early.
                          —BALTHASAR GRACIAN

An ugly girl hates the mirror.   —JAPANESE SAYING

Her features didn't seem to know the value of teamwork.
                                                  —GEORGE ADE

The most beautiful things in the world are the most useless—peacocks
and lilies, for instance.   —JOHN RUSKIN

The charming don't have to be beautiful.   —JEWISH SAYING

There is no excellent beauty that hath not some strangeness in the
proportion.   —FRANCIS BACON

Other animals take no pleasure in sense objects unless they be related
to food or sex, but man can delight in their very beauty.
                                             —THOMAS AQUINAS

Better that a girl has beauty than brains, because boys see better
than they think.   —JOSH BILLINGS

*I'm tired of all this nonsense about beauty being only skin deep.
That's deep enough. What do you want, an adorable pancreas?*
                                             —JEAN KERR

Most women are not as young as they are painted.
                                             —MAX BEERBOHM

Belief

If the stars should appear one night in a thousand years, how would
men believe and adore!   —RALPH WALDO EMERSON

A man must be orthodox upon most things or he will never have time
to preach his own heresy.   —G. K. CHESTERTON

Man prefers to believe what he prefers to be true.

—FRANCIS BACON

Men freely believe that which they desire. —JULIUS CAESAR

Everybody should believe in something; I believe I'll have another drink. —ROBERT BENCHLEY

The race of men, while sheep in credulity, are wolves for conformity.

—CARL VAN DOREN

Unbelief in one thing springs from blind belief in another.

—GEORG CHRISTOPH LICHTENBERG

Man adapts himself to everything. To one thing only does he not adapt himself: to being not clear in his own mind what he believes about things. —ORTEGA Y GASSET

The world is divided into two classes: those who believe the incredible, and those who do the improbable. —OSCAR WILDE

Lord, I do not believe; help thou my unbelief.

—SAMUEL BUTLER (AFTER AQUINAS)

Nothing is so firmly believed as what we least know. —MONTAIGNE

A belief is not true because it is useful. — HENRI FRÉDÉRIC AMIEL

Man is a credulous animal and must believe something. *In the absence of good grounds for belief, he will be satisfied with bad ones.*

—BERTRAND RUSSELL

*   *   *

Man is what he believes.　　　　　　　　　　　—CHEKHOV

To believe is very dull. To doubt is intensely engrossing.
　　　　　　　　　　　　　　　　　　—OSCAR WILDE

I never cease being dumbfounded by the totally unbelievable things people believe.　　　　　　　　　—LEO ROSTEN

I am myself a dissenter from all known religions, and I hope that every kind of religious belief will die out. I regard it as a disease, as belonging to the infancy of human reason and to a stage of development which we are now outgrowing.　　　—BERTRAND RUSSELL

Modern man . . . has not ceased to be credulous . . . the need to believe haunts him.　　　　　　　　　　—WILLIAM JAMES

Blasphemy depends upon belief, and is fading with it. If anyone doubts this, let him sit down seriously and try to think blasphemous thoughts about Thor. I think his family will find him at the end of the day in a state of some exhaustion.　　　　　　—G. K. CHESTERTON

What men really want is not knowledge, but certainty.
　　　　　　　　　　　　　　　　　—BERTRAND RUSSELL

The most costly of all follies is to believe passionately in the palpably not true. It is the chief occupation of mankind.　—H. L. MENCKEN

○ Yogi Berra ○

　　Lawrence ("Yogi") Berra was a superb baseball player and a unique verbalizer. What made many of his comments memorable is not that they were witty; they are memorable because they were so hilariously incongruous and self-contradictory, and Berra could not understand why people laughed at them.
　　During a drop in attendance at the nation's ballparks, Yogi ob-

served, "Well, if the public don't want to come out to the ballpark, nobody's going to stop them."

This is the earliest I've ever arrived late!
                    —YOGI BERRA, NOTORIOUS FOR HIS TARDINESS

"My, Mr. Berra, you look mighty cool tonight." "Thanks, ma'am. You don't look so hot yourself."   —ATTRIBUTED TO YOGI BERRA

Asked by a waitress, "Into how many slices would you like your pizza to be cut—four or eight?" Yogi screwed up his face: "Four. I'm not hungry enough to eat eight."
    Or: "*No* one goes to that restaurant anymore; it's too crowded."
    Or: "Why spend a lot for luggage? You only use it for traveling."
    Or:
Coach: "My watch has stopped. What time is it?"
Berra: "When?"

He sure did make a wrong mistake!   —YOGI BERRA

Offered a job as the manager of a baseball club, Berra was asked if he was not worried, since he had never done a minute of managing before. Berra did not bat an eye as he replied, "You'd be surprised by how much you can observe by watching."
    Perhaps his most profound observation was to a reporter who remarked how far behind Berra's team was, with only an inning left to play: "A game," intoned Berra, "isn't over till it's over."
    I most cherish the way Yogi acknowledged the honors heaped upon his many accomplishments at a "Night" in his honor. Yogi told the thousands of worshipful fans, through the microphone set up at home plate, "I just want to thank everyone who made this night necessary."
    Often kidded about his refulgent distortions of English, Yogi protested, "I didn't say everything I said!" That seems to me a reasonable explanation.
    After seeing *Doctor Zhivago*, the movie, Yogi shook his head mournfully, saying, "Man, it sure was *cold* in Russia in them days."
    He was an avid reader of comic books (possibly the only print outside of his contracts and the sports pages he read). He was often

teased about his addiction to comic books, to which Mr. Berra replied, "So if that's so silly for me to do, how come every time I put one of them comics down, some one of you guys dives to pick it up?!"

A bold radio interviewer once enlisted Yogi's interest in a pregame broadcast. "It's called free association, Yogi. I mention a name—and you just say the first thing that pops into your head! Okay?"

"Yep."

When they went on the air, the announcer explained the game to the radio audience. "I'll mention a name and Yogi is going to say the first thing that comes into his mind. That's all there is to it. . . . Ready, Yogi?"

"Sure."

"Okay. Here we go: Mickey Mantle!"

Yogi asked—"What about him?"

P.S.: This squat, short, scowling catcher was a fantastic hitter—especially of what are usually called "bad" pitches (too low, too high, beyond the outermost corners of the strike zone). An exasperated hurler, whom Yogi had murdered by hitting an assortment of supposedly bad balls, cried in frustration, "How the hell do you get that guy *out*?!"

The answer came from a veteran: "With a pistol!"

Bible

Say what you will about the Ten Commandments, you must always come back to the pleasant fact that there are only ten of them.

—H. L. MENCKEN

The Old Testament is responsible for more atheism, agnosticism, disbelief—call it what you will—than any book ever written; it has emptied more churches than all the counter attractions of cinema, motorbicycle, and golf course.

—ATTRIBUTED TO A. A. MILNE

Take away from Genesis the belief that Moses was the author, on which only the strange belief that it is the word of God has stood, and there remains nothing of Genesis but an anonymous book of stories, fables, traditionary or invented absurdities, or downright lies.

—THOMAS PAINE

The most serious doubt that has been thrown on the authenticity of the biblical miracles is the fact that most of the witnesses in regard to them were fishermen. —ARTHUR BINSTEAD

All religions issue Bibles against Satan, and say the most injurious things against him, but we never hear his side. —MARK TWAIN

The dogma of the infallibility of the Bible is no more self-evident than is that of the infallibility of the popes. —THOMAS HENRY HUXLEY

Scriptures, n. The sacred books of our holy religion, as distinguished from the false and profane writings on which all other faiths are based. —AMBROSE BIERCE

If you don't count some of Jehovah's injunctions, there are no humorists in the Bible. —MORDECAI RICHLER

Whenever we read the obscene stories, the voluptuous debaucheries, the cruel and tortuous executions, the unrelenting vindictiveness with which more than half the Bible is filled, it would be more consistent that we call it the word of a demon than the word of God. It is a history of wickedness that has served to corrupt and brutalize mankind. —THOMAS PAINE

The total absence of humor from the Bible is one of the most singular things in all literature. —ALFRED NORTH WHITEHEAD

Some of the most beautiful passages in the apostolic writings are quotations from pagan authors. —HENRY T. BUCKLE

Most people are bothered by those passages of Scripture they do not understand . . . the passages that bother *me* are those I do understand. —MARK TWAIN

Birth Control

I want to tell you a terrific story about oral contraception. I asked this girl to sleep with me and she said "No."   —WOODY ALLEN

What is the Jewish position on abortion? That a fetus is a fetus until it gets out of medical school.   —CHAIM PFLAUM

If men could get pregnant, abortion would be a sacrament.
     —FLORYNCE KENNEDY

The commonest objection to birth control is that it is against nature. (For some reason we are not allowed to say that celibacy is against nature.)   —BERTRAND RUSSELL

It is now quite lawful for a Catholic woman to avoid pregnancy by a resort to mathematics, though she is still forbidden to resort to physics or chemistry.   —H. L. MENCKEN

Boo-boos

(overheard and seen in print)

The most famous Italian composer was Libretto.   —A CHILD

In The News

He was sent to prison for strangling a woman without killing her.

The doctor felt the man's purse and said there was no hope.

The congressman . . . discussed the rise in prices and the high cost of living with several women.

Although he [Babe Herman] isn't a very good fielder, he isn't a very good hitter, either.   —RING LARDNER

A lot of people my age are dead at the present time.

They say you can't do it, but sometimes that doesn't always work.

—CASEY STENGEL

Broadcast News

"Bang! Boom! Pow!" he hissed.

The Fire Department will blow the siren fifteen minutes before the start of each fire.

He and his wife have left for Florida. We all hope they will like their trip and stay in Miami.

No one heard him laugh like that since his wife died.

The driver of the car swerved to avoid missing the woman's husband.

He's a real worker. Why, he gets up at six o'clock in the morning no matter what time it is.   —THANKS TO HYMAN KAPLAN

People in search of solitude are flocking here from the four corners of the world.   —CANADIAN HOTEL PROSPECTUS

This being Easter Sunday, we will ask Mrs. Johnson to come forward and lay an egg on the altar.   —ANONYMOUS

In The News

Mrs. and Mr. Seligman have lied most of their married life in Hartford.

The Red Cross paid for emergency care and later found a free bed for him in an institution specializing in the treatment of artcritics.

The area in which Miss [Jane] Russell was injured is famed for its beauty.

When the baby is done drinking, it must be unscrewed and laid in a cool place under a tap. If the baby does not thrive on fresh milk it should be boiled.

If we would only send young American tenors to stud abroad, they would return immensely improved.

The report was signed by five faulty members of the university.

We note with regret that Mr. Jordan is recovering after his serious accident.

Overcome by gas while taking a bath, she owes her life to the watchfulness of the janitor.

Texas is the former birthplace of President Eisenhower.

The president, who has been sick for several days, is now in bed with a coed.

His friends could give no reason why he should have committed suicide. He is single.

Mr. and Mrs. Walter F. Hill announced the coming marriage of their daughter Helene. No mate has been selected for the wedding.

In a firm voice, the bride then repeated, ". . . to love and to cherish, in sickness and in health, for poorer or richer, until debts do us part."

A seven-pound baby boy arrived last night to frighten the lives of Mr. and Mrs. Sherman Caswell.

The jury's verdict showed they were of one mind: temporarily insane.

The three-day [club] outing is climaxed by a huge picnic, which practically doubles the town population each year.

Don't fail to miss tomorrow's doubleheader.   —ANNOUNCER

In exactly thirty seconds, it will be approximately one-fifteen.
—RADIO WEATHERMAN

Beethoven had ten children; he practiced on a spinster in his attic.
—A CHILD

If his father was alive today he would be turning over in his grave.
—ANONYMOUS

Church Bulletins

The ladies of the church have cast off clothing of every kind, and they may be seen in the basement on Friday afternoon.

Thursday, at 5:00 P.M., there will be a meeting of the Little Mothers' Club. All those wishing to become little mothers, please meet the pastor in his study.

Correction: The sermon at the Presbyterian Church this coming Sunday will be *There Are No Sects in Heaven*. The subject was incorrectly printed in yesterday's edition as *There Is No Sex in Heaven*.

Radium was discovered by Madman Curry.   —A CHILD

Do you wake up feeling tired and lustless?
—RADIO ANNOUNCER FOR COMMERCIAL

It is with real regret that we learn of Mr. Wayne's recovery from an automobile accident.   —NEWS ACCOUNT

The first thing the doctor has to do when a baby is born is cut the biblical cord.   —TV PANELIST

The weather forecast: rain and slow, followed by sneet.
—RADIO REPORT

Popular authors can win the Pullet Surprise.   —A CHILD

More Church Bulletins

Miss Marcia Devin sang "I Will Not Pass This Way Again," giving obvious pleasure to the entire congregation.

The Tuesday Night Ladies' Club had a nice time at the church after their potluck supper. For the first time in several months all the members were pregnant.

Oh, you three certainly are a pair—if there ever was one!

—ANONYMOUS

He wants to be cremated, because he doesn't believe in death.

—ANONYMOUS

And at Fonseca's Pharmacy you can be sure of having your prescriptions filled with scare and kill.   —RADIO COMMERCIAL

You have been listening to a message by our honorable minister of wealth and hellfire.   —RADIO ANNOUNCER, CANADA

A girl of seventeen is much more of a woman than a boy who is seventeen.   —TV TALK SHOW

Why, some parts of the Grand Canyon are a mile deep—and two miles high.   —ANONYMOUS

The bride was wearing a gorgeous old lace gown that fell to the floor as she came down the aisle.

—SOCIETY PAGE OF MIDWESTERN NEWSPAPER

I challenge you to give me a frank, affirmative answer: yes or no!

—SAMUEL GOLDWYN

Skewered Titles

The Timing of the Screw   *Gray's Allergy*
Romeo in Juliet   *Catch Her in the Rye*
McBeth   *The Petrified Forehead*
The Merchant of Venus   *Ibsen's Goats*
Thoreau's Warden   *Robin's Son, Caruso*

Books

Be careful about reading health books. You may die of a misprint.
—MARK TWAIN

The multitude of books is making us ignorant.   —VOLTAIRE

Books are the blessed chloroform of the mind.
—ROBERT W. CHAMBERS

From the moment I picked your book up until the moment I put it down I could not stop laughing. Someday I hope to read it.
—GROUCHO MARX (LETTER TO LEO ROSTEN)

A best seller is a book which somehow sold well simply because it was selling well.   —DANIEL J. BOORSTIN

There is no such thing as a moral or an immoral book. Books are well written or badly written.   —OSCAR WILDE

Books are fatal; they are the curse of the human race. Nine tenths of existing books are nonsense, and the clever books are the refutation of that nonsense.   —BENJAMIN DISRAELI

The man who doesn't read good books has no advantage over the man who can't read them.   —MARK TWAIN

He has left off reading altogether, to the great improvement of his originality.   —CHARLES LAMB

Never read a book that is not a year old.
—RALPH WALDO EMERSON

The last thing one discovers in writing a book is what to put first.
—BLAISE PASCAL

For people who like that kind of a book, that is the kind of a book they will like.   —ABRAHAM LINCOLN

Where books are burnt, humans will be burnt in the end.
                                              —HEINRICH HEINE

Education has produced a vast population able to read but unable to distinguish what is worth reading.
                              —GEORGE MACAULAY TREVELYAN

If you drop gold and books, pick up the books first, then the gold.
                                              —JEWISH SAYING

There are books of which the backs and covers are by far the best parts.   —CHARLES DICKENS

You must not refuse to lend a book even to an enemy, for the cause of learning will suffer.
                  —A PIOUS JEW, QUOTED BY JUDAH OF REGENSBURG

A book is a mirror: If an ass peers into it, you can't expect an apostle to look out.   —GEORG CHRISTOPH LICHTENBERG

There is more treasure in books than in all the pirates' loot on Treasure Island. . . . And best of all, you can enjoy these riches every day of your life.   —WALT DISNEY

Whenever the shelves in the Library of Heaven are entirely full, and a new, worthy book appeared, all the books in the celestial collection pressed themselves closer together, and made room.
                                              —JEWISH LEGEND

Those who consider a thing proved simply because it is in print are fools.   —MAIMONIDES

Those who refuse to lend their books . . . shall be fined.
              —MINUTES, LATVIAN JEWISH COMMUNITY COUNCIL, 1736

Some scholars are like donkeys: They only carry a lot of books.
—BAHYA IBN PAQUDA

There is a great deal of difference between the eager man who wants
to read a book and the tired man who wants a book to read.
—G. K. CHESTERTON

Bores/Boredom

There is nothing so pathetic as a bore who claims attention—and gets
it.   —RIVKA KLOTCH

Bore: A person who talks when you wish him to listen.
—AMBROSE BIERCE

Every hero becomes a bore at last.   —RALPH WALDO EMERSON

The secret of being a bore is to tell everything.   —VOLTAIRE

*When a bore leaves the room, you feel as if
someone fascinating just came in.*
—JEWISH SAYING

*   *   *

Bore: One who has the power of speech but not the capacity for conversation.   —ATTRIBUTED TO BENJAMIN DISRAELI

We often forgive those who bore us, but we cannot forgive those
whom we bore.   —FRANÇOIS DE LA ROCHEFOUCAULD

Punctuality is the virtue of the bored.
            —EVELYN WAUGH

*   *   *

Dear World: I am leaving because I am bored.
            —GEORGE SANDERS (PART OF HIS SUICIDE NOTE)

Slums may well be breeding grounds of crime, but middle-class sub-
urbs are incubators of apathy and delirium.   —CYRIL CONNOLLY

The merely well-informed man is the most useless bore on God's earth.
            —ALFRED NORTH WHITEHEAD

Brains

When brains are needed, muscles won't help.   —ANONYMOUS

The human mind is our fundamental resource. —JOHN F. KENNEDY

Craft: A fool's substitute for brains.   —AMBROSE BIERCE

God looks at a man's heart before He looks at a man's brains.
            —JEWISH SAYING

I have finally come to the conclusion that a good, reliable set of bowels
is worth more to a man than any quantity of brains.
            —JOSH BILLINGS

My brain is my second favorite organ.   —WOODY ALLEN

The chief function of the body is to carry the brain around.
            —THOMAS ALVA EDISON

Bureaucracy

We have pruned and pruned our bureaucracy, and after four years we have taken a census of the government staff, and we have an increase of twelve thousand. —V. I. LENIN

The nearest approach to immortality on earth is a government bureau. —JAMES F. BYRNES

Business

The playthings of our elders are called business. —ST. AUGUSTINE

Don't steal. Thou'lt never thus compete successfully in business. Cheat. —AMBROSE BIERCE

If you laugh when you borrow, you'll cry when you pay.

No man is impatient with his creditors. —TALMUD

The world does not owe men a living, but business, if it is to fulfill its ideal, owes men an opportunity to earn a living. —OWEN D. YOUNG

People of the same trade seldom meet together, even for merriment and diversion, but the conversation ends in a conspiracy against the public, or in some contrivance to raise prices. —ADAM SMITH

C

Capitalism

Not every problem someone has with his girlfriend is necessarily due to the capitalist mode of production. —HERBERT MARCUSE

Capitalism replaced not Arcadia, but indescribable poverty, illiteracy, and economic doom.

It was under "heartless capitalism" that the earnings of the masses soared; and as men became *less* poor, their discontents grew louder, and their social protest and political power boomed into a force such as had not existed within any political system before.

—LEO ROSTEN

A socialist form of society will inevitably emerge from an equally inevitable decomposition of capitalist society. . . . Capitalism is being killed by its achievements. —JOSEPH A. SCHUMPETER

Capitalism did not arise because capitalists stole the land . . . but because it was more efficient than feudalism. It will perish because it is not merely less efficient than socialism, but actually self-destructive.

—J.B.S. HALDANE

The very claims and ambitions of the working class were and are the result of the enormous improvement of their position, which capitalism brought about.   —F. A. HAYEK

No one who buys bread knows whether the wheat from which it is made was grown by a Communist or a Republican . . . or, for that matter, by a Negro or a white. This illustrates how an impersonal market separates economic activities from political views and protects men from being discriminated against for reasons that are irrelevant to their productivity.   —MILTON FRIEDMAN

Under capitalism man exploits man; under socialism, the reverse is true.   —POLISH PROVERB

It is not from the benevolence of the butcher, the brewer, or the baker that we expect our dinner, but from their regard to their own interest.
                                                —ADAM SMITH

The capitalist achievement does not typically consist in providing more silk stockings for queens but in bringing them within the reach of factory girls, in return for steadily decreasing amounts of effort.
                                                —PETER BAUER

Celebrity

A celebrity is a person who works hard all his life to become well known, then wears dark glasses to avoid being recognized.
                                                —FRED ALLEN

A sign of celebrity is that his name is often worth more than his services.   —DANIEL J. BOORSTIN

Character/Characterizations

It is his life work to announce the obvious in terms of the scandalous.
—H. L. MENCKEN, OF A GOSSIP COLUMNIST

He had the sort of face that, once seen, is never remembered.
—OSCAR WILDE

When some English moralists write about the importance of having character, they appear to mean only the importance of having a dull character.   —G. K. CHESTERTON

The measure of a man's real character is what he would do if he knew he would never be found out.   —THOMAS BABINGTON MACAULAY

Whistler, with all his faults, was never guilty of writing a line of poetry.   —OSCAR WILDE

He is so mean, he won't let his little baby have more than one measle at a time.   —EUGENE FIELD

He only lies twice a year: in summer and in winter.
—SHOLEM ALEICHEM

You may rid your bookshelves of [Luther], but not men's minds.
—ERASMUS

Character is much easier kept than recovered.   —THOMAS PAINE

He is the kind of man who first prepares the bandage, then inflicts the wound.   —TALMUD

He is remarkably well, considering that he has been remarkably well for so many years.   —SYDNEY SMITH

She was a town-and-country soprano of the kind often used for augmenting the grief at a funeral.   —GEORGE ADE

He hasn't a single redeeming vice.   —OSCAR WILDE

Character is what you are in the dark.   —DWIGHT L. MOODY

The general is suffering from mental saddle sores.
                    —HAROLD ICKES (ON GENERAL HUGH S. JOHNSON)

Daniel Webster struck me much like a steam engine in trousers.
                    —SYDNEY SMITH

He has all the courage and resolution of a Fig Newton.
                    —LEO ROSTEN

He discloses the workings of a mind to which incoherence lends an illusion of profundity.   —T. DE VERE WHITE

He wasn't exactly hostile to facts; he was apathetic about them.
                    —WOLCOTT GIBBS

She has all the delicacy, elegance, and charm of barbed wire.
                    —LEO ROSTEN

She was always crying; in fact, she wept so much she made everybody's corns ache.   —ARTHUR ("BUGS") BAER

If he had twice as much brains, he'd be a half-wit.   —LEO ROSTEN

He lacked only a few vices to be perfect.
                    —MARQUISE DE SEVIGNE

*   *   *

I heard him speak disrespectfully of the equator.   —SYDNEY SMITH

While he was not as dumb as an ox, he was not any smarter either.
—JAMES THURBER

Too often the strong, silent man is silent only because he does not know what to say, and is reputed strong only because he has remained silent.   —WINSTON CHURCHILL

He objected to ideas only when others had them.
—A. J. P. TAYLOR (ON ERNEST BEVIN)

Characters (Famous)

Metternich comes close to being a statesman: he lies very well.
—NAPOLEON BONAPARTE

He has all of the virtues I dislike and none of the vices I admire.
—WINSTON CHURCHILL (ON STAFFORD CRIPPS)

Jerry's the only man I ever knew who can't walk and chew gum at the same time.   —LYNDON B. JOHNSON (ON GERALD FORD)

We now come to King Henry the Eighth, whom it has been too much the fashion to call "Bluff King Hal" and "Burly King Harry" and other fine names, but whom I shall take the liberty to call plainly one of the most detestable villains that ever drew breath.
—CHARLES DICKENS

Francis I was a monumental pygmy.   —NAPOLEON BONAPARTE

Lenin had many sins, but the gravest was a supreme contempt for the human race. Like Marx, he possessed an overwhelming contempt for the peasants.   —ROBERT PAYNE

Moses with his law is most terrible; there never was any equal to him in perplexing, affrighting, tyrannizing, threatening, preaching, and thundering.　　　　　　　　　　　　　　　　　—MARTIN LUTHER

One could not even dignify him with the name of stuffed shirt. He was simply a hole in the air.
　　　　　　　　　—GEORGE ORWELL (ON STANLEY BALDWIN)

Bringing Plato to the test of reason, take from him his sophisms, futilities, and incomprehensibilities, and what remains? His foggy mind is forever presenting the semblances of objects which, half seen through a mist, can be defined neither in form nor dimension.
　　　　　　　　　　　　　　　　　—THOMAS JEFFERSON

Henry James writes fiction as if it were a painful duty.
　　　　　　　　　　　　　　　　　　—OSCAR WILDE

Henry James's prose sounds as if he was being translated from the German.　　　　　　　　　　　　　　　　—LEO ROSTEN

Beneath the sophistication of his appearance and manner, he has all the unplumbable stupidities and unawareness of his class.
　　　　　　　　　—ANEURIN BEVAN (ON ANTHONY EDEN)

A day away from Tallulah [Bankhead] is like a month in the country.
　　　　　　　　　　　　　　　　　—HOWARD DIETZ

He speaks to me as if I were a public meeting.
　　　　　　　　　—QUEEN VICTORIA (ON GLADSTONE)

Fate tried to conceal him by naming him Smith.
　　　　　　—OLIVER WENDELL HOLMES (ON ADAM SMITH)

He is the greatest living master of falling without hurting himself.
　　　　—WINSTON CHURCHILL (ON RAMSAY MACDONALD)

Like Odysseus, he looked wiser when seated.
—JOHN MAYNARD KEYNES (ON WOODROW WILSON)

[Coolidge] is the first president to discover that what the American people want is to be left alone.   —WILL ROGERS

McKinley shows all the backbone of a chocolate eclair.
—THEODORE ROOSEVELT

Frank Harris is invited to all the great houses in England—once.
—OSCAR WILDE

To be a moral thief, an unblushing liar, a supreme dictator, and a cruel, self-satisfied monster, and attain, in the minds of millions, the status of a deity, is not only remarkable but a dismal reflection on the human race. She had much in common with Hitler, only no mustache.
—NOËL COWARD (ON MARY BAKER EDDY)

Bertie [Edward VII] seemed to display a deep-seated repugnance to every form of mental exertion.   —LYTTON STRACHEY

Knute Rockne wanted nothing but "bad losers." He thought good losers get into the habit of losing.   —GEORGE E. ALLEN

Bernard Shaw has discovered himself, and gave ungrudgingly of his discovery to the world.   —H. H. MUNRO ("SAKI")

It was with a sense of awe that [the Germans] turned upon Russia the most grisly of all weapons. They transported Lenin in a sealed truck, like a plague bacillus, from Switzerland into Russia.
—WINSTON CHURCHILL

Erasmus laid the egg that Luther hatched.   —ANONYMOUS

Harding was not a bad man. He was just a slob.
—ALICE ROOSEVELT LONGWORTH

Ronald Reagan has held the two most demeaning jobs in the country: president of the United States and radio broadcaster for the Chicago Cubs. —GEORGE F. WILL

Calvin Coolidge—the greatest man who ever came out of Plymouth Corner, Vermont. —CLARENCE DARROW

If my theory of relativity is proven successful, Germany will claim me as a German and France will declare that I am a citizen of the world. Should my theory prove untrue, France will say that I am a German and Germany will declare that I am a Jew. —ALBERT EINSTEIN

He is a sheep in sheep's clothing.
—WINSTON CHURCHILL (ON CLEMENT ATTLEE)

No woman has so comforted the distressed or distressed the comfortable. —CLARE BOOTHE LUCE (ON ELEANOR ROOSEVELT)

[Woodrow] Wilson . . . was a perpendicular lecturer, his talking nose and his oscillating Adam's apple moving up and down with speech. He gestured as if operating the handle of a spray pump.
—ALFRED P. DENNIS

Though I yield to no one in my admiration for Mr. Coolidge, I do wish he did not look as if he had been weaned on a pickle.
—ALICE ROOSEVELT LONGWORTH

He could not see a belt without hitting below it.
—MARGOT ASQUITH
(ON DAVID LLOYD GEORGE)

✳   ✳   ✳

Browning used poetry as a medium for writing in prose.

—Oscar Wilde

He did not care in which direction the car was traveling, so long as he remained in the driver's seat.

—Lord Beaverbrook (on David Lloyd George)

Bernard Shaw is an excellent man; he has not an enemy in the world, and none of his friends like him. —Oscar Wilde

Charity

Charity begins at home, but should not end there.   —Anonymous

He belongs to so many benevolent societies that he is destitute.

—Edgar Watson ("Ed") Howe

The longest road in the world is the one that leads from your pocket.

—Anonymous

If charity cost nothing, the world would be full of philanthropists.

—Jewish saying

To give little with a smile is better than to give much with a frown.

—Anonymous

Chastity

Chastity is a virtue in some, but in many almost a vice.

—Friedrich Wilhelm Nietzsche

Dear Lord: Give me chastity and self-restraint, but not yet.

—St. Augustine

Chastity is an insult to the Creator and an abomination to man and beast. —NORMAN DOUGLAS

Chastity: the most unnatural of the sexual perversions.
—ALDOUS HUXLEY

Chastity is no more a virtue than malnutrition.
—ALEX COMFORT

An untempted woman cannot boast of her chastity. —MONTAIGNE

The only really indecent people are the chaste. —J. K. HUYSMANS

✍ G. K. Chesterton ✍

Probably the wittiest and most versatile intellectual in England, a superb analyst, a peerless polemicist, a fearless debater, a perfectly charming essayist, an original and irresistible writer of mystery/detective stories, creator of the altogether original Father Brown, an ardent Catholic, a dazzling logician, an amusing versifier, a crusading moralist—it may be said of Gilbert Keith Chesterton, that that immense, behemothian (he surely weighed more than three hundred pounds) man of letters who toyed with a pince-nez on a long cord, that he was blessed with one of the most keen and fascinating minds of Victorian England, a mind of maximum vigor, audacity, impudence, and mockery.

You will find at least forty of his witticisms in this commonplace book. Here are more I have collected down the decades and think I simply cannot allow to remain unused:

The human race, to which many of my readers belong . . .
✍

Angels can fly because they take themselves lightly.

✍

Men who really believe in themselves are all in lunatic asylums.

✍

The Christian idea has not been tried and found wanting. It has been found difficult—and left untried.

✍

There are no uninteresting subjects; there are only uninterested people.

✍

Bigotry is the anger of people who have no opinions.

✍

No animal ever invented anything as bad as drunkenness, or as good as drink.

Perhaps Chesterton's most original insight was this: "I suspect that Mr. Shaw is the only man on earth who has never written any poetry." That idea resonates in my mind with ever-increasing aptness.

Should you yearn for an intoxicating few hours of reading, I recommend to you such collections of Chesterton's writings as *Orthodoxy*, *Heretics*, his *Autobiography*, *The Man Who Was Thursday*, *What's Wrong with the World*—and almost any book of his essays you can lay your hands on. He will make your brain cells frolic; he will tickle your ribs. He is the undisputed prince of paradox in English letters.

Children

Children begin by loving their parents. After a time they judge them. Rarely, if ever, do they forgive them.   —OSCAR WILDE

It is better that a child should cry than its parents.
                                        —MY MOTHER

Children should neither be seen nor heard from—ever.
—ATTRIBUTED TO W. C. FIELDS

Familiarity breeds contempt—and children.   —MARK TWAIN

A child is a curly, dimpled lunatic.
—RALPH WALDO EMERSON

The world of the child is much closer to the cosmic model of Einstein than the cosmic model of Einstein is to the world of adults.
—LEO ROSTEN

Reprimand your child regularly every day. You may not know why, but the kid does.   —HARRY HERSHFIELD

Little children don't let you sleep; big children won't let you live.
—JEWISH FOLK SAYING

The first half of our life is ruined by our parents and the second half by our children.   —CLARENCE DARROW

The parent who could see his boy as he really is would shake his head and say, "Willie is no good; I'll sell him."   —STEPHEN LEACOCK

You can almost be certain that the man who commits violent crimes has been treated violently as a child.   —KARL MENNINGER

If you strike a child, take care that you strike it in anger, even at the risk of maiming it for life. A blow in cold blood neither can nor should be forgotten.   —GEORGE BERNARD SHAW

Man is lucky that during childhood he cannot tell good from evil, for if he had mature powers of perception he would die of grief.
—BAHYA IBN PAQUDA

Children today are tyrants. They contradict their parents, gobble their food, and tyrannize their teachers.   —SOCRATES

Children . . . have to learn how to learn. This has to be recognized as a new problem which is only partly solved.
—MARGARET MEAD

Never lend your car to anyone to whom you have given birth.
—ERMA BOMBECK

A soiled baby, with a neglected nose, cannot be conscientiously regarded as a thing of beauty.   —MARK TWAIN

One father can support ten children, but ten children don't seem to be able to support one father.   —JEWISH SAYING

In every real man a child is hidden that wants to play.
—FRIEDRICH WILHELM NIETZSCHE

No two children are ever born into the same family. —LEO ROSTEN

A Sunday school is a prison in which children do penance for the evil conscience of their parents.   —H. L. MENCKEN

Children have more need of models than of critics.
—JOSEPH JOUBERT

A sense of humor is based on seeing and accepting human nature as stumbling, pretentious, and forever bedeviled. When I hear boys and girls call their parents "hypocrites" (a favorite word), I know I am looking at humorless—and therefore dangerous—children.
—DONALD BARR

The rich have heirs, not children.   —JEWISH SAYING

Childhood: That happy period when nightmares occur only during sleep. —CHANGING TIMES

Children without a childhood are tragic.
—MENDELE MOCHER SEFORIM

Don't threaten a child; either punish or forgive him.   —TALMUD

My eleven-year-old daughter mopes around the house all day waiting for her breasts to grow.   —BILL COSBY

Even a bad match can beget good children.   —JEWISH SAYING

When a father helps a son, both laugh; when a son must help his father, both cry.   —JEWISH SAYING

Home is the place where, when you have to go there, they have to take you in.   —ROBERT FROST

I take my children everywhere, but they always find their way back home.   —ROBERT ORBEN

Somewhere on this globe, every ten seconds, there is a woman giving birth to a child. She must be found and stopped.   —SAM LEVENSON

All children are essentially criminal.   —DENIS DIDEROT

If you're a child at twenty, you're a jackass at twenty-one.
—SHLOMO ZIPKIN

We are all geniuses up to the age of ten.   —ALDOUS HUXLEY

I see no objection in principle to censorship of the mass entertainment of the young.   —WALTER LIPPMANN

A boy is, of all wild beasts, the most difficult to manage.   —PLATO

The games of children are not sports, but should be regarded as their most serious actions.   —MONTAIGNE

The thing that impresses me most about America is the way parents obey their children.   —THE DUKE OF WINDSOR

I never met a kid I liked.   —W. C. FIELDS

Every child tends to exaggerate its own importance.   —TALMUD

What is more enchanting than the voices of young people, when you can't hear what they say?   —LOGAN PEARSALL SMITH

Jerusalem was destroyed because the children did not attend school.
                                —TALMUD

The child never learns in afterlife what it does in its first five years. The education of the child begins with conception.
                        —MOHANDAS GANDHI

The proper time to influence the character of a child is about a hundred years before he is born.   —DEAN INGE

Don't take up a man's time talking about the smartness of your children; he wants to talk to you about the smartness of his children.
                    —EDGAR WATSON ("ED") HOWE

Give me the children until they are seven and anyone may have them afterward.   —ST. FRANCIS XAVIER

I hate babies. They're so human.   —H. H. MUNRO ("SAKI")

Christianity

The study of theology, as it stands in Christian churches, is the study of nothing; it is founded on nothing; it rests on no principles; it proceeds by no authorities; it has no data; it can demonstrate nothing; and it admits to no conclusion.   —THOMAS PAINE

Archbishop: A Christian ecclesiastic of a rank superior to that attained by Christ.   —H. L. MENCKEN

Christianity has done love a great service by making it a sin.
—ANATOLE FRANCE

The chief contribution of Protestantism to human thought is its massive proof that God is a bore.   —H. L. MENCKEN

The last Christian died on the cross.
—FRIEDRICH WILHELM NIETZSCHE

There has never been a kingdom given to so many civil wars as that of Christ.   —MONTESQUIEU

It can do truth no service to blink the fact . . . that a large portion of the noblest and most valuable teaching has been the work, not only of men who did not know, but of men who knew and rejected, the Christian faith.   —JOHN STUART MILL

Every Stoic was a Stoic; but in Christendom, where is the Christian?
RALPH WALDO EMERSON

Science has done more for the development of Western civilization in one hundred years than Christianity did in eighteen hundred years.
—JOHN BURROUGHS

Christianity must be divine, since it has lasted seventeen hundred years despite the fact that it's full of villainy and nonsense.
—VOLTAIRE

I consider Christian theology to be one of the great disasters of the human race. . . . It would be impossible to imagine anything more un-Christlike than theology. Christ probably couldn't have understood it.
—ALFRED NORTH WHITEHEAD

Christian theology is not only opposed to the scientific spirit; it is opposed to every other form of rational thinking. —H. L. MENCKEN

I call Christianity the one great curse, the one enormous and innermost perversion . . . the one immortal blemish of mankind.
—FRIEDRICH WILHELM NIETZSCHE

For two thousand years Christianity has been telling us: Life is death, death is life. It is high time to consult the dictionary.
—RÉMY DE GOURMONT

There are many people who think that Sunday is a sponge to wipe out all the sins of the week.   —HENRY WARD BEECHER

The age of ignorance commenced with the Christian system.
—THOMAS PAINE

Christmas

Christmas persecutes the lonely, the frayed, and the rejected.
—JIMMY CANNON

Next to a circus there ain't nothing that packs up and tears out of town any quicker than the Christmas spirit.
—FRANK McKINNEY ("KIN") HUBBARD

Christmas is forced on a reluctant and disgusted nation by the shop-keepers and the press; on its own merits it would wither and shrivel in the fiery breath of universal hatred; and anyone who looked back to it would be turned into a pillar of greasy sausages.
—GEORGE BERNARD SHAW

Church

Depressions may bring people closer to the church, but so do funerals.
—CLARENCE DARROW

The observances of the church concerning feasts and fasts are tolerably well kept, since the rich keep the feasts and the poor the fasts.
—SYDNEY SMITH

I like convents, but I wish they wouldn't admit any women under the age of fifty. —NAPOLEON BONAPARTE

Cities

The government of cities is the one conspicuous failure of the United States. —JAMES BRYCE

The city is a human zoo, not a concrete jungle. —DESMOND MORRIS

A great city, a great solitude. —OLD TESTAMENT

Azusa is a town where a drugstore sells straw hats for horses.
—GROUCHO MARX

Well-bred Bostonians today deprecate the dourness, grimness, and bigotry of their forefathers—but they are intensely proud of them.
—DIXON WECHTER

Boston is a moral and intellectual nursery always busy applying first principles to trifles. —GEORGE SANTAYANA

New York was pandemonium with a big grin on. —TOM WOLFE

London! It has the sound of thunder. —V. S. PRITCHETT

Chicago: Miles and miles of beautiful lakefront concealing acres and acres of dreadful neighborhoods.   —LEO ROSTEN

Civil Rights

Only the spirit that is not too sure it is right speaks for the values of civility and reason.   —ARCHIBALD COX

The right to be let alone is the most comprehensive of rights and the right most valued in civilized man.   —LOUIS D. BRANDEIS

My generation has no *right* to bargain away the civil rights we inherited. We have no *right* to bribe bullies, or appease extremists, or surrender to the infantile and the paranoid. We have no *right* to be cowards.   —LEO ROSTEN

A man will fight harder for his interests than his rights.
          —NAPOLEON BONAPARTE

Civilization

Men become civilized, not in proportion to their willingness to believe, but in proportion to their readiness to doubt.   —H. L. MENCKEN

The first human who hurled an insult instead of a stone was the founder of civilization.   —ATTRIBUTED TO SIGMUND FREUD

All civilizations have been created and directed by small intellectual aristocracies, and never by people in the mass. The power of crowds is only to destroy.   —GUSTAVE LEBON

The civilized world represents the victory of persuasion over force.
          —PLATO

Men, enriched by your sweat and misery, made you superstitious not that you might fear God, but that you might fear them. —VOLTAIRE

Civilization is only the slow process of learning to be kind.
—LEO ROSTEN

Mohandas Gandhi's devastating reply to an Englishman who asked him for his opinion of Western civilization: "I would be all in favor of it."

Civilized men arrived in the Pacific armed with alcohol, syphilis, trousers, and the Bible. —HAVELOCK ELLIS

Clerics

Clergyman: A ticket speculator outside the gates of heaven.
—H. L. MENCKEN

It was hard for Satan alone to mislead the whole world, so he appointed rabbis in different localities. —NACHMAN OF BRATSLAV

As the French say, there are three sexes—men, women, and clergymen. —SYDNEY SMITH

Our rabbi is so poor that if he didn't fast every Monday and Thursday, he'd starve to death. —JEWISH SAYING

A learned bastard stands higher than an ignorant high priest.
—MIDRASH

Clergyman: An interpreter of religion who does not believe that the Bible means what it says; he is always convinced that it says what he means. —GEORGE BERNARD SHAW

I do not see by what right we send a priest to the flames who prefers the wife to the concubine. —ERASMUS

A rabbi whose congregation doesn't want to run him out of town is not a rabbi; and a rabbi whose congregation does run him out of town is not a man. —JEWISH FOLK SAYING

Communication

He can compress the most words into the smallest idea of any man I ever met. —ABRAHAM LINCOLN

A single death is a tragedy. A million deaths is a statistic. —JOSEPH STALIN

Extremists think that "communication" means agreeing with them. —LEO ROSTEN

Communists

The state is a special cudgel, nothing more. —V. I. LENIN

[Russia] seemed to me one vast prison in which the jailers were cruel bigots. When I found my friends applauding these men as liberators and regarding the regime they were creating as a paradise, I wondered . . . whether it was my friends or I who were mad. . . . —BERTRAND RUSSELL

The dictatorship of the proletariat is nothing else than power based upon force and limited by nothing—by no law and absolutely no rule! —V. I. LENIN

You cannot put theory into your soup or Marxism into your clothes. If, after forty years of communism, a person cannot have a glass of milk or a pair of shoes, he will not believe that communism is a good thing, no matter what you tell him.   —NIKITA KHRUSHCHEV

If we do not apply terror and immediate executions, we will get nowhere. It is better that a hundred innocent are killed than that one guilty person escapes.   —V. I. LENIN

[Lenin] was closer to the medieval autocrats than to Marx. . . .
          —ROBERT PAYNE

The Cuban movement is not a Communist movement. Its members are Roman Catholics, mostly.   —FIDEL CASTRO

A proletarian dictatorship is never proletarian.
          —WILL AND ARIEL DURANT

Compassion

The wretched have no compassion.   —SAMUEL JOHNSON

Confessions

I don't deserve this award, but I have arthritis, and I don't deserve that, either.   —JACK BENNY

I never gave them hell. I just tell the truth and they think it's hell.
          —HARRY S TRUMAN

I don't care what is written about me so long as it isn't true.
          —DOROTHY PARKER/KATHARINE HEPBURN/ET AL.

I am a deeply superficial person.   —ANDY WARHOL

I'd rather have two girls of seventeen than one of thirty-four.
                                                —FRED ALLEN

I never refuse. I never contradict. I sometimes forget.
                                            —BENJAMIN DISRAELI

Boys, I may not know much, but I know chicken shit from chicken
salad.   —LYNDON B. JOHNSON

For my part I would as soon be descended from [a] baboon . . . as
from a savage who delights to torture his enemies . . . treats his wives
like slaves . . . and is haunted by the grossest superstitions.
                                            —CHARLES DARWIN

I despise the pleasure of pleasing people whom I despise.
                                —LADY MARY WORTLEY MONTAGU

The reason I beat the Austrians is that they did not know the value
of five minutes.   —NAPOLEON BONAPARTE

I'm opposed to millionaires, but it would be dangerous to offer me the
position.   —MARK TWAIN

You have but two subjects, yourself and me. I am sick of both.
                        —SAMUEL JOHNSON (TO JAMES BOSWELL)

All the things I really like to do are either immoral, illegal, or fatten-
ing.   —ALEXANDER WOOLLCOTT

It used to be a good hotel, but that proves nothing—I used to be a
good boy.   —MARK TWAIN

I have just enough white in me to make my honesty questionable.   —WILL ROGERS (HE WAS PART NATIVE AMERICAN)

It is inaccurate to say I hate everything. I am strongly in favor of common sense, common honesty, and common decency. This makes me ineligible for any public office.   —H. L. MENCKEN

Success didn't spoil me; I've always been insufferable.
   —FRAN LEBOWITZ

My only policy is to profess evil and do good.
   —GEORGE BERNARD SHAW

I have always been dissatisfied with my gifts.   —SIGMUND FREUD

I hate and detest that animal called man.   —JONATHAN SWIFT

One should forgive one's enemies, but not before they are hanged.
   —HEINRICH HEINE

It took me fifteen years to discover I had no talent for writing, but I couldn't give it up because by that time I was too famous.
   —ROBERT BENCHLEY

I came to Carthage, where an unholy cauldron seethed and bubbled all around me. I was not in love, but I was in love with love.
   —ST. AUGUSTINE

I have suffered from being misunderstood, but I would have suffered a hell of a lot more if I had been understood. —CLARENCE DARROW

Everybody said I was the worst Chancellor of the Exchequer that ever was. And I am inclined to agree with them.
   —WINSTON CHURCHILL

I like the job I have now, but, if I had my life to live over again, I'd like to have ended up as a sportswriter.

                                                 —RICHARD NIXON

My movements to the chair of Government will be accompanied by feelings not unlike those of a culprit who is going to the place of his execution.   —GEORGE WASHINGTON

One good thing about being president. Nobody can tell you when to sit down.   —DWIGHT D. EISENHOWER

I thoroughly disapprove of duels. If a man should challenge me, I would take him kindly and forgivingly by the hand and lead him to a quiet place and kill him.   —MARK TWAIN

I like the sayers of No better than the sayers of Yes.

                                   —RALPH WALDO EMERSON

When choosing between two evils, I always like to take the one I've never tried before.   —MAE WEST

My one regret in life is that I'm not someone else. —WOODY ALLEN

I saved a girl from being attacked last night. I controlled myself.

                                   —RODNEY DANGERFIELD

I never would have shot her if I'd known I'd have to go through so much red tape.   —FRANK MCKINNEY ("KIN") HUBBARD

It usually takes me more than three weeks to prepare a good impromptu speech.   —MARK TWAIN

Einstein often has said to me, "I am more a philosopher than a physicist."   —LEOPOLD INFELD

I hate mankind, for I think myself one of the best of them, and I know how bad I am.   —SAMUEL JOHNSON

I have never been hurt by anything I didn't say.
                                            —CALVIN COOLIDGE

I don't drink; I don't like it—it makes me feel good.
                                            —OSCAR LEVANT

When I feel like exercising I just lie down until the feeling goes away.
                                            —ROBERT M. HUTCHINS

I've always been interested in people, but I've never liked them.
                                            —W. SOMERSET MAUGHAM

I hate the whole human race.   —GEORGE BERNARD SHAW

I am panting for nothing so much as to put that mountebank [Aristotle] to public shame.   —MARTIN LUTHER

What is my loftiest ambition? I've always wanted to throw an egg into an electric fan.   —OLIVER HERFORD

I work for a government I despise for ends I think criminal.
                                            —JOHN MAYNARD KEYNES

I go on working for the same reason that a hen goes on laying eggs.
                                            —H. L. MENCKEN

All good writers of their confessions, from Augustine on, remain a little in love with their sins.   —ANATOLE FRANCE

Confession may be good for my soul but it's bad for my reputation.   —MARK TWAIN

I often quote myself. It adds spice to my conversation.
—GEORGE BERNARD SHAW

An intimate friend and a hated enemy have always been indispensable to my emotional life.   —SIGMUND FREUD

I have never taken any exercise, except for sleeping and resting, and I never intend to take any. Exercise is loathsome.   —MARK TWAIN

Science is my passion, politics my duty.   —THOMAS JEFFERSON

I fear explanations explanatory of things explained.
—ABRAHAM LINCOLN

I have no relish for the country; it is a kind of healthy grave.
—SYDNEY SMITH

I have an intense desire to return to the womb. Anybody's.
—WOODY ALLEN

"Know thyself"? If I knew myself, I'd run away.
—JOHANN WOLFGANG VON GOETHE

I consider myself a Hindu, Christian, Moslem, Jew, Buddhist, Confucian.   —MOHANDAS K. GANDHI

Under this flabby exterior is an enormous lack of character.
—OSCAR LEVANT

I was born modest; not all over, but in spots.   —MARK TWAIN

I seldom think of politics more than eighteen hours a day.
—LYNDON B. JOHNSON

I'm no different from anybody else with two arms, two legs, and forty-two hundred hits.   —PETE ROSE

You may have noticed that the less I know about a subject, the more confidence I have, and the more new light I throw on it.

—MARK TWAIN

If I had known [about the atomic bomb] I would have become a watchmaker.

—ALBERT EINSTEIN

I have no faith, very little hope, and as much charity as I can afford.

—THOMAS HENRY HUXLEY

I love splendor, but I hate luxury.

—GLADSTONE

I should have been a country-western singer. After all, I'm older than most Western countries.

—GEORGE BURNS

Early in life I had to choose between honest arrogance and hypocritical humility. I chose honest arrogance and have seen no occasion to change.

—FRANK LLOYD WRIGHT

I am an optimist. It does not seem too much use being anything else.

—WINSTON CHURCHILL

I fired MacArthur because he wouldn't respect the authority of a president. I didn't fire him because he was a dumb son of a bitch, although he was, but that's not against the law for generals. If it was, half to three quarters of them would be in jail.

—HARRY S TRUMAN

I don't give a damn for a man that can spell a word only one way.

—MARK TWAIN

That a man can take pleasure in marching in fours to the strains of a band is enough to make me despise him.

—ALBERT EINSTEIN

I may have faults but being wrong ain't one of them.

—JIMMY HOFFA

I like long walks, especially when they are taken by people who annoy me.
                                                        —FRED ALLEN

Few people think more than two or three times a year; I have made an international reputation for myself by thinking once or twice a week.
                                        —GEORGE BERNARD SHAW

I like children. If they're properly cooked.   —W. C. FIELDS

My constitution was destroyed long ago; now I'm living under the bylaws.
                                        —CLARENCE DARROW

I have never seen a more lucid, better balanced, mad mind than mine.
                                        —VLADIMIR NABOKOV

At Harvard it took me ten years to develop a relationship of total hostility with my environment. I want you to know that here [Washington, D.C.] I have done it in eighteen months.
                                        —HENRY KISSINGER

* * *

I am a friend of the workingman, and I would rather be his friend than be one.
                                        —CLARENCE DARROW

My mother loved children—she would have given anything if I had been one.
                                        —GROUCHO MARX

When I was eleven, I thought that women were solid from the neck down.
                                        —C.E.M. JOAD

* * *

I seem to have been only like a boy, playing on the seashore and diverting myself in now and then finding a smoother pebble or a prettier shell, whilst the great ocean of truth lay all undiscovered before me.   —ISAAC NEWTON

I am convinced that both my long age and exceptional health are to be explained by an obvious fact: I never touched a cigarette, a drink, or a girl until I was almost ten years old.   —GEORGE MOORE

I'm really *smart*. I know a whole lot, but I just can't think of it.
                                                          —MOREY AMSTERDAM

I grew up with six brothers. That's how I learned to dance—waiting to get into the bathroom.   —BOB HOPE

Congress

Reader, suppose you were an idiot, and suppose you were a member of Congress—but I repeat myself.   —MARK TWAIN

Congress consists of one third, more or less, scoundrels; two thirds, more or less, idiots; and three thirds, more or less, poltroons.
                                                          —H. L. MENCKEN

Fleas can be taught nearly everything a congressman can.
                                                          —MARK TWAIN

Conscience

Living with a conscience is like driving a car with the brakes on.
                                                          —BUDD SCHULBERG

Conscience is the inner voice that warns us that someone might be looking.
                                                    —H. L. MENCKEN

                         *   *   *

The conscience is that part of the personality that dissolves in alcohol.
                                          —HAROLD D. LASSWELL

I have noticed my conscience for many years, and I know it is more trouble and bother to me than anything else I started with.
                                                    —MARK TWAIN

You can wash your hands, but not your conscience.
                                                  —YIDDISH SAYING

Conscience: That little spark of celestial fire.
                                             —GEORGE WASHINGTON

Men never do evil so fully and so happily as when they do it for conscience's sake.   —PASCAL

Conscience: the thing that acts bad when everything is feeling good.
                                                   —ANONYMOUS

An uneasy conscience is a hair in the mouth.   —MARK TWAIN

Conscience is a cur that will let you get past it but that you cannot keep from barking.   —ANONYMOUS

Conscience and cowardice are really the same things. Conscience is the trade name of the firm.   —OSCAR WILDE

Be the master of your will and the slave of your conscience.
                                                  —HASIDIC SAYING

Conservatives

Men are conservatives after dinner.   —RALPH WALDO EMERSON

Neoconservative: A liberal who has been mugged by reality.
                                                          —IRVING KRISTOL

Conservative: A statesman who is enamored of existing evils, as distinguished from the liberal, who wishes to replace them with others.
                                                          —AMBROSE BIERCE

A man who is not a Liberal at sixteen has no heart; a man who is not a Conservative at sixty has no head.   —BENJAMIN DISRAELI

Of catchwords, slogans, visions, ideal states of society, classless societies, new orders, of all the tinsel and finery with which modern political charlatans charm their jewels from the modern political savage, the Conservative has nothing to offer.   —QUENTIN HOGG

What is conservatism? Is it not adherence to the old and tried, against the new and untried?   —ABRAHAM LINCOLN

There is always a certain meanness in the argument of conservatism, joined with a certain superiority in its fact.
                                                          —RALPH WALDO EMERSON

Some fellers get credit for being conservative when they're only stupid.   —FRANK MCKINNEY ("KIN") HUBBARD

Courage

It is better to die on your feet than live on your knees.
                    —TALMUD (USED BY, AND INCORRECTLY CREDITED TO,
                        LA PASIONARIA, WOMAN LOYALIST HERO IN
                                                    SPANISH CIVIL WAR)

It is easy to be brave from a safe distance.   —AESOP

When you have no choice, at least be brave.   —JEWISH SAYING

Courage is the capacity to confront what can be imagined.

Those who have not experienced fear are not really brave.
                                                    —LEO ROSTEN

When there is no money, half is gone; when there is no courage, all is
gone.   —JEWISH SAYING

☆ Noël Coward ☆

I am baffled. I am puzzled. I stand mystified: Why are there so
few quotations from Noël Coward in this collection?

Surely one of the wittiest men of the century, a smashingly successful writer of musical comedies (with memorable lyrics as well as
captivating music), *dripping* ironies and deadly epigrams in his daily
life—epigrams that mingle elegance and scorn, uttered with the lac-
quered polish of one who views life through a malicious monocle—
Noël Coward was a ranking star of the theater and English movies,
and the darling of the bon mot circuit of Mayfair and Broadway and
Beverly Hills and Las Vegas.

Perhaps he will be best remembered for his sparkling lyrics, which
were the ne plus ultra of sophistication and social comment, plus considerable sentiment—such classics as "Mad Dogs and Englishmen,"
"Don't Put Your Daughter on the Stage, Mrs. Worthington," and "The
Stately Homes of England" (a masterpiece, to me, of unerring lampoonery). His cynicism was rooted in very keen observation of the
world around him.

Coward was a glossy, if idiosyncratic, actor, a marvelous nightclub
entertainer, a prolific playwright, and a peerless lyricist. He was the
absolute epitome of—the snob. He made not the slightest effort to
conceal or diminish his conviction that he belonged to a rare, bisexual,
superior spectrum of the theater, was a confidant of royalty, and was
a man of infinite and irresistible charm. Only Coward, I think, had the

nerve to write (in 1932!) a song called "Mad About the Boy." (It includes the first use of "gay," I think, in the current sense.)

All this said, I still cannot explain why so little of his wit gets detached from his plays or lyrics, to stand on its own, so to speak—as does the humor of Bernard Shaw or Oscar Wilde (Coward's model?). Think of how rare it is to run across a line that includes "As Noël Coward put it." . . . As rare as it is to run across one of his acidulous epigrams in this welcoming but disappointed collocation.

Crime

He who greatly excels in beauty, strength, birth, or wealth, and he, on the other hand, who is very poor, or very weak, or very disgraced, find it difficult to follow rational principles. . . . The one sort grows into violent and great criminals, the other into rogues and petty rascals.   —ARISTOTLE

The greatest crimes are caused by surfeit, not by want. Men do not become tyrants in order that they may not suffer cold. —ARISTOTLE

Every rascal is not a thief, but every thief is a rascal. —ARISTOTLE

They charged me with the commission of great crimes; but men of my stamp do not commit crimes.   —NAPOLEON

Murderer: One who is presumed to be innocent until he is proved insane.   —OSCAR WILDE

Organized crime in America takes in over forty billion dollars a year. This is quite a profitable sum, especially when one considers that the Mafia spends very little for office supplies.   —WOODY ALLEN

Much as he is opposed to lawbreaking, he is not bigoted about it.
                                                      —DAMON RUNYON

I have not yet heard one intellectually respectable defense of criminal rehabilitation.   —JAMES Q. WILSON

Innocence claims the right of speaking, as guilt invokes the privilege of silence. —JEREMY BENTHAM

There have been an increasing . . . politicalization of criminals. It's reached the point where there are no criminals in San Quentin anymore. They're all freedom fighters. —FREDERICK HACKER

All criminals turn preachers under the gallows. —ITALIAN PROVERB

Critics/Criticism

Charles Laughton commented that he was successful in the role of Captain Bligh in *Mutiny on the Bounty* because he had come from a seafaring family. "I presume," said George S. Kaufman, alluding to Laughton's portrayal of Quasimodo in *The Hunchback of Notre Dame*, "that you also came from a long line of hunchbacks."
—GEORGE S. KAUFMAN

A critic is forced to be literate about the illiterate, witty about the witless, and coherent about the incoherent.
—JOHN CROSBY

* * *

The actor who took the role of King Lear played the king as though he expected someone to play the ace. —EUGENE FIELD

I have never found in a long career of politics that criticism is ever inhibited by ignorance. —HAROLD MACMILLAN

Columbia Pictures would be smart to take that movie and cut it up into guitar picks. —IRVING CAESAR

Doris Day: The only . . . talent Miss Day possesses is that of being absolutely sanitary . . . her brow unclouded by human thought, her form unsmudged by the slightest evidence of femininity.
—JOHN SIMON

Proust . . . was mentally defective.   —EVELYN WAUGH

There was laughter in the back of the theater, leading me to the belief that someone was telling jokes back there. —GEORGE S. KAUFMAN

A critic is a man who knows the way but can't drive the car.
                                    —KENNETH TYNAN

                    *   *   *

He writes his plays for the ages—the ages between five and twelve.
        —GEORGE JEAN NATHAN (ON GEORGE BERNARD SHAW)

Sartor Resartus is simply unreadable, and for me that always sort of spoils a book.   —WILL CUPPY

Your manuscript is both good and original; but the part that is good is not original, and the part that is original is not good.
                                    —SAMUEL JOHNSON

Asking a working writer what he thinks about critics is like asking a lamppost how it feels about dogs.
        —CHRISTOPHER HAMPTON/JOHN OSBORNE

                    *   *   *

Perfectly Scandalous was one of those plays in which all of the actors unfortunately enunciated very clearly.   —ROBERT BENCHLEY

[Book review, in entirety]: Rhetoric.   —H. D. LASSWELL

During a performance of a very bad play, George S. Kaufman leaned forward and politely asked the lady in front of him if she would mind putting on her hat.   —GEORGE S. KAUFMAN

Hamlet is a coarse and barbarous play. . . . One might think the work is a product of a drunken savage's imagination.   —VOLTAIRE

[Of Pope's translation of Homer]: A portrait endowed with every merit excepting that of likeness to the original. —EDWARD GIBBON

Bad as the play was, her acting was worse. It was a masterpiece of failure.   —GEORGE BERNARD SHAW

I have no doubt that this book will fill a much-needed void.
          —BOSTON BOOK REVIEW

He doesn't act on stage—he behaves.   —OSCAR WILDE

Criticism is prejudice made plausible.   —H. L. MENCKEN

For people who like that kind of a book, that is the kind of a book they will like.   —ABRAHAM LINCOLN

The scenery in the play was beautiful, but the actors got in front of it.   —ALEXANDER WOOLLCOTT

Henry James's prose reads as though it has been translated from the German.   —LEO ROSTEN

Mr. Henry James writes fiction as if it were a painful duty.
          —OSCAR WILDE

Once you've put one of his books down, you simply can't pick it up again.   —MARK TWAIN (ON HENRY JAMES)

She runs the gamut of emotions from A to B.
          —DOROTHY PARKER [OF KATHARINE HEPBURN'S
          FIRST APPEARANCE ON BROADWAY]

The covers of this book are too far apart.   —AMBROSE BIERCE

It is much easier to be critical than to be correct.
                                          —BENJAMIN DISRAELI

There has never been set up a statue in honor of a critic.
                                          —JEAN SIBELIUS

From the moment I picked your book up until the moment I put it down, I could not stop laughing. Someday I hope to read it.
                        —GROUCHO MARX (LETTER TO LEO ROSTEN)

Cult

A cult is a religion with no political power.   —FISCHEL PFEIFFER

Curses

> *Curses:* May all your teeth fall out—except one:
> to get toothaches.
> ☞
> May his stomach churn like a music box.
> ☞
> May his buttocks drop off!
> ☞
> May you live in interesting times.
> ☞
> May onions grow in his navel.
> ☞
> May he own five ships of gold—all wrecked.
> ☞
> I would like to treat him like a treasure; bury him
> with care and affection.

Cynics

The cynic puts all human actions into two classes: openly bad and secretly bad.   —Henry Ward Beecher

The Ancient Mariner would not have taken so well if it had been called *The Old Sailor*.   —Samuel Butler

Cynic: A man who, when he smells flowers, looks around for a coffin.
                        —H. L. Mencken

Nice guys finish last.   —Leo Durocher

What God does is best—probably.   —Jewish saying

Give me six lines written by the most honest man; I will find something in them to hang him.   —Richelieu

The only thing speed is good for is catching flies.   —Hilda Kvetch

I have received no more than one or two letters that were worth the postage.   —Henry David Thoreau

> Cynic: *A blackguard whose faulty vision sees things as they are, not as they ought to be.*
>   —Ambrose Bierce

*   *   *

People think I am cynical when I am only trying to be clinical.
                        —Leo Rosten

Well-washed and well-combed domestic pets grow dull; they miss the stimulus of fleas.   —Francis Galton

The bee isn't really that busy; it just can't buzz any slower.
—FRANK MCKINNEY ("KIN") HUBBARD

You can fool most of the people most of the time. —P. T. BARNUM

April fool: A joke repeated 365 times a year. —SHOLEM ALEICHEM

If you give a man enough rope he'll hang you. —LEO ROSTEN

Civil War: A conflict that cost more than ten billion dollars. For less than half, the freedom of all the four million slaves could have been purchased. —CHARLES AND MARY BEARD

The speed of a runaway horse counts for nothing. —JEAN COCTEAU

It's going to be fun to watch and see how long the meek can keep the earth after they inherit it.
—FRANK MCKINNEY ("KIN") HUBBARD

* * *

No one ever went broke underestimating the taste of the American public. —H. L. MENCKEN/GEORGE ADE/P. T. BARNUM

We all have the strength to endure the misfortunes of others.
—FRANÇOIS DE LA ROCHEFOUCAULD

If, by ill luck, people understood each other, they would never agree. —BAUDELAIRE

The power of accurate observation is commonly called cynicism by those who have not got it. —GEORGE BERNARD SHAW

The cynics are right nine times out of ten. —H. L. MENCKEN

Faithfulness is to the emotional life what consistency is to the life of the intellect—simply a confession of failure.   —OSCAR WILDE

The most melancholy of human reflections, perhaps, is that, on the whole, it is a question whether the benevolence of man does more harm or good.   —WALTER BAGEHOT

The fellow who laughs last may laugh best, but he gets the reputation of being very slow-witted.   —LEO ROSTEN

Most conversations are an exchange of propitiating noises.
                                           —HAROLD D. LASWELL

A cynic is a man who knows the price of every-thing and the value of nothing.
                                           —OSCAR WILDE

                        *   *   *

The brain is a wonderful organ: It starts working the moment you get up in the morning and does not stop until you get into the office.
                                           —ROBERT FROST

A little sincerity is a dangerous thing, and a great deal of it is absolutely fatal.   —OSCAR WILDE

Insincerity is merely a method by which we can multiply our personalities.   —OSCAR WILDE

In the misfortune of our best friends we find something that is not displeasing to us.   —FRANÇOIS DE LA ROCHEFOUCAULD

No one ever won an interview.   —GARSON KANIN

The world is populated in the main by people who should not exist.
                                           —GEORGE BERNARD SHAW

The paths of glory may lead but to the grave (mused Thomas Gray), but what paths do not?   —LEO ROSTEN

Pain may be purely mental, caused by the good fortune of another.
—AMBROSE BIERCE

We must beware of needless innovations, especially when guided by logic.   —WINSTON CHURCHILL

Adam was the luckiest man: he had no mother-in-law.
—MARK TWAIN

What a glorious garden of wonders this world would be to anyone who was lucky enough to be unable to read.
—G. K. CHESTERTON (ON SEEING TIMES SQUARE,
ALL LIGHTED UP, FROM THE TIMES TOWER)

♦ Jerome ("Dizzy") Dean ♦

I have referred to the freewheeling syntax and loopy neologisms with which Samuel Goldwyn enriched demotic English. Many others from the world of entertainment (vaudeville, pugilism, the circus, wrestling, football, baseball—oh, *yes, baseball*!) have created small wonders of creative phrasing, revised idioms, outlandish similes, unearthly metaphors, *und zo weiter*.

One unique languageer from the baseball diamond has always stayed high in my affections. He was sui generis, to put it mildly. Indeed, one of my fondest wishes is that I could have sat in on an informal discussion of art or philosophy or batting averages or—oh, *you* name it!—among Dizzy Dean and, say, Casey Stengel and Salvador Dali and "Kin" Hubbard and Red Smith.

A self-anointed hick, and a wordmonger of considerable cunning (and a keen sense of publicity), Jerome "Dizzy" Dean was a baseball pitcher extraordinaire. He would offer radio and newspaper reporters various and bizarre versions of an event or comment. When caught in a fib (or ten or twenty), Ole Diz would say with a grin, "Them ain't *lies*, fellas; them's scoops."

His atrocious grammar was authentic. He had the barest rudiments of instruction, up to the third grade in a Chickawallah, Arkansas, elementary school. But he was a marvel on the mound, with

116

chutzpa to match his magic with a baseball. He would publicly announce to upcoming batters what his next pitch would be; he would order his outfielders to leave their posts because "none of them batters is going to hit the ball out of this here infield." He would announce at the beginning of a season how many games he and his almost equally talented brother Paul ("Daffy"), another pitcher, would win—and they usually did.

Once, running the bases, Dizzy was hit by a "beanball." He was rushed to the nearest hospital. The headline that added to his luster was:

X RAY OF DEAN'S HEAD SHOWS NOTHING*

When he was only thirty, the incomparable Dean's career on the diamond ended. Unfazed, Ole Diz became—a sports announcer, surely the most unusual reporter any radio station ever employed.

Diz loved talking on radio (or anywhere else), and he cheerfully tortured pronunciation, ignored syntax, and rearranged conventional grammar. So wacky (and colorful) were his solecisms that English teachers and parents protested, alarmed by the effect Dizzy, a legend and a hero to millions of boys, was having on the English tongue. He would invent participles, triple-split infinitives, and otherwise redesign conventional, long-established usages.

Once he said that a runner had "slud" into third ("slud" being the plausible past tense of "slide"). He pronounced the names of players with complete indifference to how they pronounced their own names.

Finally, when told by the St. Louis Board of Education that due to massive audience protests, Mr. Dean would no longer adorn the radio with his originality, he said with a shrug, "Okay. But you should remember that a lot of folks that ain't sayin' 'ain't' these days ain't eatin,' either."

My favorite specimen of Dizzy's delightful diction will always give me comfort in the long, dark hours of the night. One afternoon, in the St. Louis dugout, the intrepid Dean rattled off a soliloquy that contained one particularly godawful error in English.

A teammate said with a snicker, "Diz, you sure don't know the king's English!"

Without a moment's hesitation, the master retorted, "I sure do, bub—and so is the queen!"

People who keep harping on the deplorable state of our schools should realize that we are not turning out pitchers like that anymore.

---

* Incidentally, the same story was told about Yogi Berra, and many a bush leaguer.

Death

Death: *To stop sinning suddenly.*
                    —ELBERT HUBBARD

*   *   *

Plan for this world as if you expect to live forever; but plan for the hereafter as if you expect to die tomorrow.   —IBN GABIROL

We rejoice over a birth and mourn over a death. But we should not. For when a man is born, who knows what he will do or how he will end? But when a man dies, we may rejoice—if he left a good name and this world in peace.   —ADAPTED FROM MIDRASH

The reports of my death are greatly exaggerated.   —MARK TWAIN

My wallpaper is killing me. One of us must go.
          —OSCAR WILDE (AS HE LAY DYING
                    IN A HOTEL IN PARIS)

*   *   *

Here I am, dying of a hundred good symptoms.
                    —ALEXANDER POPE

I submit to you that if a man hasn't discovered something he will die for, he isn't fit to live.   —MARTIN LUTHER KING, JR.

You need a religion if you are terrified of death.   —GORE VIDAL

It's astonishing how important a man becomes when he dies.
                    —YIDDISH SAYING

I wonder where the *bad* people are buried.
—CHARLES LAMB, AGE NINE,
AFTER WANDERING THROUGH A GRAVEYARD

All things considered, I'd rather be in Philadelphia.
—W. C. FIELDS (HIS CHOSEN EPITAPH)

Shrouds have no pockets.   —FOLK SAYING

There is no answer to death, nor to many of the problems that perplex us; there are only rueful accommodations to reality. —LEO ROSTEN

No young man believes he will ever die.   —WILLIAM HAZLITT

[He] is one of those people who would be enormously improved by death.   —H. H. MUNRO ("SAKI")

Death is the vast perhaps. —RABELAIS
*   *   *

Death: A fate worse than life.   —J. J. FURNAS

Man comes into the world with an *oy!* and leaves with a *gevalt!*
—YIDDISH SAYING

I don't believe in an afterlife, although I am bringing a change of underwear.   —WOODY ALLEN

It costs a lot of money to die comfortably.   —SAMUEL BUTLER

Death: A low chemical trick played on everybody except sequoia trees.
—J. J. FURNAS

Death: The debt you pay nature.   —FROM THE LATIN

The goal of all life is death.   —SIGMUND FREUD

Man lives freely only by his readiness to die.
                                        —MOHANDAS K. GANDHI

A man who lost his brother was asked, "What was the cause of his death?" and replied, "Life."   —IBN ZABARA

When good Americans die, they go to Paris; when bad Americans die, they go to America.
                                        —OSCAR WILDE

*   *   *

In case my life should end with the cannibals, I hope they will write on my tombstone, "We have eaten Dr. Schweitzer. He was good to the end."   —ALBERT SCHWEITZER

Definitions of Distinction

Coward: One who in a perilous emergency thinks with his legs.
                                        —AMBROSE BIERCE

Cemetery: *An isolated spot, usually in a suburb, where mourners swap lies.*
                                        —AMBROSE BIERCE

*   *   *

This is the final test of a gentleman: his respect for those who can be of no possible service to him.   —WILLIAM LYON PHELPS

Destiny: A tyrant's authority for crime and a fool's excuse for failure.
—AMBROSE BIERCE

Metallurgist: Someone who is allergic to metal.   —LEO ROSTEN

Gentleman: One who never strikes a woman without provocation.
—H. L. MENCKEN

Melancholy is the pleasure of being sad.   —VICTOR HUGO

A celebrity is one who is known to many persons he is glad he doesn't know.   —H. L. MENCKEN

An appeaser is one who feeds a crocodile, hoping it will eat him last.
—WINSTON CHURCHILL

Artificial insemination: *Copulation without representation.*
—*PLAYBOY*

*   *   *

He seemed such a nice old gentleman, I thought I would give him my autograph as a souvenir.
—ADOLF HITLER (AFTER "ACCEPTING" NEVILLE CHAMBERLAIN'S "PEACE INITIATIVE" AT MUNICH, 1938)

A gentleman is one who never hurts anyone's feelings unintentionally.
— OLIVER HERFORD/OSCAR WILDE/ET AL.

Patience: A minor form of despair, disguised as a virtue.
—AMBROSE BIERCE

Hobson's choice: Mrs. Hobson.   —LEO ROSTEN

Politeness . . . is fictitious benevolence.   —SAMUEL JOHNSON

Cauliflower is nothing but cabbage with a college education.
     —MARK TWAIN

What we call public opinion is generally public sentiment.
     —BENJAMIN DISRAELI

     *   *   *

An exaggeration is a truth that has lost its temper.
     —KAHLIL GIBRAN

Accuracy: To a newspaper what virtue is to a lady.
     —JOSEPH PULITZER

Mark Twain: He was the Lincoln of literature.
     —WILLIAM DEAN HOWELLS

Positive: Being mistaken at the top of one's voice.
     —AMBROSE BIERCE

Superhighway: A prison in motion.   —CLIFTON FADIMAN

Bigotry: Being certain of something you know nothing about.
     —ANONYMOUS

Bigot: One who is obstinately attached to an opinion you do not entertain.   —AMBROSE BIERCE

Present: That part of eternity dividing the domain of disappointment from the realm of hope.   —AMBROSE BIERCE

Originality: Only an unaccustomed method of tickling the world.
                                         —GEORGE BERNARD SHAW

The demagogue is one who preaches doctrines he knows to be untrue
to men he knows to be idiots.   —H. L. MENCKEN

Fanaticism consists of redoubling your effort when you have forgotten
your aim.   —GEORGE SANTAYANA

Cheese: Milk's leap toward immortality.   —CLIFTON FADIMAN

Middle age: The time when you think that in a week or two you'll feel
as good as ever.   —DON MARQUIS

> *You can know a man by three signs: his tips,
> his tippling, and his temper.*
>   —ADAPTED FROM THE TALMUD

                     ✳   ✳   ✳

Camel: A horse that was designed by a committee.   —ANONYMOUS

Hypochondriac: Someone who feels bad when he feels good because
he knows he'll feel worse when he feels better.   —ANONYMOUS

Bachelor: A man who comes to work each morning from a different
direction.   —SHOLEM ALEICHEM

Home: The place where you can scratch anyplace you itch.
                                          —FRONTIER HUMOR

When a man wants to murder a tiger he calls it sport; when a tiger
wants to murder him, he calls it ferocity.
                                         —GEORGE BERNARD SHAW

Conversation usually consists of a series of propitiating noises.
                                          —H. D. LASSWELL

Egotist: One more interested in himself—than in me.
—AMBROSE BIERCE

Rare volume: A returned book.   —HARRY HERSCHELOVITZER

Tact: *Thinking all you say without saying all you think.*

* * *

Barometer: An ingenious instrument that indicates what kind of weather we are having.   —AMBROSE BIERCE

Despair is the conclusion of fools.   —BENJAMIN DISRAELI

Consistency is the last refuge of the unimaginative.
—ATTRIBUTED TO OSCAR WILDE

Assassination is the extreme form of censorship.
—GEORGE BERNARD SHAW

* * *

Falsies: Hidden persuaders.   —ATTRIBUTED TO MAE WEST

Pomposity is only the failure of pomp.   —G. K. CHESTERTON

The only certainty is that nothing is certain.   —PLINY THE ELDER

Centimeter: A parking meter that takes pennies.   —LEO ROSTEN

Accordion: A stomach Steinway.   —P. G. WODEHOUSE

The age of discretion is reached when one has learned to be indiscreet discreetly.   —ANONYMOUS

Savage nation: One that doesn't wear uncomfortable clothes.
—FINLEY PETER DUNNE ("MR. DOOLEY")

Tourist: *Someone who goes three thousand miles to get a picture of himself in front of his car.*
—ROBERT BENCHLEY

* * *

OUT OF THE MOUTHS OF BABES

Italics: The language spoken by ancient Italians.   —A CHILD

Vesuvius: The volcano where the creator usually smokes.
—A CHILD

Version: The mother of Jesus.   —A CHILD

Coincide: What you should do when it starts pouring.
—A CHILD

Antidote: The medicine that kills dotes.   —A CHILD

Giraffes: They are a rich source of necks.   —A CHILD

Vituperation: Satire, as understood by dunces.   —AMBROSE BIERCE

Imagination: What prevents us from being as happy in the arms of a chambermaid as in the arms of a duchess.   —SAMUEL JOHNSON

Puritanism: *The haunting fear that someone, somewhere, may be happy.*
—H. L. MENCKEN

* * *

Kleptomaniac: A person who helps himself because he can't help himself.   —HENRY MORGAN

Gossip: Nature's telephone.   —SHOLEM ALEICHEM

Yawn: A silent shout.   —G. K. CHESTERTON

The optimist thinks that this is the best of all possible worlds, and the pessimist knows it.   —J. ROBERT OPPENHEIMER

Destiny is an invention of the cowardly and the resigned.
                                        —IGNAZIO SILONE

*All men are ordinary men; the extraordinary
men are those who know it.*
                    —G. K. CHESTERTON

               *   *   *

The golden rule is that there are no golden rules.
                                    —GEORGE BERNARD SHAW

City life: Millions of people being lonesome together.
                                    —HENRY DAVID THOREAU

Fanatic: A man who does what God would do—if He only had the facts straight.   —FINLEY PETER DUNNE ("MR. DOOLEY")

Eccentric: A man too rich to be called crazy.   —LEO ROSTEN

Courtesy: Acceptable hypocrisy.   —AMBROSE BIERCE

The celebrity is the person who is known for his well-knownness.
                                    —DANIEL J. BOORSTIN

Every definition is dangerous. —ERASMUS

Platitude: A remark that is too true to be good. —ANONYMOUS

Parking space: An unoccupied place on the other side of the street.
—ANONYMOUS

Positive: Being mistaken at the top of one's voice.
—AMBROSE BIERCE

Democracy

The people are to be taken in very small doses.
—RALPH WALDO EMERSON

Even though counting heads is not an ideal way to govern, at least it is better than breaking them. —LEARNED HAND

*Equality may perhaps be a right, but no power
on earth can ever turn it into a fact.*
—HONORÉ DE BALZAC

* * *

Man's capacity for justice makes democracy possible, but man's inclination to injustice makes democracy necessary.
—REINHOLD NIEBUHR

Democracy is based upon the conviction that there are extraordinary possibilities in ordinary people. —HARRY EMERSON FOSDICK

Vox populi, vox *humbug*.
                —WILLIAM TECUMSEH SHERMAN

*   *   *

You can't fool *all* the people *all* the time—but it isn't necessary to—in order to get power.   —LEO ROSTEN

Democracy is good. I say this because other systems are worse.
                                           —JAWAHARLAL NEHRU

Democracy is more vindictive than cabinets. The wars of people will be more terrible than those of kings.
                                —WINSTON CHURCHILL

Men have always found it easy to be governed. What is hard is for them to govern themselves.   —MAX LERNER

No party is as bad as its leaders.   —WILL ROGERS

America is still a government of the naive, by the naive, and for the naive. He who does not know this, nor relish it, has no inkling of the nature of this country.   —CHRISTOPHER MORLEY

With all my admiration and love for democracy, I am not prepared to accept the statement that the largest number of people are always right.   —JAWAHARLAL NEHRU

A free society is a society where it is safe to be unpopular.
                                           —ADLAI STEVENSON

Sure the people are stupid; the human race is stupid. Sure Congress is an inefficient instrument of government. But the people are not stupid enough to abandon representative government for any other kind, including government by the guy who knows.

—BERNARD DEVOTO

*   *   *

In a democracy both deep reverence and a sense of the comic are requisite.

—CARL SANDBURG

The people no longer believe in principles, but will probably periodically believe in saviors.

—JACOB BURCKHARDT

Democracy becomes a government of bullies tempered by editors.

—RALPH WALDO EMERSON

Of the many things we have done to democracy in the past, the worst has been the indignity of taking it for granted.

—MAX LERNER

"As I would not be a slave, so I would not be a master." Whatever differs from this, to the extent of the difference, is no democracy.

—BARBARA JORDAN

Democracy is the surrogate faith of intellectuals deprived of religion.

—JOSEPH SCHUMPETER

Your Constitution is all sail and no anchor.

—THOMAS BABINGTON MACAULAY

If one man offers you democracy and another offers you a bag of grain, at what stage of starvation will you prefer the grain to the vote?
                    —BERTRAND RUSSELL

                *   *   *

Democracy means government by the uneducated, while aristocracy means government by the badly educated.   —G. K. CHESTERTON

The tendency of democracies is, in all things, to mediocrity.
                    —JAMES FENIMORE COOPER

The democratic faith is this: that the most terribly important things must be left to ordinary men themselves—the mating of the sexes, the rearing of the young, the laws of the state.
                    —G. K. CHESTERTON

When I was a boy I was told that anybody could become president; I'm beginning to believe it.   —CLARENCE DARROW

That all men are created equal is a proposition to which, at ordinary times, no sane individual has ever given his assent.
                    —ALDOUS HUXLEY

Democracy is the theory that the common people know what they want, and deserve to get it good and hard.   —H. L. MENCKEN

Democracy means government by discussion, but it is only effective if you can stop people talking.   —CLEMENT ATTLEE

I must follow them. I am their leader.
          —ANDREW BONAR LAW, PRIME MINISTER, GREAT BRITAIN

Anybody that wants the presidency so much that he'll spend two years organizing and campaigning for it is not to be trusted with the office. —DAVID BRODER.

The genius of impeachment lay in the fact that it could punish the man without punishing the office.
—ARTHUR M. SCHLESINGER, JR.

If, to please the people, we offer what we ourselves disapprove, how can we afterward defend our work? Let us raise a standard to which the wise and honest can repair. —GEORGE WASHINGTON

The majority, compose them how you will, are a herd, and not a very nice one.
—WILLIAM HAZLITT

*   *   *

Democracy substitutes election by the incompetent many for appointment by the corrupt few. —GEORGE BERNARD SHAW

Democracy . . . is the only form of government that is founded on the dignity of man. Not the dignity of some men, of rich men, of educated men, or of white men, but of all men. Its sanction is not the sanction of force, but the sanction of human nature. —ROBERT M. HUTCHINS

Television is democracy at its ugliest. —PADDY CHAYEVSKY

A government that robs Peter to pay Paul can, as a rule, calculate on the support of Paul. —GEORGE BERNARD SHAW

A democracy is a government in the hands of men of low birth, no property, and vulgar employments. —ARISTOTLE

As I see it, democracy encourages the nimble charlatan at the expense of the thinker, and prefers the plausible wizard with quack remedies to the true statesman.

—JAMES JEANS

*   *   *

There is somebody wiser than any of us, and that is everybody.

—NAPOLEON BONAPARTE

Votes are collared under democracy, not by talking sense but by talking nonsense.

—H. L. MENCKEN

The sober second thought of the people is seldom wrong.

—MARTIN VAN BUREN

*   *   *

The principle of majority rule is the mildest form in which force of numbers can be exercised. It is a pacific substitute for civil war.

—WALTER LIPPMANN

The first of all democratic doctrines is that all men are interesting.

—G. K. CHESTERTON

The presidency has become a cross between a popularity contest and a high-school debate, with an encyclopedia of clichés as the first prize.

—SAUL BELLOW

A president's hardest task is not to do what is right, but to know what is right.

—LYNDON B. JOHNSON

*   *   *

Universal suffrage is the government of a house by its nursery.
—OTTO VON BISMARCK

Democracy . . . is a charming form of government, full of variety and disorder, and dispensing a sort of equality to equals and unequals alike. —PLATO

If there is a country in the world where concord, according to common calculation, would be least expected, it is America. Made up, as it is, of people from different nations, accustomed to different form and habits of government, speaking different languages, and more different in their modes of worship, it would appear that the union of such a people was impracticable. But by the simple operation of constructing government on the principles of society and the rights of man, every difficulty retires, and the parts are brought into cordial unison.
—THOMAS PAINE

* * *

There's no underestimating the intelligence of the American public.
—H. L. MENCKEN

I do not believe in the collective wisdom of individual ignorance.
—THOMAS CARLYLE

It would be folly to argue that the people cannot make political mistakes. They can and do make grave mistakes. They know it, they pay the penalty, but compared with the mistakes which have been made by every kind of autocracy, they are unimportant.
—CALVIN COOLIDGE

America is the place where you cannot kill your government by killing the men who conduct it.   —WOODROW WILSON

America has believed that in differentiation—not in uniformity—lies the path of progress. It acted on this belief, it has advanced human happiness, and it has prospered.   —LOUIS BRANDEIS

If there were a people consisting of gods, they would be governed democratically. So perfect a government is not suitable to men.
                    —JEAN-JACQUES ROUSSEAU

Nothing can be more abhorrent to democracy than to imprison a person or keep him in prison because he is unpopular. This is really the test of civilization.   —WINSTON CHURCHILL

Corruption, the most infallible symptom of constitutional liberty.
                    —EDWARD GIBBON

In our country we have those three unspeakably precious things: freedom of speech, freedom of conscience, and prudence never to practice either.
                    —MARK TWAIN

*   *   *

Democracy: The recurrent suspicion that more than half the people are right more than half the time.   —E. B. WHITE

Democracy is also a form of religion; it is the worship of jackals by jackasses.   —H. L. MENCKEN

Democracy is the form of government in which the free are rulers.   —ARISTOTLE

Descriptions Worth Remembering

She is intolerable, but that is her only fault.   —TALLEYRAND

The butler entered the room, a solemn procession of one.
—P. G. WODEHOUSE

Why don't you get a haircut? You look like a chrysanthemum.
—P. G. WODEHOUSE

My handwriting looks as if a swarm of ants, escaping from an ink bottle, had walked over a sheet of paper without wiping their legs.
—SYDNEY SMITH

The White House is the finest jail in the world.
—HARRY S TRUMAN

*   *   *

He is too illiterate, unread, unlearned for his station and reputation.
—JOHN ADAMS (ON GEORGE WASHINGTON)

[On the death of a promiscuous actress]: She sleeps alone at last.
—ROBERT BENCHLEY

*   *   *

If you weren't such a great man you'd be a terrible bore.
—MRS. WILLIAM GLADSTONE (TO HER HUSBAND)

He has no more privacy than a goldfish.   —H. H. MUNRO ("SAKI")

She was a town-and-country soprano of the kind often used for augmenting the grief at a funeral.   —GEORGE ADE

Richard Nixon is a no-good lying bastard. He can lie out of both sides of his mouth at the same time, and if he ever caught himself telling the truth, he'd lie just to keep his hand in.   —HARRY S TRUMAN

He called upon God the way a baseball manager sends in a pinch hitter.   —LEO ROSTEN

When you look like your passport photo, it's time to go home.
                                        —ATTRIBUTED TO ERMA BOMBECK

The difference between Balfour and Asquith is that Arthur is wicked and moral, Asquith is good and immoral.   —WINSTON CHURCHILL

> *While he was not dumber than an ox, he was not any smarter, either.*
> —JAMES THURBER

*   *   *

He knew the precise psychological moment when to say nothing.
                                                         —OSCAR WILDE

Freud is the father of psychoanalysis. It has no mother.
                                               —GERMAINE GREER

Groucho Marx was the Voltaire of vaudeville. —LEO ROSTEN

Gertrude Stein is the mama of dada.   —CLIFTON FADIMAN

T. E. Lawrence: An adventurer with a genius for backing into the limelight.   —LOWELL THOMAS

Stalin: Genghis Khan with a telephone.   —ANONYMOUS

Why do you sit there looking like an envelope without any address on it?   —MARK TWAIN

He is insane, but he has lucid moments, when he is merely stupid.
—HEINRICH HEINE

Barring that natural expression of villainy which we all have, the man looked honest enough. —MARK TWAIN

He has the kind of face that looks as if it hasn't been lived in yet.
—ANONYMOUS (OF DAN QUAYLE)

I think that I am superior to the common run of men in noticing things which easily escape attention, and in observing them carefully. My industry has been nearly as great as it could have been in the observation and collection of facts. —CHARLES DARWIN

There is a marvelous dumb sagacity about him, like that of a miraculous dog, and he gets to the truth in ways as dark as those of the heathen Chinee. —THOMAS HUXLEY (OF DARWIN), FROM OBITUARY NOTICE TO THE ROYAL SOCIETY

Put three grains of sand inside a vast cathedral, and the cathedral will be more closely packed with sand than space is with stars.
—JAMES JEANS

Masochist: Someone who is only happy when miserable.
— ANONYMOUS

There is a certain mystery about Lincoln, as there is about every great and simple man; a mystery too simple, it may be, to be found out. —JOSEPH F. NEWTON

There is only the difference of a letter between the beginning and the end of life—creation and cremation. —HERBERT BEERBOHM TREE

Luther sinned in two respects: He knocked off the crown of the Pope and attacked the bellies of the monks. —ERASMUS

I often say of George Washington that he was one of the few in the whole history of the world who was not carried away by power.

—ROBERT FROST

Hypochondriac: A person with an infinite capacity for faking pains.

—*MODERN MEDICINE*

I love fools' experiments. I am always making them.

—CHARLES DARWIN

*   *   *

Nowadays a parlor maid as ignorant as Queen Victoria was when she came to the throne would be classed as mentally defective.

—GEORGE BERNARD SHAW

Calvin Coolidge didn't say much, and when he did he didn't say much.

—WILL ROGERS

His face was filled with broken commandments.

—JOHN MASEFIELD

His face looks like a slateful of wrong answers.

—ARTHUR ("BUGS") BAER

Even at sixty-five he seems precocious.   —LEO ROSTEN

No one is as deaf as the man who will not listen.

—JEWISH FOLK SAYING

He is forever poised between a cliché and an indiscretion.

—HAROLD MACMILLAN (OF ANTHONY EDEN)

The essence of this man is loneliness.
—HENRY KISSINGER (OF RICHARD NIXON)

He sometimes sounds like an ambulatory Library of Congress.
—LEO ROSTEN (ON H. D. LASSWELL)

Working with Julie Andrews is like getting hit over the head with a valentine.
—CHRISTOPHER PLUMMER

*   *   *

Those comfortably padded lunatic asylums which are known, euphemistically, as the stately homes of England.   —VIRGINIA WOOLF

Mr. Wilson bores me with his Fourteen Points. Why, God Almighty has only ten.   —GEORGES CLEMENCEAU

He is the purest figure in history.
—WILLIAM GLADSTONE (ON GEORGE WASHINGTON)

A hypocrite is a person who—but who isn't?   —DON MARQUIS

He [Gladstone] made his conscience not his guide but his accomplice.
—BENJAMIN DISRAELI

How can I talk to a fellow [Woodrow Wilson] who thinks himself the first man in two thousand years to know anything about peace on earth?   —GEORGES CLEMENCEAU

A vacuum with nipples.
—OTTO PREMINGER
(OF MARILYN MONROE)

*   *   *

An empty taxi stopped, and Jack Warner got out.
—HOLLYWOOD SAYING, ALSO IN REFERENCE
TO OTHER PRODUCERS

In short, when you have penetrated through all the circles of power and splendor, you were not dealing with a gentleman, at last, but with an impostor and a rogue.
—RALPH WALDO EMERSON (OF NAPOLEON)

People said that my language was bad, but Jesus, you should have heard LBJ!   —RICHARD NIXON (ON LYNDON B. JOHNSON)

Caesar was too old to find his amusement in conquering the world. Such a game was all right for Augustus or Alexander. They were still young and difficult to control. But Caesar ought to have been more mature.   —PASCAL

Impostor: A rival aspirant to public honors.   —AMBROSE BIERCE

The swaggering underemphasis of New England.
—HEYWOOD BROUN

Mr. Shaw is (I suspect) the only man on earth who has never written any poetry.   —G. K. CHESTERTON

Politeness: The most acceptable hypocrisy.   —AMBROSE BIERCE

For seventeen years he did nothing at all but kill animals and stick in stamps.   —HAROLD NICOLSON (ON GEORGE V)

Mr. Attlee is a very modest man. But then he has much to be modest about.   —WINSTON CHURCHILL

It isn't only the things he doesn't know, it's the things he does know that aren't true.   —SIGMUND FREUD (ON HAVELOCK ELLIS)

He [Alexander Woollcott] wasn't exactly hostile to facts, but he was apathetic about them. —WOLCOTT GIBBS

He errs, as other men do, but he errs with integrity.
—BENJAMIN FRANKLIN
(OF GEORGE WASHINGTON)

* * *

It's our fault. We should have given him better parts!
—JACK WARNER (ON HEARING THAT RONALD REAGAN HAD BEEN ELECTED GOVERNOR OF CALIFORNIA)

She was the type that would wake up in the morning and immediately start apologizing. —WOODY ALLEN

Well, if Gladstone fell into the Thames, that would be a misfortune; and if anybody pulled him out, that, I suppose, would be a calamity. —BENJAMIN DISRAELI

A hippie wears his hair long like Tarzan, walks like Jane, and smells like Cheetah. —BUSTER CRABBE

President Johnson was given to stretching the truth to as thin a soup as was necessary to feed a lot of people. He never proposed marriage to me, but he sometimes made me feel I might be an illegitimate son.
—BILL MOYERS

* * *

Clark Gable's ears make him look like a taxicab with the doors open.
—HOWARD HUGHES

You look wise; pray, correct that error. —CHARLES LAMB

I am dying, sir, of a hundred good symptoms.   —ALEXANDER POPE

The more things a man is ashamed of, the more respectable he is.
                                    —GEORGE BERNARD SHAW

   The best of men cannot suspend their fate;
   The good die early, and the bad die late.   —DANIEL DEFOE

Of all the benefits which virtue confers on us, the contempt of death
is one of the greatest.   —MONTAIGNE

*When Heywood Broun is all dressed up, he
looks like an unmade bed.*
                            —DOROTHY PARKER
              *   *   *

Those who have endeavored to teach us to die well, have taught few
to die willingly.   —SAMUEL JOHNSON

The right honorable gentleman's smile is like the fittings on a coffin.
              —BENJAMIN DISRAELI (ON SIR ROBERT PEEL)

How holy people look when they are seasick!   —SAMUEL BUTLER

McKinley has no more backbone than a chocolate éclair.
              —THEODORE ROOSEVELT (ON MCKINLEY'S RELUCTANCE
                            TO GO TO WAR WITH SPAIN, 1898)

Let us endeavor so to live that when we come to die even the undertaker will be sorry.   —MARK TWAIN

A sophisticated rhetorician intoxicated with the exuberance of his own
verbosity
         —BENJAMIN DISRAELI (OF A MEMBER OF THE OPPOSITION)

She is a cross between Little Nell and Lady Macbeth.
—ALEXANDER WOOLLCOTT (OF DOROTHY PARKER)

He is a sheep in sheep's clothing.
—WINSTON CHURCHILL
(OF CLEMENT ATTLEE OR STAFFORD CRIPPS)

A shy, faunlike creature with a keen sense of double-entry bookkeeping.
—ALEXANDER WOOLLCOTT (OF HARPO MARX)

Cromwell said to the Scotch before the Battle of Dunbar: "I beseech you in the bowels of Christ, think it possible that you may be mistaken." It is a pity that Cromwell never addressed the same remark to himself.
—BERTRAND RUSSELL

He is a pleasant man, who, without any important qualifications for the office, would very much like to be president.
—WALTER LIPPMANN (OF FRANKLIN D. ROOSEVELT, 1932)

One of the crying needs of the time is for a suitable burial service for the admittedly damned.
—H. L. MENCKEN

✳   ✳   ✳

The reason so many people turned up at his funeral is that they wanted to make sure he was dead.
—ATTRIBUTED TO SAMUEL GOLDWYN, LOUIS B. MAYER,
HARRY COHN, AND SEVERAL OTHER PRODUCERS

Adolf Hitler: A combination of initiative, perfidy, and epilepsy.
—LEON TROTSKY

Devil

An apology for the Devil: It must be remembered that we have only heard one side of the case. God has written all the books.
—SAMUEL BUTLER/MARK TWAIN

In all theologies, the devil figures as a male.
—DON MARQUIS

*   *   *

One can just as well hold God responsible for the existence of the devil as for the evil he personified.   —SIGMUND FREUD

Give the devil his due, but be very careful that there ain't much due him.   —JOSH BILLINGS

Mass movements can rise and spread without a belief in God, but never without a belief in a devil.   —ERIC HOFFER

The devil's boots don't creak.   —SCOTTISH PROVERB

The belief in a supernatural source of evil is not necessary; men alone are quite capable of every wickedness.
—JOSEPH CONRAD

In Haiti, when they make statues of Christ and Satan, they make Christ black and Satan white.   —BERTRAND RUSSELL

Satan seduces us in this world, and accuses us in the next.
—TALMUD

The devil tempted Christ, but it was Christ who tempted the devil to tempt him.   —SAMUEL BUTLER

Dictatorship

No despotism is more terrible than the tyranny of neurosis. No punishment is more pitiless, more harsh and cunning and malevolent, than that which we inflict upon ourselves. —Leo Rosten

Whenever you have an efficient government you have a dictatorship.
—Harry S Truman

*　　*　　*

Where all think alike, no one thinks very much.
—Walter Lippmann

Dictators ride to and fro upon tigers which they dare not dismount. And the tigers are getting hungry. —Winston Churchill

Diet

If you give food to a small child, you must tell its mother.
—Talmud

Eat a third, drink a third, and leave a third of your stomach empty; then, should anger seize you, there will be room for its rage.
—adapted from Talmud

I'm on a seafood diet. I see food and I eat it.
—Variously ascribed

I found there was only one way to look thin—hang out with fat people.
—Rodney Dangerfield

Water, taken in moderation, cannot hurt anybody.
                              —MARK TWAIN

*   *   *

I've been on a diet for two weeks and all I've lost is two weeks.
                              —TOTIE FIELDS

Tell me what you eat and I will tell you what you are.
                              —ANTHELME BRILLAT-SAVARIN

Eat, drink, and be merry, for tomorrow we may diet.
                              —HARRY KURNITZ

No matter what kind of diet you are on, you can usually eat as much as you want of anything you don't like.   —WALTER SLEZAK

Nothing in the world arouses more false hopes than the first four hours of a diet.
                              —ANONYMOUS

*   *   *

Diplomacy/Diplomats

Consul: In American politics, a person who, having failed to secure an office from the people, is given one by the administration on condition that he leave the country.   —AMBROSE BIERCE

Diplomacy: Lying in state.   —OLIVER HERFORD

Diplomacy is a continuation of war by other means.   —ZHOU ENLAI

Diplomat: *In the United States his social life can be defined in three words—protocol, alcohol, and Geritol.*

—ADLAI STEVENSON

*   *   *

When a diplomat says yes he means perhaps; when he says perhaps he means no; when he says no he is no diplomat.   —ANONYMOUS

A diplomat is a man who always remembers a woman's birthday but never remembers her age.

—ROBERT FROST/FRANÇOIS DE LA ROCHEFOUCAULD/ET AL.

No one, not even the most malevolent democrat, has any idea how much nullity and charlatanism there is in diplomacy.

—OTTO VON BISMARCK

Sincere diplomacy is no more possible than dry water.

—JOSEPH STALIN

The first requirement of a statesman is that he be dull. This is not always easy to achieve.   —DEAN ACHESON

It is amazing how wise statesmen can be when it is ten years too late.

—DAVID LLOYD GEORGE

Diplomacy is the art of saying "nice doggie" until you can find a rock.

—WILL ROGERS

*   *   *

Disease

The art of medicine consists of amusing the patient while nature cures the disease.   —VOLTAIRE

If I had my way I'd make health catching instead of disease.

—ROBERT INGERSOLL

*   *   *

Stubbornness is a disease.   —IDA F. ROSTEN

Insomnia: A contagious disease transmitted from babies to parents.

Physicians think they do a lot for a patient when they give his disease a name.   —IMMANUEL KANT

The desire to take medicine is perhaps the greatest feature that distinguishes man from animals.   —WILLIAM OSLER

Where there is no wine, drugs are necessary.   —TALMUD

Divorce

Getting divorced just because you don't love a man is almost as silly as getting married just because you do.   —ZSA ZSA GABOR

Divorce dates from just about the same time as marriage. I think that marriage is a few weeks older.   —VOLTAIRE

Divorces are made in heaven. —OSCAR WILDE

The happiest time of anyone's life is just after the first divorce.
—JOHN KENNETH GALBRAITH

I should like to add an eighth sacrament to those of the Roman Church—the sacrament of divorce. —SAMUEL BUTLER

To a wedding, walk; to a divorce, run. —SHOLEM ALEICHEM

Tears fall on God's altar for whoever divorces his first wife.
—TALMUD

For some reason, we see divorce as a signal of failure despite the fact that each of us has a right and an obligation to rectify any other mistake we make in life. —JOYCE BROTHERS

When a divorced man marries a divorced woman, four get into bed.
—TALMUD

Clergymen can marry you, but if you find you have made a mistake, in order to get unmarried you have to hire a lawyer.
—ELBERT HUBBARD

When I can no longer bear to think of the victims of broken homes, I begin to think of the victims of intact ones. —PETER DE VRIES

Doctors

There are only two sorts of doctors: those who practice with their brains, and those who practice with their tongues.

—WILLIAM OSLER

* * *

It was not until I had attended a few postmortems that I realized that even the ugliest human exteriors may contain the most beautiful viscera, and was able to console myself for the facial drabness of my neighbors in omnibuses by dissecting them in my imagination.

—J.B.S. HALDANE

A physician gets no pleasure out of the health of his friends.

—MONTAIGNE

Only a physician can commit homicide with impunity.

—PLINY THE ELDER

I am dying with the help of too many physicians.

—ALEXANDER THE GREAT

Doctors pour drugs of which they know little, to cure diseases of which they know less, into human beings of whom they know nothing.

—VOLTAIRE

A physician who treats himself has a fool for a patient.*

—WILLIAM OSLER

We have not lost faith, but we have transferred it from God to the medical profession.   —GEORGE BERNARD SHAW

Before undergoing a surgical operation, arrange your temporal affairs. You may live.
—AMBROSE BIERCE

*   *   *

The door that is not opened for a beggar will open for a doctor.

—TALMUD

* —and a fool for a doctor.

Doctors are just the same as lawyers; the only difference is that lawyers merely rob you, whereas doctors rob you and kill you, too.
—ANTON CHEKHOV

Specialist: A man who knows more and more about less and less.
—WILLIAM J. MAYO/NICHOLAS MURRAY BUTLER

The greatest discoveries of surgery are anesthesia, asepis, and roentgenology—and none was discovered by a surgeon.
—MARTIN HENRY FISCHER

Dogma

Dogmatism: That wretched disease that rivets a man so firmly to his own belief that he becomes incapable of conceiving other men may believe otherwise.
—MONTAIGNE

Truths turn into dogmas the moment they are disputed.
—G. K. CHESTERTON

Dogs

Man is a dog's ideal of what God should be. —HOLBROOK JACKSON

The more I see of men the more I admire dogs.
—MARQUISE DE SEVIGNE

The great pleasure of a dog is that you may make a fool of yourself with him and not only will he not scold you, but he will make a fool of himself, too. —SAMUEL BUTLER

If man's best friend is a dog, his worst is a dogma. —LEO ROSTEN

If you pick up a starving dog and make him prosperous, he will not bite you; that is the principal difference between a dog and a man.
—MARK TWAIN

Biting dogs don't bark.   —LEO ROSTEN

Two dogs can kill a lion.   —JEWISH PROVERB

Dreams

This world is a dream—but please don't wake me up.
—OLD WOMAN'S SAYING

The dumplings in a dream are not dumplings, but dreams.
—TALMUD

Thieves have easy jobs but bad dreams.   —JEWISH SAYING

A dream is a disguised fulfillment of a suppressed or repressed wish. . . . Dreams are guardians of sleep, not its disturbers.
—SIGMUND FREUD

Men see in their dreams only that which is suggested by their own thoughts.   —TALMUD

In dreams, desire tends to satisfy itself in imagery, for the higher faculties no longer inhibit the passions.   —PLATO

In sleep, it is not we who sin—but our dreams.   —TALMUD

In dreams we see ourselves naked and acting out our real characters, even more clearly than we see others awake.   —THOREAU

The interpretation of dreams is the royal road to a knowledge of the unconscious activities of the mind.   —SIGMUND FREUD

We use up too much artistic effort in our dreams.
                                —FRIEDRICH WILHELM NIETZSCHE

I could be bounded in a nutshell and count my-
self a king of infinite space were it not that I
have bad dreams.
                                                —SHAKESPEARE

                     *   *   *

A dream not interpreted is like a letter not read.
                                —ADAPTED FROM TALMUD

It is in sleep that the wild beast in our nature stands up and walks about naked and there is no conceivable folly or shame or crime, however unnatural, not excepting incest or patricide, of which such a nature may not be guilty.   —PLATO

Drink

The worst thing about some men is that when they are not drunk they are sober.   —WILLIAM BUTLER YEATS

A woman drove me to drink, and I never even
had the courtesy to thank her.
                                          —W. C. FIELDS

                     *   *   *

A saloon can't corrupt a good man, and a synagogue can't reform a bad one.   —JEWISH FOLK SAYING

When I drink, I think; and when I think, I drink.
—FRANÇOIS RABELAIS

The drunkard smells of whiskey—but so does the bartender.
—JEWISH SAYING

There should be asylums for habitual teetotalers, but they would probably relapse into teetotalism as soon as they came out.
—SAMUEL BUTLER

Wine hath drowned more men than the sea.
—THOMAS FULLER

*   *   *

When schnapps [liquor] goes in, judgment goes out.
—JEWISH SAYING

Melancholy, indeed, should be diverted by every means but drinking.
—SAMUEL JOHNSON

I'm not so think as you drunk I am.   —JOHN SQUIRE

I always keep a supply of stimulant handy in case I see a snake, which I also keep handy.   —W. C. FIELDS

I'm only a beer teetotaler, not a champagne teetotaler; I don't like beer.   —GEORGE BERNARD SHAW

I have been brought up and trained to have the utmost contempt for people who get drunk.   —WINSTON CHURCHILL

Drinking makes such fools of people, and people are such fools to begin with, that it's compounding a felony.   —ROBERT BENCHLEY

Never accept a drink from a urologist.
     —ERMA BOMBECK'S FATHER

*   *   *

Somebody left the cork out of my lunch.   —W. C. FIELDS

The Talmud declares that wine, in moderation, unfolds a man's brain; a teetotaler rarely possesses great wisdom. —THE KORETSER RABBI

Drunkenness exiles a man from his family.   —JEWISH SAYING

I drink to make other people seem more interesting.
     —GEORGE JEAN NATHAN

It's better to be dead drunk than dead hungry.   —FOLK SAYING

The cost of living has gone up another dollar a quart.
     —W. C. FIELDS

A drunkard can't help harming someone.   —FOLK SAYING

When wine goes in, secrets come out.   —ANONYMOUS

When one man tells you you're drunk, hesitate; when two tell you, think it over; when three tell you—lie down.   —TALMUD

One reason I don't drink is that I want to know when I am having a good time.
     —LADY ASTOR

*   *   *

Economics

There's no such thing as a free lunch. —MILTON FRIEDMAN

Man is an animal that makes bargains; no other animal does this—no dog exchanges bones with another. —ADAM SMITH

Blaming a storekeeper for high prices is like blaming the thermometer for the fever it records. Boycotting the storekeeper is like breaking the thermometer to cure the fever. —MILTON FRIEDMAN

We have a love-hate relationship with inflation. We hate inflation, but we love everything that causes it. —WILLIAM SIMON

Economists now say we move in cycles instead of running around in circles. It sounds better, but it means the same.

—ANONYMOUS

* * *

Income tax has made more liars out of the American people than golf.
—WILL ROGERS

The government never knows whether it is going to stop inflation, only whether it hopes and intends to stop inflation.
—W. ALLEN WALLIS

Property is necessary, but it is not necessary that it should remain forever in the same hands. —RÉMY DE GOURMONT

If all economists were laid end to end, they would not reach a conclusion. —GEORGE BERNARD SHAW

Planned economy: Where everything is included in the plans except economy. —CAREY McWILLIAMS

In a bureaucratic system, useless work drives out useful work.
—MILTON FRIEDMAN

A financier is a pawnbroker with imagination.
—SIR ARTHUR WING PINERO

The merchant has no country. —THOMAS JEFFERSON

Inflation is the one form of taxation that can be imposed without legislation. —MILTON FRIEDMAN

We cannot depend on [any] government to liquidate the welfare state. . . . In the end, it will be market forces that will make the welfare state yield to private choice and technical advance.
—ARTHUR SELDON

Contact with the West most often resulted in the elimination of the worst epidemic and endemic diseases, the mitigation or disappearance of famines, and a general improvement in the material standard of living for all. —P. T. BAUER

The supposed exploitation derives from the fact that the poorer nations export raw commodities to the industrialized nations. Since they have nothing else to export, and since these exports are paid for, this is a perfectly natural and not at all unhealthy state of affairs. For the better part of the nineteenth century the United States was in exactly this condition.   —IRVING KRISTOL

The taxpayer—that's someone who works for the federal government but doesn't have to take a civil service examination.
                                              —RONALD REAGAN

When large numbers of men are unable to find work, unemployment results.   —CALVIN COOLIDGE

There are two times in a man's life when he should not speculate: when he can't afford it, and when he can.   —MARK TWAIN

Government is not the solution (to our economic problems); government is the problem.
        —MILTON FRIEDMAN (IN THE 1930S)

            *   *   *

A little inflation is like a little pregnancy—it keeps on growing.
                                              —LEON HENDERSON

What this country needs is a good five-cent nickel.
                                     —FRANKLIN PIERCE ADAMS

Businessmen possess "a mean rapacity and monopolizing spirit. . . . They seldom meet without [concocting] a conspiracy against the public."   —ADAM SMITH

The ideas of economists and political philosophers, both when they are right and when they are wrong, are more powerful than is commonly understood. Indeed, the world is ruled by little else.
                                       —JOHN MAYNARD KEYNES

Practical men, who believe themselves to be quite exempt from any intellectual influences, are usually the slaves of some defunct economist.   —JOHN MAYNARD KEYNES

Far from the West having caused the poverty of the Third World, contact with the West has been the principal agent of material progress there.   —P. T. BAUER

We have no acts of Parliament against combining to lower the price of work, but many against combining to raise it.   —ADAM SMITH

If you ask economists whether price controls are a good thing, about 90 percent would say no, absolutely not. What appears to be disagreement really is not because it involves others—sometimes columnists or journalists—talking like economists.   —MILTON FRIEDMAN

An economist's guess is liable to be as good as anybody else's.
                                        —WILL ROGERS

*   *   *

Inflation is taxation without representation.   —MILTON FRIEDMAN

The invisible hand in politics operates in the opposite direction to the invisible hand in the market.   —MILTON FRIEDMAN

When you have 7 percent unemployed, you have 93 percent working.
                                        —JOHN F. KENNEDY

*   *   *

It is doubtful that the government knows much more than the public does about how government [economic] policies will work.
                                        —W. ALLEN WALLIS

Far from being harmful to society, the miser is a benefactor, increasing our buying power each time he engages in hoarding.

—WALTER BECK

One man's wage rise is another man's price increase.

—HAROLD WILSON

*   *   *

No nation was ever ruined by trade.   —BENJAMIN FRANKLIN

There are two problems in my life: The political ones are insoluble, and the economic ones are incomprehensible.

—ALEC DOUGLAS-HOME

Education

Academic vows: poverty, bibliography, and jargon.   —LEO ROSTEN

As much as the living are to the dead.

—ARISTOTLE, ASKED HOW MUCH EDUCATED MEN WERE
SUPERIOR TO THOSE UNEDUCATED

A pedant's solution to a problem is to recite a bibliography.

—LEO ROSTEN

Education: The inculcation of the incomprehensible into the indifferent by the incompetent.   —JOHN MAYNARD KEYNES

When you educate a man you educate an individual; when you educate a woman you educate a whole family.   —ROBERT M. MACIVER

If you think education is expensive, try ignorance.

—DEREK BOK

I have never let my schooling interfere with my education.

—MARK TWAIN

All my life, as down an abyss without a bottom, I have been pouring vanloads of information into that vacancy of oblivion I call my mind.   —LOGAN PEARSALL SMITH

Learning is achieved only in company.   —TALMUD

Education is the established church of the United States. It is one of the religions that Americans believe in. It has its own orthodoxy, its pontiffs, and its noble buildings.   —MICHAEL SADLIER

Grammar school never taught me anything about grammar.

—ISAAC GOLDBERG

Nothing in education is so astonishing as the amount of ignorance it accumulates in the form of inert facts.

—HENRY ADAMS

✳   ✳   ✳

The ill-tempered cannot teach.   —HILLEL

Education: The path from cocky ignorance to miserable uncertainty.

—MARK TWAIN

It has been said that we have not had the three *r*'s in America, we had the six *r*'s: remedial readin', remedial 'ritin', and remedial 'rithmetic.   —ROBERT M. HUTCHINS

Learning is one thing that can't be bequeathed.
                    —ADAPTED FROM SAYINGS OF THE FATHERS

*A learned blockhead is a greater blockhead
than an ignorant one.*
                    —BENJAMIN FRANKLIN

*   *   *

You can't expect a boy to be depraved until he has been to a good
school.   —H. H. MUNRO ("SAKI")

Education: A succession of eye-openers each involving the repudiation
of some previously held belief.   —GEORGE BERNARD SHAW

He is to be educated not because he is to make shoes, nails, and pins,
but because he is a man.   —WILLIAM ELLERY CHANNING

The three major administrative problems on a campus are sex for the
students, athletics for the alumni, and parking for the faculty.
                    —ROBERT M. HUTCHINS

Education is the best provision for old age.   —ARISTOTLE

Public schools: A place of detention for children placed in the care of
teachers who are afraid of the principal, principals who are afraid of
the school board, school boards who are afraid of the parents, parents
who are afraid of the children, and children who are afraid of nobody.
                    —ANONYMOUS

I prefer the company of peasants because they have not been educated
sufficiently to reason incorrectly.   —MONTAIGNE

The college graduate is presented with a sheepskin to cover his intellectual nakedness.   —ROBERT M. HUTCHINS

How is it that little children are so intelligent and men so stupid? It must be education that does it.

—ALEXANDRE DUMAS, *fils*

Learning is not child's play; we cannot learn without pain.

—ARISTOTLE

You ain't learnin' nothin' when you're talkin'.

—LYNDON B. JOHNSON

I respect faith, but doubt is what gets you an education.

—WILSON MIZNER

The ratio of literacy to illiteracy is constant, but nowadays the illiterates can read.

—ALBERTO MORAVIA

✳   ✳   ✳

The average Ph.D. thesis is nothing but the transference of bones from one graveyard to another.   —J. FRANK DOBIE

Everybody who is incapable of learning has taken to teaching.

—OSCAR WILDE

Universities are full of knowledge; the freshmen bring a little in and the seniors take none away, so knowledge accumulates.

—ABBOTT LAWRENCE LOWELL

Open your discourse with a jest, and let your hearts laugh a little; then become serious.   —TALMUD

Much have I learned from my teachers, more from my colleagues, but most from my students. —TALMUD

Soap and education are not as sudden as a massacre, but they are more deadly in the long run. —MARK TWAIN

One must learn to think well before learning to think; afterward it proves too difficult. —ANATOLE FRANCE

Men are born ignorant, not stupid; they are made stupid by education. —BERTRAND RUSSELL

I honestly believe it is better to know nothing than to know what ain't so. —JOSH BILLINGS/WILL ROGERS/"KIN" HUBBARD

Education: That which reveals to the wise, and conceals from the stupid, the vast limits of their knowledge. —MARK TWAIN

My education was dismal. I went to a series of schools for mentally disturbed teachers. —WOODY ALLEN

The lecture method of instruction is based on the idea that the instructors' notebook can be transferred to the notebook of the student without passing through the brain of the student—or the teacher. —DARRELL HUFF

He who is dying of hunger must be fed rather than taught. —THOMAS AQUINAS

God said: You must teach, as I taught, without a fee.

—TALMUD

*   *   *

In the first place, God made idiots; this was for practice. Then he made school boards.   —MARK TWAIN

Academic tenure encourages pedants to become fossils.
                                         —LEO ROSTEN

He who can, does; he who cannot, teaches.
                              —GEORGE BERNARD SHAW

Education: What remains after you have forgotten all that you have been taught.   —LORD HALIFAX

It should be possible to explain the laws of physics to a barmaid.
                              —ALBERT EINSTEIN

* * *

Education is the process of casting false pearls before the real swine.
                         —ATTRIBUTED TO PROF. IRWIN EDMAN

Education: A race against catastrophe.   —H. G. WELLS

A university is what a college becomes when the faculty loses interest in students.   —JOHN CIARDI

He who refuses to learn deserves extinction.   —HILLEL

All men by nature desire to know.   —ARISTOTLE

Education: That which discloses to the wise and disguises from the foolish their lack of understanding.
                         —AMBROSE BIERCE/MARK TWAIN

The world itself rests upon the breath of the children in our schools.
                                         —TALMUD

Education is the ability to listen to almost anything without losing your temper or your self-confidence.   —ROBERT FROST

Those who educate children well are more to be honored than they who produce them; for these only gave them life, those the art of living well.
                    —ARISTOTLE

*   *   *

The aim of education should be to teach the child to think, not what to think.   —JOHN DEWEY

The roots of education are bitter, but the fruit is sweet.
                    —ARISTOTLE

I had, out of my sixty teachers, a scant half dozen who couldn't have been supplanted by phonographs.   —DON HEROLD

There are two kinds of arguments, the true and the false. The young should be instructed in both—but the false first.   —PLATO

Egotism

One of my chief regrets during my years in the theater is that I couldn't sit in the audience and watch me.
                    —JOHN BARRYMORE

*   *   *

We have an innate propensity to get ourselves noticed, and noticed favorably, by our kind.   —WILLIAM JAMES

If I cannot brag of knowing something, then I brag of not knowing it;
at any rate, brag.   —RALPH WALDO EMERSON

To love oneself is the beginning of a lifelong romance.
                                          —OSCAR WILDE

Take egotism out, and you would castrate the benefactors.
                                          —RALPH WALDO EMERSON

Conceit: *That which causes more conversation
than wit.*

Egotist: *A person of low taste, more interested
in himself than in me.*
                                          —AMBROSE BIERCE

*   *   *

He who despises himself nevertheless esteems himself as a self-
despiser.   —FRIEDRICH WILHELM NIETZSCHE

Self-love is proof against cudgel blows but not against pinpricks.
                                 —FRIEDRICH WILHELM NIETZSCHE

Emotions

The advantage of the emotions is that they lead us astray.
                                          —OSCAR WILDE

Emotion has taught mankind to reason.
                                          —VAUVENARGUES

*   *   *

If, after I depart this vale, you remember me and have thought to please my ghost, forgive some sinner and wink at a homely girl.
—H. L. Mencken

The hardest thing is to disguise your feelings when you put a lot of relatives on the train for home.   —Anonymous

Envy

Don't envy a sinner; you don't know what awaits him.
—adapted from Ben Sirach

Malice may be sometimes out of breath, but never envy.
—Lord Halifax

Envy is hatred without a cure.
—Bahya Ben Asher

*   *   *

Men are not against you; they are merely for themselves.
—Gene Fowler

Our nature is inseparable from desires, and the very word "desire" ... implies that our present felicity is not complete.
—Thomas Hobbes

Epigrams

(ALL BY LEO ROSTEN)

The one thing curiosity can*not* be is—idle.

It is the weak who are cruel; kindness is to be expected only from the strong.

People debase the pursuit of happiness into the narcotic pursuit of "fun."

Courage is the capacity to confront what can be imagined.

Those who do not know fear cannot be brave.

Don't blame God; He's only human.

Rome wasn't burned in a day.

Most men never mature; they simply grow taller.

Give a man enough rope and he'll hang you.

Those who lead processions shouting, "All power to the people!" want power to be given to—those who shout "All power to the people!"

Where there's a will, there's a wail.

Flying saucers are an optical conclusion.

He who laughs last, lasts.

The hardest part of growing up is learning how to *wait*.

He is by all odds the most interesting man he has ever met.

Passion, like politics, makes very strange bedfellows.

He has all the wit and charm of a damp sock.

Although not inept, he is not ept, either.

Miracles only testify to the limits of our knowledge.

Everyone had an unhappy childhood.

No one knows how a society really works.

The most satisfactory technique in making love is to be in love with the one you are making love to.

People who are never unhappy are crazy.

Most social scientists mistake jargon for insight.

If you want to be popular, just ask people for advice; don't take it, just ask for it.

There is a destiny that ends our shapes.

Epitaphs

The rarest quality in an epitaph is truth.
—HENRY DAVID THOREAU

Satire does not look pretty on a tombstone.   —CHARLES LAMB

H. L. Mencken: A writer who denounces life and makes you want to live.   —WALTER LIPPMANN

An inscription which hopes that virtues acquired by death will have a retroactive effect.   —AMBROSE BIERCE

I die adoring God, loving my friends, not hating my enemies, and detesting superstition.   —VOLTAIRE

He is a good man—according to his epitaph.   —JEWISH SAYING

If you take epitaphs seriously, we ought to bury the living and resurrect the dead.
—MARK TWAIN

*   *   *

EPITAPHS SELECTED BY A HANDFUL OF CELEBRITIES:

Here lies a nuisance dedicated to sanity. —DAVID LOW

All things considered, I'd rather be in Philadelphia. —W. C. FIELDS

Here lies that part of J.R.L.
That hampered him from doing well.
—JAMES RUSSELL LOWELL

William Powell: Excuse me for not rising.

H. G. Wells: I *told* you so, dammit!

Dorothy Parker: Excuse my dust.

Jack Benny: Did you hear about my operation?

Milton Berle: This one's on me.

Robert Benchley: All of this is over my head.

Alfred Hitchcock: I'm involved in a plot.

Leo Rosten: This is much too deep for me.

A hypochondriac: I kept *telling* you I was sick!

Nunnally Johnson: I *thought* there was a funny taste about that last one.

Equality

There isn't a parallel of latitude but thinks it would have been the equator if it had had its rights.

—MARK TWAIN

*   *   *

The worst form of inequality is to try to make unequal things equal.
—ARISTOTLE

That all men are equal is a proposition to which, at ordinary times, no sane individual has ever given his assent.   —ALDOUS HUXLEY

It is to be regretted that the rich and powerful too often bend the acts of government to their selfish purposes. . . . Equality of talents, of education, or of wealth cannot be produced by human institutions.
—ANDREW JACKSON

Some will always be above others. Destroy the inequality today, and it will appear again tomorrow.   —RALPH WALDO EMERSON

The principle that all people are fundamentally equal is an axiom I can accept as a religious mandate but not as an educational one.
—DAVID RIESMAN

Nature has never read the Declaration of Independence. It continues to make us unequal.

—WILL DURANT

*   *   *

By nature all men are equal in liberty, but not in other endowments.
—THOMAS AQUINAS

We who are liberal and progressive know that the poor are our equals in every sense except that of being equal to us. —LIONEL TRILLING

All men are equal—all men, that is to say, who possess umbrellas.
—E. M. FORSTER

All animals are equal, but some animals are more equal than others.
—GEORGE ORWELL

Evil

When choosing between two evils, I always like to take the one I've never tried before. —MAE WEST

There is only one good—knowledge; and only one evil—ignorance.
—SOCRATES

Evil is sweet in the beginning but bitter in the end. —TALMUD

This world was created for those who are ashamed to do evil.
—INTRODUCTION TO *TIKUNE ZOHAR*

It is a sin to believe evil of others, but it is seldom a mistake.
—H. L. MENCKEN

* * *

The mercy of the wicked is cruel. —OLD TESTAMENT

I prefer the wicked rather than the foolish. The wicked sometimes rest. —ALEXANDRE DUMAS, *PÈRE*

It is easier to denature plutonium than to denature the evil spirit of man. —ALBERT EINSTEIN

Evolution

We are descended not only from monkeys, but from monks.
—ELBERT HUBBARD

Experience/Adversity

Experience is only half of experience.   —GOETHE

Experience is the name people give their mistakes.
                                —TALMUD/OSCAR WILDE

> *The cat, having sat upon a hot stove lid, will*
> *not sit upon a hot stove lid again. But he won't*
> *sit upon a cold stove lid, either.*
>   —MARK TWAIN

                    *   *   *

The only thing experience teaches us is that experience teaches us
nothing.   —ANDRÉ MAUROIS

Experience increases our wisdom but doesn't reduce our follies.
                                —JOSH BILLINGS

> *Experience is not what happens to a man. It is*
> *what a man does with what happens to him.*
>   —ALDOUS HUXLEY

                    *   *   *

Experience is the comb that Nature gives us when we are bald.
                                —RUSSIAN PROVERB

Experience never errs; what alone may err is our judgment, which
predicts effects that cannot be produced in our experiments.
                                —LEONARDO DA VINCI

Few men are worthy of experience. The majority let it corrupt them.
                                —JOUBERT

Facts

Get your facts first, and then you can distort them as much as you please.　　　　　　　　　　　　　　　　　—MARK TWAIN

Generally the theories we believe we call facts,
and the facts we disbelieve we call theories.
　　　　　　　　　　　　　—FELIX COHEN

*　　*　　*

Faith

We only speak of faith when we wish to substitute emotion for evidence.　　　　　　　　　　　　　　—BERTRAND RUSSELL

The way to see by Faith is to shut the Eye of Reason.
　　　　　　　　　　　　　—BENJAMIN FRANKLIN

There are those who scoff at the schoolboy, calling him frivolous and shallow. Yet it was the schoolboy who said, "Faith is believing what you know ain't so."   —MARK TWAIN

Logic is like the sword—those who appeal to it shall perish by it. Faith is appealing to the living God, and one may perish by that, too, but somehow one would rather perish that way than the other, and one has got to perish sooner or later.   —SAMUEL BUTLER

With faith, there are no questions; without faith, there are no answers.
                                          —THE CHOFETZ CHAIM

You can do very little with faith, but you can do nothing without it.
                                          —SAMUEL BUTLER

Faith is much better than belief. Belief is when someone else does the thinking.   —BUCKMINSTER FULLER

Aristotle has said that man is a thinking animal; all my life I have been searching for evidence to support this.
                                          —BERTRAND RUSSELL

                          *   *   *

How many things that served us yesterday as articles of faith, today are fables.   —MONTAIGNE

Faith: An illogical belief in the improbable.   —H. L. MENCKEN

We may define "faith" as a firm belief in something for which there is no evidence. When there is evidence, no one speaks of "faith." We do not speak of a faith that two and two are four or that the earth is round.   —BERTRAND RUSSELL

Faith must trample under foot all reason, sense, and understanding.
                                          —MARTIN LUTHER

Faith can move mountains, but not furniture. —ANONYMOUS

Faith is that quality that enables us to believe what we know to be untrue. —ANONYMOUS

Fame

Glory [is the] most useless, frivolous, and false coin that passes current among us. —MONTAIGNE

If fame is to come only after death, I am in no hurry for it. —MARTIAL

Celebrities are known primarily for their well-knownness. And we imitate them as if they were cast in the mold of greatness. —DANIEL J. BOORSTIN

Our very efforts to debunk celebrities . . . are self-defeating. They increase our interest in the fabrication. —DANIEL J. BOORSTIN

Fame is the perfume of heroic deeds. —SOCRATES

Fame is a vapor, popularity an accident; the only earthly certainty is oblivion. —MARK TWAIN

Fanatics

Fanatics are picturesque; and mankind prefers observing poses to listening to reason. —FRIEDRICH WILHELM NIETZSCHE

A fanatic is a man who does what he thinks the Lord would do if He knew the facts of the case. —FINLEY PETER DUNNE ("MR. DOOLEY")

Fanaticism consists in redoubling your effort when you have forgotten your aim.   —GEORGE SANTAYANA

Defoe says that there were a hundred thousand country fellows ready to fight to the death against popery, without knowing whether popery was a man or a horse.   —WILLIAM HAZLITT

Fashion

When in doubt, wear red.   —BILL BLASS

Women's styles may change but their designs remain the same.
                                                    —OSCAR WILDE

High heels were invented by a woman who had been kissed on the forehead.   —CHRISTOPHER MORLEY

Fashion is something barbarous, for it produces innovation without reason and imitation without benefit.
                                            —GEORGE SANTAYANA

Fashion is a form of ugliness so intolerable that we have to alter it every six months.   —OSCAR WILDE

Her hat is a creation that will never go out of style; it will just look ridiculous year after year.   —FRED ALLEN

Only men who are not interested in women are interested in women's clothes; men who like women never notice what they wear.
                                                    —ANATOLE FRANCE

All women's dresses are merely variations on the eternal struggle between the admitted desire to dress and the unadmitted desire to undress. —LIN YUTANG

I have heard with admiring submission the lady who declared that the sense of being perfectly well dressed gives a feeling of inward tranquillity which religion is powerless to bestow.
—RALPH WALDO EMERSON

He who goes against fashion is himself its slave.
—LOGAN PEARSALL SMITH

I dress for women—and I undress for men.
—ANGIE DICKINSON

*   *   *

A fashionable woman is always in love with herself.
—FRANÇOIS DE LA ROCHEFOUCAULD

She wore far too much rouge and not quite enough clothes; that is always a sign of despair in a woman. —OSCAR WILDE

I never expected to see the day when girls would get sunburned in the places they do now. —WILL ROGERS

Fashions, after all, are only induced epidemics.
—GEORGE BERNARD SHAW

The trick of wearing mink is to look as though you are wearing a cloth coat. The trick of wearing a cloth coat is to look as though you are wearing mink. —PIERRE BALMAIN

Fashion: That, not necessarily beautiful, which makes what preceded it look stodgy, foolish, or inexpensive. —LEO ROSTEN

Fear

Fear the man who fears you.   —HASIDIC SAYING

Men are moved by only two things: fear and self-interest.
                                —NAPOLEON BONAPARTE

It is better to be frightened now than killed hereafter.
                                —WINSTON CHURCHILL

The thing of which I have most fear is fear.
                    —MONTAIGNE/HENRY DAVID THOREAU/
                        FRANKLIN D. ROOSEVELT

Early and provident fear is the mother of safety.
                    —EDMUND BURKE/CF. WINSTON CHURCHILL

I came to believe it not true that "the coward dies a thousand deaths, the brave man only one." I think it is the other way around: It is the brave who die a thousand deaths. For it is imagination, and not just conscience, which doth make cowards of us all. Those who do not know fear are not really brave.   —LEO ROSTEN

We're afraid of truth, afraid of fortune, afraid of death, and afraid of each other.   —RALPH WALDO EMERSON

Fear only two: God, and the man who has no fear of God.
                                —HASIDIC SAYING

No one loves the man whom he fears.   —ARISTOTLE

Hope is ambiguous, but fear is precise.   —LEO ROSTEN

Flattery

We sometimes imagine we hate flattery, but we only hate the way we are flattered. —FRANÇOIS DE LA ROCHEFOUCAULD

If you can't love, learn how to flatter.
—JEWISH SAYING

* * *

A flatterer is a friend who is your inferior, or pretends to be so.
—ARISTOTLE

Many know how to flatter but few know how to praise.
—ANONYMOUS

Flatterer: One who says things to your face that he wouldn't say behind your back. —ANONYMOUS

What really flatters a man is that you think him worth flattering.
—GEORGE BERNARD SHAW

Nature has hardly formed a woman ugly enough to be insensible to flattery upon her person. —LORD CHESTERFIELD

Flattery is all right if you don't inhale.
—ADLAI E. STEVENSON

* * *

Baloney is the . . . lie laid on so thick you hate it. Blarney is flattery laid on so thin you love it. —FULTON J. SHEEN

Folk Sayings

The man who is destined to drown will drown in a glass of water.

—JEWISH SAYING

*   *   *

What was hard to endure is sweet to recall.

—CONTINENTAL PROVERB

Little dogs make the most noise.   —MAORI SAYING

If cats wore gloves, they would catch no mice.   —HINDU SAYING

Other men's misfortunes are not hard to bear.

—TALMUD/ROCHEFOUCAULD/SWIFT/WILDE/EMERSON

No barber cuts his own hair.   —TURKISH SAYING

Ten excuses are less persuasive than one.

—JEWISH SAYING

*   *   *

If a horse had anything to say, he would speak up.

—JEWISH SAYING

The man who looks for easy work always goes to bed tired.

—JEWISH SAYING

He who climbs Mt. Fuji once is a wise man; he who climbs it twice is a fool.   —JAPANESE SAYING

When there's a wind, garbage flies high.   —JEWISH SAYING

No one needs help to get into trouble.   —Maori saying

He who has butter on his bread should not go into the sun.
                              —Yiddish proverb

* * *

There is no cloth so fine that moths are unable to eat it.
                              —Chinese saying

If you have money, men think you are wise, handsome, and able to sing like a bird.   —Jewish saying

The hardest work of all is to do nothing.   —Jewish saying

Any man can count his own teeth.   —Italian proverb

It is easier to guard a sack full of fleas than a girl in love.
                              —Jewish saying

He that's born to be hanged needn't fear water.   —Irish proverb

A broken clock is still better than one that goes wrong; at least it is right twice a day.   —Jewish saying

Indecision is like the stepchild: If he doesn't wash his hands, he is called dirty; if he does, he is wasting water.
                              —African proverb

* * *

If you do not ask their help, all men are good-natured.
                              —Chinese proverb

A toothache makes you forget a headache.   —Yiddish saying

An ugly patch is nicer than a beautiful hole.   —JAPANESE PROVERB

In time even a bear can learn to dance.   —RUSSIAN SAYING

Locks keep out only the honest.   —JEWISH SAYING

A full bag is heavy to carry, but an empty one is heavier.
                                                 —CHINESE SAYING

A wooden bed is better than a golden coffin.   —RUSSIAN PROVERB

The daughters of the rich are always beautiful.   —ARABIC SAYING

Any man surrounded by dwarfs looks like a giant. —JEWISH SAYING

Out of snow, you can't make cheesecake.
                                   —JEWISH SAYING
                    ✳   ✳   ✳

He's half a millionaire: He has the air, but not the million.
                                             —MY UNCLE

Do no good—and you will suffer no ingratitude.
                                    —ARABIAN PROVERB

Every shut eye ain't asleep.
            —AFRICAN AMERICAN PROVERB
                    ✳   ✳   ✳

Where there's too much, something is missing.   —YIDDISH SAYING

The one-eyed need sleep, too.   —JEWISH SAYING

Some things are clever only the first time.   —JEWISH SAYING

In the eyes of its mother every beetle is a gazelle.
—MOROCCAN PROVERB

*I felt sorry for myself because I had no shoes
—until I met a man who had no feet.*
—JEWISH FOLK SAYING

✳   ✳   ✳

Food/Diets

I am convinced digestion is the great secret of life.
—SYDNEY SMITH

My illness is due to my doctor's insistence that I drink milk, a whitish fluid they force down helpless babies.   —W. C. FIELDS

Artichoke: That vegetable of which one has more at the finish than at the start of a dinner.   —LORD CHESTERFIELD

Oyster: A slimy, gobby shellfish which civilization gives men the hardihood to eat without removing its entrails! The shells are something given to the poor.   —AMBROSE BIERCE

Chop: A piece of leather skillfully attached to a bone and administered to the patients at restaurants. —AMBROSE BIERCE

Everything you see I owe to spaghetti.   —SOPHIA LOREN

I will not eat oysters. I want my food dead—not sick, not wounded—dead.   —WOODY ALLEN

Hunger finds no fault with the cookery.   —HENRY GEORGE BOHN

Isn't there any other part of the matzo you people eat?
                                    —Priest, at kosher restaurant

No man is lonely while eating spaghetti.   —Frank Morley

Fools/Folly

Against stupidity, the Lord Himself is helpless.   —Talmud

The fools who sing all summer weep all winter.   —Jewish saying

Better a witty fool than a foolish wit.   —Shakespeare

Wise men talk because they have something to say, fools because they
have to say something.   —Plato

Who loves not women, wine, and song remains a fool his whole life
long.   —Martin Luther

The conceited man is not a sinner but a fool. —the Chofetz Chaim

A fool measures water with a sieve.   —Jewish saying

Don't approach a goat from the front, a horse from the back, or a fool
from any side.   —Jewish saying

God created the flirt as soon as He made the fool.   —Victor Hugo

You can educate a fool but you can't make him think.

—YIDDISH SAYING

*   *   *

In life, each of us must sometime play the fool.   —YIDDISH SAYING

A fool who wants to hang himself grabs a knife.   —JEWISH SAYING

That fools are fond of sweets is a discovery of the wise.

—JEWISH SAYING

There are two kinds of fools: those who can't change their opinions and those who won't.

—JOSH BILLINGS

*   *   *

A fool can ask more questions in an hour than ten wise men can answer in a year.   —JEWISH SAYING

Fortune, seeing she could not make fools wise, has made them lucky.

—MONTAIGNE

Most fools think they are only ignorant.

—BENJAMIN FRANKLIN

*   *   *

The world is in the hands of fools.   —TALMUD

It has been said that there is no fool like an old fool, except a young fool. But the young fool has first to grow up to be an old fool to realize what a damn fool he was when he was a young fool.

—HAROLD MACMILLAN

✳   ✳   ✳

He who holds hopes for the human condition is a fool.

—ALBERT CAMUS

There are two kinds of fools; one says, "This is old, therefore it is good"; the other says, "This is new, therefore it is better."

—WILLIAM RALPH INGE

Wise men think out their thoughts; fools proclaim them.

—HEINRICH HEINE

Nature never blunders: When she makes a fool, she means it.

—JOSH BILLINGS

There are four types of men in this world:

The man who knows, and knows that he knows; he is wise, so consult him.
The man who knows, but doesn't know that he knows; help him not forget what he knows.
The man who knows not, and knows that he knows not; teach him.
Finally, there is the man who knows not but pretends that he knows; he is a fool, so avoid him.

—IBN GABIROL

Foreign Affairs/Foreign Policy

We have no commission from God to police the world.
—Benjamin Harrison

This is the devilish thing about foreign affairs—they are foreign and will not always conform to our whim. —James Reston

We are the greatest power in the world. If we behave like it.
—Walt W. Rostow

* * *

You call that statesmanship? I call it an emotional spasm.
—Aneurin Bevan, on unilateral disarmament

Freedom

The basic test of freedom is perhaps less in what we are free to do than in what we are free not to do. —Eric Hoffer

If people have to choose between freedom and sandwiches, they will take sandwiches.
—Lord Boyd Orr

* * *

The truly free man is the one who will turn down an invitation to dinner without giving an excuse.
—Jules Renard, attributed to Oscar Wilde

The most "secure" of human institutions is a prison, but who would choose to live in one? —Leo Rosten

Man is condemned to be free. —Jean-Paul Sartre

While the right to talk may be the beginning of freedom, the necessity of listening is what makes the right important.
—WALTER LIPPMANN

American freedom consists largely in talking nonsense.
—EDGAR WATSON ("ED") HOWE

It is better to die on your feet than to live on your knees.
—DOLORES IBARRURI/TALMUD

A slave is a free man if he is content with his lot; a free man is a slave if he seeks more than that.   —ANONYMOUS

Necessity is the plea for every infringement of human freedom. It is the argument of tyrants; it is the creed of slaves.   —WILLIAM PITT

Those who expect to reap the blessings of freedom must, like men, undergo the fatigue of supporting it.   —TOM PAINE

Freedom of expression is the indispensable condition of nearly every other form of freedom.   —BENJAMIN N. CARDOZO

I know of no example in time or place of a society that has been marked by a large measure of political freedom, and that has not also used something comparable to a free market.   —MILTON FRIEDMAN

Freudian Slips

Not a day goes by without thousands of people making millions of Freudian slips—errors in speech or writing or conduct which convey unexpected opinions—unexpected because true. "Slips of the tongue" have long, buried histories. Volumes can be printed about Freudian slips; among my favorites are the following:

The all-girl orchestra was rather weak in the bras section.

Mr. and Mrs. Oliver Sloane request the pleasure of your presents at the marriage of their daughter . . .

Telegram to wife: HAVING WONDERFUL TIME, DARLING. WISH YOU WERE HER. (Signed) Johnny

The bride and her mother were in the deceiving line.

Upon arriving at the Honolulu airport, two men were given coveted lays by Hawaiian maidens.

The protesting students insisted that before they were arrested they only intended to show their opposition to the speaker by pissing.

They were married and lived happily even after.

Friends

A friend that ain't in need is a friend indeed.
—FRANK MCKINNEY "KIN" HUBBARD

God gives us relatives; thank God we can choose our friends.
—ADDISON MIZNER/ETHEL MUMFORD

False friends are like migratory birds: They fly away in cold weather.
—HASIDIC SAYING

We cherish our friends not for their ability to amuse us, but for ours to amuse them.
—EVELYN WAUGH

*　*　*

You, sir, are a foul-weather friend. —BERNARD BARUCH

May God defend me from my friends; I can defend myself from my enemies. —VOLTAIRE

The good fellow to everyone is a good friend to no one.
—JEWISH SAYING

A friend you have to buy; enemies you get for nothing.
—JEWISH SAYING

Future

The future ain't what it used to be.
—ATTRIBUTED TO YOGI BERRA/PAUL VALERY/CASEY STENGEL

If you want a picture of the future, imagine a boot stomping on a human face—forever. —GEORGE ORWELL

G

Gambling

The gambling known as business looks with austere disfavor upon the business known as gambling. —AMBROSE BIERCE

The best throw with the dice is to throw them away. —ANONYMOUS

No wife can endure a gambling husband, unless he is a steady winner.
—LORD THOMAS ROBERT DEWAR

There is no gambling like politics. —BENJAMIN DISRAELI

The urge to gamble is so universal and its practice so pleasurable that I assume it must be evil.

—HEYWOOD BROUN

* * *

Gambling promises the poor what property performs for the rich—
something for nothing.   —GEORGE BERNARD SHAW

Genius

To the question, "Do you think genius is hereditary?" he replied, "I
can't tell you; heaven has granted me no offspring."
                                    —JAMES MCNEILL WHISTLER

There is no great genius without a mixture of madness.
                                    —ARISTOTLE/SENECA

In every work of genius we recognize our rejected thoughts.
                                    —RALPH WALDO EMERSON

The difference between genius and stupidity is that genius has
its limits.   —ANONYMOUS

Doing easily what others find difficult is talent; doing what is
impossible for talent is genius.   —AMIEL

What is genius? It is the power to be a boy again at will.
                                    —JAMES M. BARRIE

Genius is 1 percent inspiration and 99 percent perspiration.
                                    —THOMAS ALVA EDISON

We are all geniuses up to the age of ten.   —ALDOUS HUXLEY

The function of genius is not to give new answers, but to pose new
questions which time and mediocrity can resolve.
                                    —H. R. TREVOR-ROPER

Churchill was fundamentally what the English call unstable: by which they mean anybody who has that touch of genius which is inconvenient in normal times. —HAROLD MACMILLAN

Genius is born—not paid. —OSCAR WILDE

God

God sneezed. What could I say to Him? —HENNY YOUNGMAN

I cannot believe in a God who wants to be praised all the time. —FRIEDRICH WILHELM NIETZSCHE

Those who set out to serve both God and Mammon soon discover that there is no God. —LOGAN PEARSALL SMITH

I have never understood why it should be considered derogatory to the Creator to suppose that he has a sense of humor. —WILLIAM RALPH INGE

God is closest to those with broken hearts. —JEWISH SAYING

I tremble for my country when I reflect that God is just. —THOMAS JEFFERSON

I would not marry God. —MAXINE ELLIOTT

Why attack God? He may be as miserable as we are. —ANONYMOUS

God will forgive me: *C'est son métier* ("It's his business"). —HEINRICH HEINE (DURING FINAL DAYS)

God is subtle, but He is not malicious. . . . I cannot believe that
God plays dice with the world.   —ALBERT EINSTEIN

If you gain, you gain all; if you lose, you lose nothing. Wager,
then, without hesitation, that He exists.   —BLAISE PASCAL

What thinking man is there who still requires the hypothesis of
a God?   —FRIEDRICH WILHELM NIETZSCHE

We are told that when Jehovah created the world he saw that it was
good; what would he say now?   —GEORGE BERNARD SHAW

I would believe only in a God that knows how to dance.
                            —FRIEDRICH WILHELM NIETZSCHE

*God may be dead, but fifty thousand social
workers have risen to take his place.*
                            —J. D. MCCOUGHEY

*   *   *

If God lived on earth, people would knock out all His windows.
                            —MY FATHER

If you talk to God, you are praying; if God talks to you, you have
schizophrenia.   —THOMAS SZASZ

If God did not exist, it would have been necessary to invent Him.
                            —VOLTAIRE

The most haunting (and courageous) comment I have ever heard
about the Almighty, more powerful than any of the heretical broad-
sides hurled by H. L. Mencken, Voltaire, Stendhal, or the relentless
George Bernard Shaw, is this old saying of the Jews: "Dear God: If
You forgive us, we will forgive You."   —LEO ROSTEN

It is a curious thing that God learned Greek when he wished to turn author—and that he did not learn it better.
—FRIEDRICH WILHELM NIETZSCHE

A baby is God's opinion that the world should go on.
—CARL SANDBURG

When God wants to break a man's heart, he gives him a lot of sense.
—JEWISH SAYING

God seems to have left the receiver off the hook, and time is running out.
—ARTHUR KOESTLER

We are most unfair to God: we do not allow Him to sin.
—FRIEDRICH WILHELM NIETZSCHE

If God really thinks well of the human race . . . why did he not proceed, as in Genesis, to create man at once? What was the point of the ichthyosaurs, dinosaurs, diplodochi, mastodons, and so on?
—BERTRAND RUSSELL

If triangles made a god, they would give him three sides.
—BARON DE MONTESQUIEU

Dear God: You help strangers, so why not me?   —JEWISH SAYING

An honest God is the noblest work of man.
—ROBERT G. INGERSOLL

One half of the world does not believe in God, and the other half does not believe in me.
—OSCAR WILDE

Few men dare publish to the world the prayers they make to Almighty God.   —MONTAIGNE

Which is it: Is man one of God's blunders, or is God one of man's blunders?   —FRIEDRICH WILHELM NIETZSCHE

Nothing appears more to impugn divine providence in human affairs than the affliction of the innocent.

—THOMAS AQUINAS

* * *

The chief contribution of Protestantism to human thought is its massive proof that God is a bore.   —H. L. MENCKEN

Our Heavenly Father invented man because he was disappointed in the monkey.   —MARK TWAIN

I fear God, yet am not afraid of him.   —SIR THOMAS BROWNE

He was a wise man who invented God.   —PLATO

The only excuse for God is that he doesn't exist.   —STENDHAL

The chicken probably came before the egg because it is hard to imagine God wanting to sit on an egg.   —ANONYMOUS

It is impossible to believe that the same God who permitted His own son to die a bachelor regards celibacy as an actual sin.

—H. L. MENCKEN

* * *

I have been reading the Old Testament, a most bloodthirsty and perilous book for the young. Jehovah is beyond doubt the worst character in fiction. —EDWARD ARLINGTON ROBINSON

Dear God: Help me get up; I can fall down by myself.
—JEWISH SAYING

When the gods wish to punish us they answer our prayers.
—OSCAR WILDE

O Lord, glance down from heaven and take a real look at Your world!
—JEWISH SAYING

When a woman gets too old to be attractive to man she turns to God.
—HONORÉ DE BALZAC

God created only one man so that no one could call virtue or vice hereditary. —TALMUD

It is impossible to imagine the universe run by a wise, just, and omnipotent God, but it is quite easy to imagine it run by a board of gods. If such a board actually exists it operates precisely like the board of a corporation that is losing money.
—H. L. MENCKEN

Father expected a good deal of God. He didn't actually accuse God of inefficiency, but when he prayed, his tone was loud and angry, like that of a dissatisfied guest in a carefully managed hotel. —CLARENCE DAY

Every day people are straying away from the church and going back to God. —LENNY BRUCE

Men, enriched by your sweat and misery, made you superstitious not that you might fear God, but that you might fear them.
—VOLTAIRE

The idea of a Supreme Being who creates a world in which one creature is designed to eat another in order to subsist, and then passes a
law saying "Thou shalt not kill," is so monstrously, immeasurably,
bottomlessly absurd that I am at a loss to understand how mankind
has entertained or given it house room all this long.

—PETER DE VRIES

God: The most popular scapegoat for our sins.   —MARK TWAIN

If the [Greek] gods steal, by whom shall their believers swear?

—APOCRYPHA

In German the word *sein* signifies both things: to be, and to belong
to Him.   —FRANZ KAFKA

The only thing that stops God sending a second Flood is that the first
one was useless.   —NICHOLAS CHAMFORT

Dear God, I know you will provide, but why don't you provide *until*
you provide?   —YIDDISH SAYING

One on God's side is a majority.   —WENDELL PHILLIPS

*All sentences that start with "God forbid" de-
scribe what is possible.*

—JEWISH SAYING

*   *   *

I do not believe in God. I believe in cashmere.   —FRAN LEBOWITZ

My prayer to God is a very short one: "O Lord, make my enemies look ridiculous!" God has granted it.

—VOLTAIRE

*   *   *

God requires no synagogue—except in the heart. —HASIDIC SAYING

If God, as some now say, is dead, He no doubt died of trying to find an equitable solution to the Arab-Jewish problem.   —I. F. STONE

If only God would give me some clear sign! Like making a large deposit in my name at a Swiss bank.   —WOODY ALLEN

God said, "Let us make man in our own image"; and man said, "Let us make God in our image."   —DOUGLAS JERROLD

God is always on the side of the big battalions.   —VOLTAIRE

We praise God not for his benefits, but for our own.

—THOMAS AQUINAS

★ Samuel Goldwyn ★

Goldwyn's faux pas were numerous, funny, and sometimes hilarious. They were not wit. They were boners or, more precisely, boo-boos.

Among the best known are these:

★

To friends and employees at the dock who had come to see the Goldwyns off on a trip to Europe, Mr. G. stood at the rail, waving and calling out, *"Bon voyage! Bon voyage!"*

★

Considering the purchase of a successful play by Lillian Hellman, to be made into a movie, one of Goldwyn's staff protested, "But Mr. Goldwyn, you don't want to buy that property!"

"Why not?"

"Well, the story is about two women who—who are lesbians!"

Mr. Goldwyn cried, "So, we'll make them Americans!" (The movie he made was called *We Three*.)

★

To a newspaper reporter, "If I was in this business for the business, I wouldn't be in this business!" (also attributed to Joseph Schenck).

★

Walking out of a conference of movie producers considering plans to negotiate with one of the unions: "Gentlemen, you can count me out."

★

Simon Michael Bessie, at that time a young publisher at Harper & Row, swears to me that he had sent a forthcoming novel to Mr. G., offering movie rights. Days passed. Weeks passed. No word from Goldwyn. Bessie made phone calls, sent telegrams, and used other pressures to get Mr. Goldwyn to give him an answer on whether he was interested in bidding for the movie rights. On the phone, finally, Goldwyn said, "I'll give it to you straight, Mike. About that property. I could give you a positive 'yes' and I don't want to give you a positive 'no.' But Mike, I *will* give you a positive 'maybe.'"

★

About Ben Hecht, Mr. Goldwyn told a dinner table, "The money he's asking for a screenplay is scandalous. I'm paying him a *fortune*—but he's worth it."

★

Year after year after year, Hollywood regaled itself with laughter about boners attributed to Goldwyn. I say attributed because some (perhaps many) of the malaprops attributed to Goldwyn had been committed by others.

★

Mr. Goldwyn was visiting a friend in Connecticut. The friend had just installed an old sundial in his garden. "What's that?" asked Goldwyn.

"It's a sundial."

"What? What does it *do*?" asked Goldwyn.

"It uses the shadow of this piece to tell roughly what time it is. See—here is noon; here, say, three o'clock, and so on."

"My goodness!" clucked Mr. Goldwyn. "What will they think up next?"

Goldwyn's chief of publicity was "Jock" Lawrence. He was a patsy for wit and had a passion for Jewish humor. I got to know Jock quite well. We often lunched at an excellent restaurant on Hollywood Boulevard, often with one or two friends. Jock dispensed "Goldwynisms" right and left. Apparently Mr. Goldwyn did not at all mind the laughter over his (or adopted) verbal distortions; publicity is publicity.

The lunches were full of wit, wisecracks, and funny anecdotes— which I would read in one or another column in the weeks that followed.

I cannot swear to this, but I remember Jock's asking Goldwyn, "So what would Hyman Kaplan say if someone asked him a question to which the answer was "Impossible"?

"Mr. Kaplan would never say that," Goldwyn said (with confidence). "He would say, 'In two words; "Um, possible!"' "

That solecism has been bandied about the world ever since, as a prime example of Goldwyn's propensity to invent colorful and novel English phrasings.

P.S.: One should never forget Goldwyn's outstanding excellence as a producer. The man, for all his lack of education (total), was a superb judge of stories and style. He knew that the script is the decisive element: No star or director could make a memorable film from a mediocre script. He bought the best books, for which he paid top money, chose the best writers, and paid them royally. His choice of directors (the real key to movies) was faultless. It was not hyperbole to say of his films, "They have 'the Goldwyn touch.' "

Among Goldwyn's best movies (and the best of Hollywood's Golden Age) were (and remain) *The Best Years of Our Lives* and *Wuthering Heights*.

Good Deeds

The man who gives little with a smile gives more than the man who gives much with a frown.   —JEWISH SAYING

Happy is the man whose deeds are greater than his learning.
                                        —MIDRASH

One can always be kind to people about whom one cares nothing.
                                        —OSCAR WILDE

*   *   *

Good men need no monuments; their acts remain their shrines.
                    —ADAPTED FROM *MISHNEH SHEKALIM*

Gossip

Women tell everybody not to tell anybody.   —ANONYMOUS

Gossip is what no one claims to like—but everybody enjoys.
                                        —JOSEPH CONRAD

Gossip is the art of saying nothing in a way that leaves practically nothing unsaid.   —WALTER WINCHELL

Gossipers start with praise and end with derogation.
                                        —MIDRASH

*   *   *

Great minds discuss ideas; average minds discuss events; small minds discuss people.   —ANONYMOUS

Gossip is vice enjoyed vicariously.   —ELBERT HUBBARD

She told him it was terrible to hear such things as he told her and to please go ahead.   —GEORGE ADE

There isn't much to be seen in a little town, but what you hear makes up for it.   —FRANK MCKINNEY ("KIN") HUBBARD

Conversation: When three women stand on the corner talking. Gossip is when one of them leaves.   —HERB SHRINER

Hearts that are delicate and kind, and tongues that are neither—these make the finest company in the world.
       —LOGAN PEARSALL SMITH

It is perfectly monstrous the way people go about nowadays saying things against one, behind one's back, that are absolutely and entirely true.   —OSCAR WILDE

Gossip is nature's telephone.   —SHOLEM ALEICHEM

Men govern nothing with more difficulty than their tongues, and can moderate their desires more than their words.   —SPINOZA

If all men knew what each said of the other, there would not be four friends in the world.   —BLAISE PASCAL

Loose tongues are worse than wicked hands.   —JEWISH SAYING

What is candor to your face is slander behind your back.
       —TALMUD

*   *   *

The only time people dislike gossip is when you gossip about them.
                                                                —WILL ROGERS

Government

Many people want the government to protect the consumer. A much more urgent problem is to protect the consumer from the government.
                                                         —MILTON FRIEDMAN

A government that is big enough to give you all you want is big enough to take it all away.   —BARRY GOLDWATER

Any party which takes credit for the rain must not be surprised if its opponents blame it for the drought.
                                                —DWIGHT D. MORROW

                    *   *   *

Modern government is made possible by two sentimentalist fallacies. One is that because there is majority rule, government acts only for the interests of majorities. The second is that government is disinterested and so does not have the human tendency to maximize one's own interests. Jackson knew better.   —GEORGE F. WILL

It is perfectly true that the government is best which governs least. It is equally true that that government is best which provides most.
                                                            —WALTER LIPPMANN

It could probably be shown by facts and figures that there is no distinctly native American criminal class except Congress.
                                                              —MARK TWAIN

The art of government consists in taking as much money as possible from one class of citizens to give to the other.   —VOLTAIRE

Society is produced by our wants and government by our wickedness.

—THOMAS PAINE

*   *   *

. . . but when the laws undertake to add to these natural and just advantages . . . to make the rich richer and the potent more powerful, the humble members of society . . . who have neither the time nor the means of securing like favors to themselves, have a right to complain of the injustice of their government.   —GEORGE F. WILL

Pray for political stability, for if not for fear of the government men would swallow each other alive.   —*SAYINGS OF THE FATHERS*

Popular government has not yet been proved to guarantee, always and everywhere, good government.   —WALTER LIPPMANN

I am against all efforts to make men virtuous by law. I believe that the government . . . is simply a camorra of incompetent and mainly dishonest men, transiently licensed to live by the labor of the rest of us.   —H. L. MENCKEN

More freedom for the government means less security for the rest of us.   —ALAN REYNOLDS

A good government remains the greatest of human blessings and no nation has ever enjoyed it.   —WILLIAM R. INGE

Government is like a baby. An alimentary canal with a big appetite at one end and no sense of responsibility on the other.   —RONALD REAGAN

I don't make jokes; I just watch the government and report the facts.   —WILL ROGERS

It is dangerous to be right when the government is wrong.
—VOLTAIRE

The man to be elected should be the best man for the task, not necessarily the person with the finest character, or the most full of charity.
—THOMAS AQUINAS

The art of government is the organization of idolatry.
—GEORGE BERNARD SHAW

The danger is not that a particular class is unfit to govern. Every class is unfit to govern.
—LORD ACTON

*　　*　　*

Governments never learn. Only people learn. —MILTON FRIEDMAN

Nothing appears more surprising to those who consider human affairs with a philosophical eye, than the ease with which the many are governed by the few.
—DAVID HUME

Today, if you invent a better mousetrap, the government comes along with a better mouse.
—RONALD REAGAN

I really could not think of a good reason. . . . A little vagueness goes a long way in this business.
—JERRY BROWN, GOVERNOR OF CALIFORNIA

To leave positions of great responsibility and authority is to die a little.
—DEAN ACHESON

*　　*　　*

Government has no other end but the preservation of property.
—JOHN LOCKE

If people say that here and there someone had been taken away and mistreated, I can only reply: You can't make an omelette without breaking eggs. —HERMANN GÖRING (ALSO LENIN)

Reader, suppose you were an idiot; and suppose you were a member of Congress: But I repeat myself. —MARK TWAIN

The selfish wish to govern is often mistaken for a holy zeal in the cause of humanity. —ELBERT HUBBARD

Every decent man is ashamed of the government he lives under. —H. L. MENCKEN

Every form of government tends to perish by excess of its basic principles. —WILL DURANT

I think the world is run by C students. —ANONYMOUS

The government solution to a problem is usually as bad as the problem. —MILTON FRIEDMAN

I am persuaded that there is absolutely no limit to the absurdities that can, by government action, come to be generally believed.
—BERTRAND RUSSELL

✳   ✳   ✳

Governments tend not to solve problems, only to rearrange them. —RONALD REAGAN

The best minds are not in government. If they were, business would hire them away. —RONALD REAGAN

A government is the only known vessel that leaks from the top.
                                        —James Reston

That government is best which governs least.
                                        —Henry David Thoreau

*I'd rather entrust the government of the United
States to the first four hundred people listed in
the Boston telephone directory than to the faculty of Harvard University.*
                    —William F. Buckley, Jr.

              *   *   *

Those who promise us paradise on earth never produced anything but
a hell.   —Karl Popper

The pleasure of governing must certainly be exquisite if we may judge
from the vast numbers who are eager to be concerned with it.
                                        —Voltaire

All government—indeed, every human benefit and enjoyment and
every prudent art—is founded on compromise and barter.
                                        —Edmund Burke

Governments exist to protect the rights of minorities.
                                        —Wendell Phillips

Those who set out nobly to be their brother's keeper sometimes end
up by becoming his jailer. Every emancipation has in it the seeds of
a new slavery, and every truth easily becomes a lie.   —I. F. Stone

*The urge to save humanity is almost always a
false front for the urge to rule.*
                                        —H. L. Mencken

              *   *   *

Graffiti

Only within the past two decades have the wit, frivolity, illumination, and sheer truthfulness of graffiti come into their own. I celebrate but a few stellar examples.

On church steps: You make God sick.

On dormitory bulletin board:
    She offered her honor, so
    I honored her offer.
    And all night long
    I was on her and off her.

In auto repair shop: He who looketh upon a woman loseth a fender.

In Los Angeles: I shot an arrow into the air, and it stuck there.

On wall at Brooklyn College:
    KAFKA
    is a
    KVETCH.

Chalked on wall:
    Get out of Angola!

Below that, in another hand:
    WHAT'S HER LAST NAME?

On church bulletin board: If Jesus was a Jew, how come he has a Puerto Rican name?

On college wall:
    God
    is
    Dead!
        —Nietzsche
And underneath:
    No. Nietzsche
        is Dead.
            —God

On garage for trucking firm:
　WE NEVER SLEEP
Someone added:
　NEITHER DO YOUR NEIGHBORS!

In college dorm:
　A little coitus
　Never hoitus.

On mirror above washbasin in a men's room:
　THINK!
Underneath this, a wag had printed an arrow, pointing downward, and one word:
　THOAP.

On college wall:
　Just because you're paranoid, don't think they don't hate you.

Gratitude

Benefactors seem to love those whom they benefit more than those who receive benefits love their benefactors.　　　—ARISTOTLE

Gratitude, like love, is never a dependable international emotion.
　　　　　　　　　　　　　　　　　　　—JOSEPH ALSOP

Gratitude, in most men, is only a strong secret hope of greater favors.
　　　—FRANÇOIS DE LA ROCHEFOUCAULD

✳　　✳　　✳

Nothing tires a man more than to be grateful all the time.
　　　　　　　　　　　　—EDGAR WATSON ("ED") HOWE

Grief

Time takes away the grief of men.   —ERASMUS

There are people who have an appetite for grief; pleasure is not strong enough, and they crave pain.   —RALPH WALDO EMERSON

A man is very apt to complain of the ingratitude of those who have risen far above him.   —SAMUEL JOHNSON

If we could not forget, we would never be free from grief.
                    —ADAPTED FROM BAHYA IBN PAQUDA

                    ✳   ✳   ✳

All things grow with time—except grief.   —JEWISH SAYING

Guilt

[Freud] found guilt the core, the center, and the censor of civilization. The repression of our instinctual demands makes human society possible. Guilt is our helmsman and our scourge.   —LEO ROSTEN

The truly innocent are those who not only are guiltless themselves but who think others are.   —JOSH BILLINGS

The guilty man who denies his guilt doubles it.
                                        —TALMUD

                    ✳   ✳   ✳

The feeling of guilt has aptly been termed one of America's few remaining surplus commodities. Ubiquitous and repeated allegations that the West is responsible for the poverty of the so-called Third World both reflect and strengthen this feeling of guilt.
                                        —PETER BAUER

H

Happiness

Amusement is the happiness of those who cannot think.
—ALEXANDER POPE

There are those sublimely cursed by discontent, and to them happiness comes only when they push their brains and hearts to the farthest reaches of which they are capable.   —LEO ROSTEN

Men can only be happy when they do not assume that the object of life is happiness.   —GEORGE ORWELL

Anyone who is happy all the time is nuts.   —LEO ROSTEN

Some cause happiness wherever they go; others whenever they go.
—OSCAR WILDE

Happiness is good health plus a bad memory.   —INGRID BERGMAN

Happiness is not good for work.   —CHARLES DARWIN

If you wish to be happy yourself, you must resign yourself to seeing others also happy. —BERTRAND RUSSELL

A lifetime of happiness! No man alive could bear it; it would be hell on earth. —GEORGE BERNARD SHAW

Happiness is never my aim. Like Einstein, I am not happy and do not want to be happy. I have neither time nor taste for such comas, attainable at the price of a pipeful of opium or a glass of whiskey, though I have experienced a very superior quality of it two or three times in dreams. —GEORGE BERNARD SHAW

While we pursue happiness, we flee from contentment.
HASIDIC SAYING

It is neither wealth nor splendor, but tranquillity and occupation which give happiness. —THOMAS JEFFERSON

Once in every man's youth there comes the hour when he must learn, what no one ever yet believed save on the authority of his own experience: that the world was not created to make him happy.
—GEORGE MACAULAY TREVELYAN

Too much fun is of all things the most loathsome. Mirth is better than fun, and happiness is better than mirth. —WILLIAM BLAKE

Happiness is having a large, loving, caring, close-knit family in another city.
—GEORGE BURNS

✳   ✳   ✳

Most men debase "the pursuit of happiness" by transforming it into a narcotic pursuit of "fun." —LEO ROSTEN

It's pretty hard to tell what does bring happiness; poverty and wealth have both failed.   —FRANK McKINNEY ("KIN") HUBBARD

Happiness: A good bank account, a good cook, and a good digestion.   —JEAN-JACQUES ROUSSEAU

Someone has said that the ideal life is to live in an English country home, engage a Chinese cook, marry a Japanese wife, and take a French mistress.   —LIN YUTANG

There is no duty we so much underrate as the duty of being happy.
                    —ROBERT LOUIS STEVENSON

A peasant and a philosopher may be equally *satisfied*, but not equally *happy*. Happiness consists in the multiplicity of agreeable consciousness.   —SAMUEL JOHNSON

All happy families are alike, but each unhappy family is unhappy in its own way.   —TOLSTOY

I can sympathize with people's pains, but not with their pleasure. There is something curiously boring about somebody else's happiness.
                    —ALDOUS HUXLEY

*   *   *

There is no cure for birth or death save to enjoy the interval.
                    —GEORGE SANTAYANA

There is no happiness; there are only moments of happiness.
                    —SPANISH PROVERB

The only really happy folk are married women and single men.
                    —H. L. MENCKEN

Happiness is not a goal, it is a by-product. —ELEANOR ROOSEVELT

It's a short way from happiness to sorrow, but a long way from sorrow
to happiness.   —MY FATHER

Hate

One does not hate so long as one despises.
                        —FRIEDRICH WILHELM NIETZSCHE

I have never considered myself at all a good hater—although I recognize that from moment to moment [hate] has added stimulus to
pugnacity.   —WINSTON CHURCHILL

There are few who would not rather be hated than laughed at.
                                        —SYDNEY SMITH

If you are fair, your fairness will destroy your hate.
                                        —JEWISH SAYING

Man is a hating rather than a loving animal.
                                —REBECCA WEST

It does not matter much what a man hates provided he hates
something.   —SAMUEL BUTLER

Impotent hatred is the most horrible of all emotions; one should hate
nobody whom one cannot destroy.   —GOETHE

Few people can be happy unless they hate some other person, nation,
or creed.   —BERTRAND RUSSELL

A man who hates men is hated by them.   —IBN GABIROL

Love blinds us to faults, but hatred blinds us to virtues. —Iba Ezra

Hatred is an element of the relentless hatred that impels us over and beyond the natural limitations of man and transforms us into effective, violent, selected, and cold killing-machines.   —Che Guevara

Passionate hatred can give meaning and purpose to an empty life.
—Eric Hoffer

Heart

Any wound is better than a wound in the heart. —Old Testament

If you want to live in this world, equip yourself with a heart that can endure suffering.   —Midrash

Heaven

Heaven: *The Coney Island of the Christian imagination.*
—Elbert Hubbard

*   *   *

A worm in a jar of horseradish thinks he's in Paradise.
—Jewish saying

At any rate there will be no wedding presents in heaven.
—Samuel Butler

My idea of heaven is eating *pâtés de foi gras* to the sound of trumpets.
—Sydney Smith

Heaven, as conventionally conceived, is a place so inane, so dull, so useless, so miserable, that nobody has ever ventured to describe a whole day in heaven, though plenty of people have described a day at the seaside.
—GEORGE BERNARD SHAW

*   *   *

When a man appears before the Throne of Judgment, the first question he will be asked is not "Have you believed in God?" or "Have you prayed and observed the ritual?"—but "Have you dealt honorably with your fellow man?"
—TALMUD

In heaven all the interesting people are missing.
—FRIEDRICH WILHELM NIETZSCHE

*   *   *

We send missionaries to China so the Chinese can get to heaven, but we won't let them into our country.
—PEARL S. BUCK

When I reflect on the number of disagreeable people who I know have gone to a better world, I am moved to lead a different life.
—MARK TWAIN

Baptism: A sacred rite of such efficacy that he who finds himself in heaven without having undergone it will be unhappy forever.
—AMBROSE BIERCE

Hell

Maybe this world is another planet's hell.
—ALDOUS HUXLEY

Men have feverishly conceived a heaven only to find it insipid, and a hell to find it ridiculous.
—GEORGE SANTAYANA

I don't want to express an opinion. . . . I have friends in both places.
—MARK TWAIN (ASKED WHAT HE THOUGHT
ABOUT THE EXISTENCE OF HEAVEN OR HELL)

Hell hath no fury like a liberal scorned.   —DICK GREGORY

I desire to go to Hell, not Heaven. In Hell I shall enjoy the company of popes, kings, and princes, but in Heaven there are only beggars, monks, hermits, and apostles.
—NICCOLÒ MACHIAVELLI

*   *   *

One cannot walk through a mass-production factory and not feel that one is in Hell.   —W. H. AUDEN

Hell is a half-filled auditorium.   —ROBERT FROST

A perpetual holiday is a good working definition of hell.
—GEORGE BERNARD SHAW

We all hope he is where we all know he ain't.
—ANONYMOUS SHLEPPER

If I owned Texas and Hell, I would rent out Texas and live in Hell.
—PHILIP SHERIDAN

*   *   *

There are no fans in hell.   —ARAB PROVERB

Hell can lie between the lashes of a beautiful woman's eyes.
—ANONYMOUS

Here's to Hell! May we have as good a time being there as we had getting there. —YUSSEL SHNOOK

Heredity

We need not worry so much about what man descends from—it's what he descends to that shames the human race. —MARK TWAIN

Man does not transmit a single acquired memory to his progeny. The son of the greatest mathematician does not inherit even the multiplication table. —ANONYMOUS

If we are honest we have to admit that we will never fully know what happened to our ancestors in their journey toward modern humanity. —RICHARD LEAKEY

One of life's greatest mysteries is how the boy who wasn't good enough to marry your daughter can be the father of the smartest grandchild in the world. —JEWISH SAYING

Heresy

Heresy is only another word for freedom of thought. —GRAHAM GREENE

The appellation of heretics has always been applied to the less numerous party. —EDWARD GIBBON

Hero

Being a hero is about the shortest-lived profession on earth.
—WILL ROGERS

Concerning the statement that no man is a hero to his valet: This is
not because the hero is no hero, but because the valet is a valet.
—FRIEDRICH HEGEL

A hero is no braver than an ordinary man, but he is brave five minutes
longer.   —RALPH WALDO EMERSON

Hero: A man who is afraid to run away.   —ENGLISH PROVERB

One murder makes a villain; millions, a hero.
—NAPOLEON BONAPARTE

History

The history of mankind is little else than a narrative of designs which
have failed and hopes that have been disappointed.
—SAMUEL JOHNSON

What can we see in the longest kingly line in Europe, save that it
runs back to a successful soldier?   —WALTER SCOTT

History teaches us that men and nations behave wisely once they have
exhausted all other alternatives.   —ABBA EBAN

Every great event has been a capital misfortune. History has kept no
account of times of peace and tranquillity; it relates only ravages and
disasters.   —VOLTAIRE

History is, indeed, little more than the register of the crimes, follies, and misfortunes of mankind.   —EDWARD GIBBON

The very ink with which history is written is merely fluid prejudice.   —MARK TWAIN

The Holy Roman Empire was neither holy, nor Roman, nor an empire.
     —VOLTAIRE

Civil confusions often spring from trifles but decide great issues.
     —ARISTOTLE

You don't change the course of history by turning the faces of portraits to the wall.   —JAWAHARLAL NEHRU

Anecdotes are the gleaming toys of history.
     —WINSTON CHURCHILL

*   *   *

History, a distillation of rumor.   —THOMAS CARLYLE

History would be a wonderful thing—if it were only true.
     —LEO TOLSTOY

Only the future will tell us whether it would not have been better if neither I nor Rousseau had ever lived.   —NAPOLEON BONAPARTE

There is no record in history of a nation that ever gained anything valuable by being unable to defend itself.   —H. L. MENCKEN

God cannot alter the past; that is why he is obligated to connive at the existence of historians.   —SAMUEL BUTLER

Until history is interesting, it is not written.
—RALPH WALDO EMERSON

History is always written wrong, and so always needs to be rewritten.
—GEORGE SANTAYANA

*　*　*

Italy had a Renaissance, Germany had a Reformation, but France had Voltaire.　　　　　　　　　　　　　　—WILL DURANT

Had Cleopatra's nose been shorter, the whole face of the world would have been different.
—BLAISE PASCAL

*　*　*

The ignorance of French society gives one a rough sense of the infinite.　　　　　　　　　　　—JOSEPH ERNEST RENAN

We learn from history that we do not learn from history.
—GEORGE WILHELM FRIEDRICH HEGEL AND
HALF A DOZEN OTHERS

Republics end through luxury, monarchy through poverty.
—MONTESQUIEU

Those we call the ancients were really new in everything.
—BLAISE PASCAL

Any event, once it has occurred, can be made to appear inevitable by a competent historian.
—LEE SIMONSON

*　*　*

We owe to the Middle Ages the two worst inventions of humanity—
gunpowder and romantic love.   —ANDRÉ MAUROIS

The fate of a nation has often depended upon the good or bad digestion
of a prime minister.   —VOLTAIRE

All history, in short, is little else than a long succession of useless
cruelties.   —VOLTAIRE

History is a bucket of ashes.   —CARL SANDBURG

*I have written too much history to have faith
in it; and if anyone thinks I'm wrong, I am
inclined to agree with him.*
                                —HENRY ADAMS

*   *   *

There is no Gibbon but Gibbon, and Gibbon is his prophet. The solemn
march of his cadences, the majestic impropriety of his innuendo are
without rivals in the respective annals of British eloquence and British
indelicacy.   —PHILIP GUEDALLA

History repeats itself; historians repeat each other.
                                —PHILIP GUEDALLA

History is nothing but a pack of tricks that we play upon the dead.
                                —VOLTAIRE

The historian is a prophet looking backward.
                                —FRIEDRICH VON SCHLEGEL

Hollywood

Hollywood is a community of people who work and live in fantasy. It is to be expected that their life should take on the attributes of the fantastic.   —LEO ROSTEN

As in all times, the incomes of leading actors are very high . . . and the morals are what might be expected of men moving from place to place, fluctuating between luxury and poverty, and too high-strung to be capable of a stable and normal life. . . . They lived with characteristic superiority to the morals of their time.   —WILL DURANT

Moviemakers are prone to depression when they are alone; hence they do not like to be alone. Anxiety, like misery, loves company.
                                                —LEO ROSTEN

Beverly Hills is very exclusive. For instance, their fire department won't make house calls.   —WOODY ALLEN

In Hollywood, anxiety serves as a restraint on excessive elation and as a kind of penance for extravagances of income, spending, and conduct.   —LEO ROSTEN

Hollywood: An emotional Detroit.   —LILLIAN GISH

Hollywood is a sewer with services from the Ritz Carlton.
                                          —WILSON MIZNER

Hollywood is a great place to live—if you happen to be an orange.   —FRED ALLEN

The only "ism" Hollywood believes in is plagiarism.
                                          —DOROTHY PARKER

A good deal of Hollywood's amorous acrobatics is deliberately engi-
neered by publicity offices and press agents. Romantic hoopla is un-
equaled as a method of "building up" personalities quickly.

—LEO ROSTEN

To say that "yes-men" are unnecessary in Hollywood is like saying
that gondoliers are unnecessary in Venice.   —LEO ROSTEN

Hollywood is the only place in the world where
an amicable divorce means each one gets 50
percent of the publicity.
                              —LAUREN BACALL

*   *   *

I went around the world last year, and you want to know something?
It hates each other.   —HOLLYWOOD PRODUCER

Youth is at a premium in Hollywood. . . . The movie people—famous,
pampered, rich—are very *young* to be so famous, so pampered, and
so rich.   —LEO ROSTEN

Hollywood: A dreary industrial town controlled by hoodlums of enormous wealth.   —ATTRIBUTED TO S. J. PERELMAN

Producers shouldn't get ulcers; they should *give* them.
                              —SAMUEL GOLDWYN

In Hollywood, everyone goes to a therapist, is a therapist, or is a
therapist going to a therapist.   —TRUMAN CAPOTE

Gary Cooper and Greta Garbo may be the same
person. Have you ever seen them together?
                              —ERNST LUBITSCH

*   *   *

Studio heads have foreheads by dint of electrolysis.
—S. J. PERELMAN

In Hollywood a starlet is the name for any woman under thirty who is not actively employed in a brothel.
—BEN HECHT

Strip away the phony tinsel of Hollywood and you find the real tinsel underneath.   —OSCAR LEVANT

Hollywood: Ten million dollars' worth of intricate and highly ingenious machinery, functioning elaborately to put skin on baloney.
—GEORGE JEAN NATHAN

You can take all the sincerity in Hollywood, place it in the navel of a fruit fly, and still have room enough for three caraway seeds and an agent's heart.   —FRED ALLEN

[Observing the large crowd at Louis B. Mayer's funeral:] It only goes to show that when you give the public what it wants, it will turn out.
—RED SKELTON

You had to stand in line to hate him [speaking of Harry Cohn, movie producer].   —HEDDA HOPPER; (ALSO SAID OF LOUIS B. MAYER)

The fallacy of our stereotypes about Hollywood:

- *Uneducated captains of industry are praised as "self-made men," uneducated movie executives are dismissed as "illiterates."*
- *Erratic bankers are called "eccentric," but erratic moviemakers are called "crazy."*
- *Indiscretions of Park Avenue are winked at as all-too-human peccadilloes, those of Beverly Hills are paraded forth as proof of licentiousness.*

—LEO ROSTEN

I don't want any yes-men around me. I want everybody to tell me the truth even if it costs them their jobs!   —SAMUEL GOLDWYN

An associate producer is the only guy in Hollywood who will associate with a producer.   —FRED ALLEN

What I like about Hollywood is that one can get along quite well by knowing two words of English: "swell" and "lousy."   —VICKY BAUM

The fortuitous arrangement of facial components may be enough to shoot a name onto the theater marquees. It is no wonder that Hollywood is a perpetual magnet to hope.   —LEO ROSTEN

Homosexuals

The love that previously dared not speak its name has now grown hoarse from screaming it.   —ROBERT BRUSTEIN

I thought men like that shot themselves.   —KING GEORGE V

Boys will be boys these days, and so, apparently, will girls.
                                                    —JANE HOWARD

I wish everybody would go back into the closet!   —ANONYMOUS

I don't hate homosexuals. I love homosexuals. It's the sin of homosexuality I hate.   —ANITA BRYANT

I'd rather be black than gay because when you're black you don't have to tell your mother.   —CHARLES PIERCE

If homosexuality were normal, God would have created Adam and Bruce.   —ANITA BRYANT

Honesty

A daughter-in-law is always a bit of a mother-in-law.
                                        —YIDDISH SAYING

There's one way to find out if a man is honest: Ask him. If he says "yes," you know he is a crook.
                    —GROUCHO MARX/MARK TWAIN/W. C. FIELDS

A man is not honest simply because he never had a chance to steal.
                                        —JEWISH SAYING

When ancient opinions and rules of life are taken away, the loss cannot possibly be estimated. From that moment we have no compass to govern us, nor can we know distinctly to what port to steer.
                                        —EDMUND BURKE

Hope

Vows begin when hope dies.   —LEONARDO DA VINCI

We promise according to our hopes and perform according to our fears.   —FRANÇOIS DE LA ROCHEFOUCAULD

Hope is itself a species of happiness, and perhaps the chief happiness we could thus afford.   —SAMUEL JOHNSON

Hope returns with the sun.   —JUVENAL

Hope is the only universal liar who never loses his reputation for veracity.   —ROBERT INGERSOLL

It is good to hope but bad to depend on it. —YIDDISH SAYING

Hope is the feeling that the feeling you have isn't permanent.
—JEAN KERR

Too much hope can drive you crazy.   —JEWISH SAYING

Hope is a good breakfast, but it is a bad supper.
—FRANCIS BACON

The miserable have no other medicine but only hope.
—SHAKESPEARE

Human Behavior

It is absurd to divide people into good and bad. People are either charming or tedious.   —OSCAR WILDE

Modesty died when clothes were born.   —MARK TWAIN

What a chimera is man! What a novelty, what a monster, what a chaos, what a contradiction, what a prodigy! . . . depository of truth, and sewer of uncertainty and terror, the glory and the shame of the universe.   —BLAISE PASCAL

Man: *A reasoning rather than a reasonable animal.*
—ALEXANDER HAMILTON

*   *   *

Most men are within a finger's breadth of being mad.   —DIOGENES

Most men are trash.   —SIGMUND FREUD

A man will fight harder for his interests than for his rights.
                                        —NAPOLEON BONAPARTE
                    (CF. ARISTOTLE/ MACHIAVELLI/ BIERCE/ MENCKEN)

If you stop and think about it, you'll realize that three out of four
persons do not know exactly what they're doing a large part of the
time.   —GELETT BURGESS

Man: The glory, jest, and riddle of the world.   —ALEXANDER POPE

> *Man is a clever animal who behaves like an*
> *imbecile.*
>   —ALBERT SCHWEITZER

              *   *   *

"Every man has his price." This is not true. But for every man there
exists a bait that he cannot resist swallowing.
                            —FRIEDRICH WILHELM NIETZSCHE

Before a man speaks it is always safe to assume that he is a fool. After
he speaks, it is seldom necessary to assume it.
                            —H. L. MENCKEN/OSCAR WILDE

> *An idealist is one who, on noticing that a rose*
> *smells better than a cabbage, concludes that it*
> *will also make better soup.*
>   —H. L. MENCKEN

              *   *   *

Nobody ever forgets where he buried the hatchet.
—FRANK McKINNEY ("KIN") HUBBARD

What can procure digestion? Exercise. What will recruit strength? Sleep. What will alleviate incurable evils? Patience.   —VOLTAIRE

Few radicals have good digestions.   —SAMUEL BUTLER

The nature of men and women—their essential nature—is so vile and despicable that if you were to portray a person as he really is, no one would believe you.   —W. SOMERSET MAUGHAM

There is nothing more demoralizing than a small but adequate income.
—EDMUND WILSON

Everything comes to him who hustles while he waits.
—THOMAS ALVA EDISON

The great masses of the people . . . will more easily fall victims to a great lie than to a small one.   —ADOLF HITLER

When people are free to do as they please, they usually imitate each other.   —ERIC HOFFER

When we are free to act, we are also free to refrain from acting, and where we are able to say "no" we are also able to say "yes."
—ARISTOTLE

Some folks can look so busy doing nothin' that they seem indispensable.
—FRANK McKINNEY ("KIN") HUBBARD

*   *   *

It is often temperament that makes men brave and women chaste.
—FRANÇOIS DE LA ROCHEFOUCAULD

Matters change and morals change; men remain.
—JOHN GALSWORTHY

Men make mistakes not because they think they know when they do
not know, but because they think others do not know.
—SHOLEM ALEICHEM

No one is conceited before one o'clock.   —SYDNEY SMITH

He is Man, the most terrible of the beasts.   —G. K. CHESTERTON

By nature we like the familiar and dislike the strange.
—MAIMONIDES

Men can forget anything—except when to eat.   —JEWISH SAYING

Man's capacity for sacrifice, for devotion and compassion and that
most miraculous of all virtues—simple decency—can forever hearten
and surprise us.   —LEO ROSTEN

Man is the missing link between apes and human beings.
—KONRAD LORENZ

Darwinian man, though well behaved, is at best only a monkey
shaved.   —W. S. GILBERT

Some folks seem to have descended from the chimpanzee later
than others.   —FRANK McKINNEY ("KIN") HUBBARD

If men talked about only what they understood, the silence would
become unbearable.   —MAX LERNER

Kindness is in our power, but fondness is not.   —SAMUEL JOHNSON

People who bite the hand that feeds them usually lick the boot that kicks them. —ERIC HOFFER

There is luxury in self-reproach. When we blame ourselves we feel no one else has a right to blame us. —OSCAR WILDE

I believe the best definition of man is the ungrateful biped.
—DOSTOYEVSKY

* * *

Few things are harder to put up with than the annoyance of a good example. —MARK TWAIN

Rich people are wise, handsome—and sing like angels. —JEWISH SAYING

No doubt Jack the Ripper excused himself on the grounds that it was human nature. —A. A. MILNE

When a man knows he is to be hanged in a fortnight, it concentrates his mind wonderfully. —SAMUEL JOHNSON

I think I think; therefore, I think I am.
—AMBROSE BIERCE

* * *

To hunger for use and to go unused is the worst hunger of all. —LYNDON B. JOHNSON

No man does anything from a single motive. —SAMUEL TAYLOR COLERIDGE

All that I care to know is that a man is a human being—that is enough for me; he can't be any worse. —MARK TWAIN

The deepest principle of human nature is the craving to be appreciated.   —WILLIAM JAMES

All human actions have one or more of these seven causes: chance, nature, compulsion, habit, reason, passion, desire.
                                        —ARISTOTLE

*   *   *

It is the weak who are cruel, and gentleness is to be expected only from the strong.
                                        —LEO ROSTEN

Nothing will dispel enthusiasm like a small admission fee.
                            —FRANK MCKINNEY ("KIN") HUBBARD

To a drunkard, no liquor is bad; to a merchant, no money is tainted; to a lecher, no woman is ugly.   —TALMUD

You can understand people better if you look at them—no matter how old or important or impressive they may be—as if they are children. For most men never mature; they simply grow taller.
                                        —LEO ROSTEN

Humility

Too humble is half proud.   —ANONYMOUS

When you turn proud, remember that a flea preceded you in the order of divine creation.   —TOSEPHTA

Don't be humble. You're not that great.
                            —GOLDA MEIR (TO MOSHE DAYAN)

Humor

The secret source of humor is not joy but sorrow; there is no humor in heaven. —MARK TWAIN

Analyzing humor is like dissecting a frog. Few people are interested and the frog dies. —E. B. WHITE

Men will confess to treason, murder, arson, false teeth, or a wig. How many of them will own up to a lack of humor?
—FRANK MOORE COLBY

* * *

There seems to be no limits to which humorless people will not go to analyze humor. It seems to worry them. They can't believe that anything could be so funny just on its own hook.
—ROBERT BENCHLEY

A joke is an epitaph on an emotion.
—FRIEDRICH WILHELM NIETZSCHE

Adam was the only man who, when he said a good thing, knew that nobody had said it before him. —MARK TWAIN

The educational process has long been associated only with the glum. We speak of the "serious" student. Our time presents a unique opportunity for learning by means of humor—a perceptive or incisive joke can be more meaningful than platitudes lying between the covers.
—MARSHALL MCLUHAN

Humor is an affirmation of dignity, a declaration of man's superiority to all that befalls him. —ROMAIN GARY

Humor is emotional chaos remembered in tranquillity.
—JAMES THURBER

A humorist is a man who feels bad but who feels good about it.
—DON HEROLD

A life without humor is like a life without legs.
—FRANK MOORE COLBY

Hunger

When hunger comes through the door, love flees through the window.
—JEWISH SAYING

He that is good for making excuses is seldom good for anything else.
—BENJAMIN FRANKLIN

Husbands

The man who enters his wife's dressing room is either a philosopher or an imbecile.   —HONORÉ DE BALZAC

It's as hard to get a man to stay home after you've married him as it was to get him to go home before you married him.
—HELEN ROWLAND

A henpecked husband gets no relief in court.   —TALMUD

A husband is always a sensible man; he never thinks of marrying.
—ALEXANDRE DUMAS, *FILS*

If there were no husbands, who would look after our mistresses?
—GEORGE MOORE

Thy wife is short, so bend down and consult her. —TALMUD

The majority of husbands remind me of an orangutan trying to play the violin.
—HONORÉ DE BALZAC

* * *

It is better to have an ugly wife for one's self than a beautiful wife for others. —ANONYMOUS

Never feel remorse for what you have thought about your wife. She has thought much worse things about you. —JEAN ROSTAND

The death of a woman is felt by no one so much as her husband.
—TALMUD

When a man is too good for this world, it's too bad for his wife.
—ANONYMOUS

Hypocrisy

Hypocrisy is the homage that vice pays to virtue.
—FRANÇOIS DE LA ROCHEFOUCAULD

A hypocrite is a person who—but who isn't? —DON MARQUIS

Politeness is the most acceptable hypocrisy. —AMBROSE BIERCE

Idealists/Idealism

Idealism is the noble toga that political gentlemen drape over their
will to power. —ALDOUS HUXLEY

It takes no brain to be idealistic. —LEO ROSTEN

The idealists who make a revolution are bound to be disappointed. . . .
For at best their victory never dawns on the shining new world they
had dreamed of, cleansed of all human meanness. Instead it dawns on
a familiar, workaday place, still in need of groceries and sewage dis-
posal. The revolutionary state, under whatever political label, has to
be run not by violent romantics but by experts in marketing, sanitary
engineering, and the management of bureaucracies. For the Byrons
among us, this discovery is a fate worse than death.
—JOHN FISCHER

Positive ideals are becoming a curse, for they can seldom be achieved
without someone being killed or maimed or interned.
—E. M. FORSTER

Most idealists mistake ideals for ideas.   —LEO ROSTEN

Idealism is fine, but as it approaches reality the cost becomes prohibitive.   —WILLIAM F. BUCKLEY, JR.

Idealism increases in direct proportion to one's distance from the problem.   —JOHN GALSWORTHY

No folly is more costly than the folly of intolerant idealism.
            —WINSTON CHURCHILL

Ideas

An idea isn't responsible for the people who believe in it.
            —DON MARQUIS

His mind is open; yes, it is so open that nothing is retained; ideas simply pass through him.   —FRANCIS HERBERT BRADLEY

Only the wise possess ideas; the greater part of mankind are possessed by them.   —SAMUEL TAYLOR COLERIDGE

Greater than the tread of mighty armies is an idea whose time has come.   —VICTOR HUGO

Man is ready to die for an idea, provided that idea is not quite clear to him.   —PAUL ELDRIDGE/BERTRAND RUSSELL

There's an element of truth in every idea that lasts long enough to be called corny.   —IRVING BERLIN

The ideas of economists and political philosophers, both when they are right and when they are wrong, are more powerful than is commonly understood. Indeed, the world is ruled by little else.
                              —JOHN MAYNARD KEYNES

Ideas are like beards: Men do not have them until they grow up.
                              —VOLTAIRE

The man who strikes first admits that his ideas have given out.
                              —CHINESE PROVERB

One of the greatest pains to human nature is the pain of a new idea.
                              —WALTER BAGEHOT

To die for an idea is to place a pretty high price upon conjecture.
                              —ANATOLE FRANCE

To die for an idea—it is unquestionably noble. But how much nobler it would be if men died for ideas that were true. —H. L. MENCKEN

Very simple ideas lie within the reach only of complex minds.
                              —RÉMY DE GOURMONT

Idiocies

Music is essentially useless, as life is.   —GEORGE SANTAYANA

Americans are broad-minded people. They'll accept the fact that a person can be an alcoholic, a dope fiend, a wife beater, and even a newspaperman, but if a man doesn't drive there's something wrong with him.
                              —ART BUCHWALD

*   *   *

Gaiety is the most outstanding feature of the Soviet Union.
                                                —JOSEPH STALIN

Heavier-than-air flying machines are impossible.   —LORD KELVIN

When the president does it, that means it's not illegal.
                                                —RICHARD NIXON

We affirm that the ludicrous use of the Western hat stands in the way
of our independence and is contrary to the will of God.
                                                —AYATOLLAH KHOMEINI

*One must avoid praying when one feels an urge
to urinate or defecate or when one is wearing
socks that are too tight.*
                                    —AYATOLLAH KHOMEINI

*   *   *

I would have made a good pope.   —RICHARD NIXON

I often think how much easier the world would have been to manage
if Herr Hitler and Signor Mussolini had been at Oxford.
                                                —LORD HALIFAX

We're more popular than Jesus Christ now. I don't know which will
go first: rock 'n' roll or Christianity.   —JOHN LENNON

Let's go to the circus tomorrow, if—God willing—we're alive; and if
not, let's go Tuesday.   —JEWISH WITTICISM

Ignorance

*Everybody is ignorant, only on different
subjects.*
                                    —WILL ROGERS

*   *   *

Your ignorance cramps my conversation.   —ANTHONY HOPE

Nothing in the world is more dangerous than sincere ignorance and conscientious stupidity.   —MARTIN LUTHER KING, JR.

Even supposing knowledge to be easily attainable, more people would be content to be ignorant than would take even a little trouble to acquire it.   —SAMUEL JOHNSON

In a long experience in politics, I have never found that criticism is ever inhibited by ignorance.
          —HAROLD MACMILLAN

*   *   *

War is peace. Freedom is slavery. Ignorance is strength.
          —GEORGE ORWELL (THE TEACHINGS OF BIG BROTHER)

Imagination

There is a boundary to men's passions when they act from feelings; but none when they are under the influence of imagination.
          —EDMUND BURKE

Imagination is nature's equal, sensuality her slave.
          —GOETHE

*   *   *

To know is nothing at all; to imagine is everything.
          —ANATOLE FRANCE/ALBERT EINSTEIN

Put off your imagination, as you put off your overcoat, when you enter the laboratory. But put it on again, as you put on your overcoat, when you leave. —CLAUDE BERNARD

Were it not for imagination, a man would be as happy in the arms of a chambermaid as of a duchess. —SAMUEL JOHNSON

His imagination resembled the wings of an ostrich. It enabled him to run, though not to soar.
—THOMAS BABINGTON MACAULAY

* * *

The deaf imagine what they cannot hear. —JEWISH SAYING

Immortality

If I have any beliefs about immortality, it is that certain dogs I have known will go to heaven, and very, very few persons.
—JAMES THURBER

The first requisite for immortality is death. —STANISLAW J. LEC

I don't want to achieve immortality through my work. . . . I want to achieve it through not dying. —WOODY ALLEN

Millions long for immortality who do not know what to do with themselves on a rainy Sunday afternoon.
—SUSAN ERTZ

* * *

The only thing wrong with immortality is that it tends to go on forever. —HERB CAEN

Good deeds bring a man immortality. —THE SASSOVER RABBI

Infidelity

A man can have two, maybe three love affairs while he's married. After that it's cheating.   —YVES MONTAND

As to fidelity, there is no animal in the world so treacherous as man.
                                        —MONTAIGNE

Insanity

We are all born mad. Some remain so.
                    —SAMUEL BECKETT

*   *   *

The human race consists of the dangerously insane and such as are not.   —MARK TWAIN

Even paranoids have real enemies.   —DELMORE SCHWARTZ

Insanity: A perfectly rational adjustment to an insane world.
                                        —R. D. LAING

When dealing with the insane, the best method is to pretend to be sane.   —HERMANN HESSE

All of us are crazy in one way or another.
                    —YIDDISH SAYING

*   *   *

The men who really believe in themselves are all in lunatic asylums.
                                        —G. K. CHESTERTON

Insanity is hereditary. You get it from your children.
—Sam Levenson

There is but an inch of difference between the cushioned chamber and the padded cell. —G. K. Chesterton

Every man has a sane spot somewhere.
—Robert Louis Stevenson

✳   ✳   ✳

There is about every madman a singular sensation that his body has walked off and left the important part of him behind.
—G. K. Chesterton

Show me a sane man and I will cure him for you. —C. G. Jung

I learned that in some way, however small and secret, each of us is a little mad. If we want to stay sane we must moderate our demands —on ourselves and on others. —Leo Rosten

There nearly always is method in madness; it's what drives men insane—being methodical. —G. K. Chesterton

If a man is in a minority of one, we lock him up.
—Oliver Wendell Holmes, Jr.

Insults

There [of a passing starlet] goes the good time that was had by all.
—Bette Davis

✳   ✳   ✳

If there's ever a price on your head, take it.

What were you when you were alive?

You have a ready wit. Let me know when it's ready.

You have a wonderful head on your shoulders; too bad it's not on your neck.

—HENNY YOUNGMAN

He has all the characteristics of a dog—except loyalty.

—SAM HOUSTON

Intelligence/Intellectuals

So far as I can remember, there is not one word in the Gospels in praise of intelligence.   —BERTRAND RUSSELL

An intellectual is a man who takes more words than necessary to tell more than he knows.   —DWIGHT D. EISENHOWER

Has anyone checked the intelligence of people who devise intelligence tests?

If religion is the opiate of the masses, jargon is the opiate of the intellectuals.

—LEO ROSTEN

What is a highbrow? He is a man who has found something more interesting than women.
—EDGAR WALLACE/
FRED ALLEN/MORT SAHL

*   *   *

Intellectuals (especially professors) tend to become silly because they are never called upon to make decisions upon which very much depends. —LEO ROSTEN

Only the shallow know themselves. —OSCAR WILDE

First-rate brains hang around with first-rate brains; second-rate brains hang around with third-rate brains. —LEO ROSTEN

The most terrible of all intellectual weapons ever wielded by man [was] the mockery of Voltaire. —TALLEYRAND

The masses have not always felt themselves to be frustrated and exploited. But the intellectuals who formulated their views for them have always told them that they were, without necessarily meaning anything precise. —JOSEPH A. SCHUMPETER

When I see no way of teaching a truth save one that will please one intelligent man but will offend ten thousand fools, I address myself to the one and ignore the censure of the thousands. —MAIMONIDES

The more unintelligent a man is, the less mysterious existence seems to him. —ARTHUR SCHOPENHAUER

You don't need intelligence to have luck, but you do need luck to have intelligence. —JEWISH SAYING

History does repeat itself; not, as Karl Marx quipped, as farce, but in what I, for one, can only mourn as the recurring lunacy of the intelligentsia. —LEO ROSTEN

*We should take care not to make the intellect
our god; it has, of course, powerful muscles, but
no personality.*
                                        —ALBERT EINSTEIN

                    *   *   *

Whenever the cause of the people is entrusted to professors, it is lost.
                                        —V. I. LENIN

A highbrow is a person educated beyond his intelligence.
                                        —BRANDER MATTHEWS

A spirit of national masochism prevails, encouraged by an effete corps
of impudent snobs who characterize themselves as intellectuals.
                                        —SPIRO T. AGNEW

Compromise is odious to passionate natures because it seems a surrender; and to intellectual natures because it seems a confusion.
                                        —GEORGE SANTAYANA

There is nobody so irritating as somebody with less intelligence and
more sense than we have.   —DON HEROLD

Intellectuals cannot tolerate the chance event, or the unintelligible;
they have a nostalgia for the absolute, for a universally comprehensive
scheme.   —RAYMOND ARON

The trouble with the world is that the stupid are cocksure and the
intelligent full of doubt.   —BERTRAND RUSSELL

*You will always find some Eskimo ready to in-
struct the Congolese on how to cope with heat
waves.*
                                        —STANISLAW J. LEC

                    *   *   *

Intuition

Intuition is the source of scientific knowledge. —ARISTOTLE

It is by logic that we prove, but by intuition that we discover. To know how to criticize is good, but to know how to create is better.
—HENRI POINCARÉ

Intuition is reason in a hurry. —HOLBROOK JACKSON

Ironies

Autobiography is an unrivaled vehicle for telling the truth about other people. —PHILIP GUEDALLA

My sympathy often goes out for the humble decimal point. He has a pathetic and hectic life wandering around among regimented ciphers, trying to find some of the old places he used to know when budgets were balanced. —HERBERT HOOVER

There is no satisfaction in hanging a man who does not object to it.
—GEORGE BERNARD SHAW

A little inaccuracy saves a world of explanation. —C. E. AYRES

Jealousy

The man who loves without jealousy does not truly love.   —ZOHAR

Love may be blind, but jealousy sees too much.   —ANONYMOUS

Jews

One who belongs to the most vilified and persecuted minority in history [Jews] is not likely to be insensible to the freedom guaranteed by our Constitution.   —FELIX FRANKFURTER

It is to the Jews that humanity owes the deepest debt of gratitude, and it is on them that humanity has inflicted the deepest wrongs.
—F. W. FARRAR

Jews favor paradox because they know that only paradox can do justice to the injustices of life.   —LEO ROSTEN

May the children of the stock of Abraham who dwell in this land continue to merit and enjoy the good will of the other inhabitants—while every one shall sit in safety under his own vine and fig tree and there shall be none to make him afraid.

—GEORGE WASHINGTON

* * *

Dear God: If you really loved the Jews, why did you make them your "chosen people"? —JEWISH SAYING

Marx's hatred of Jews was a canker which neither time nor experience ever eradicated from his soul. —SAUL K. PADOVER

Hilaire Belloc (or A. N. Ewer) coined this famous quatrain:

How odd
of God
To choose
The Jews.

This jingle was answered by some unknown wag:

Not news,
Not odd,
The Jews
Chose God.

To which a Jew responded:

Not odd
Of God:
Goyim
Annoy 'im.

Any Jew can be a cantor, except that at this moment he happens to be hoarse. —JEWISH SAYING

If a Jew breaks his leg, he thanks God that he did not break both legs; if he breaks both legs, he thanks God he did not break his neck.
—FOLK SAYING

Every Jew has his own brand of madness.   —JEWISH SAYING

Since I'm only half Jewish, can I join if I only play nine holes?
—SENATOR BARRY GOLDWATER
(ON BEING BLACKBALLED BY A
GOLF CLUB IN PHOENIX, ARIZONA)

*   *   *

We [Jews] must not appoint a leader in any community without first consulting the people.   —TALMUD

They are not Jews in America; they are American citizens.
—WOODROW WILSON

When a poor Jew eats a chicken, *one* of them is sick.
—JEWISH FOLK SAYING

Nations that persecute Jews never last long.   —JEWISH PROVERB

The real slavery in Egypt was this: The Israelites learned to endure it.   —SIMCHA BUNIN

Study and prayer, or (better) study-prayer, was the most potent mortar in Jewish life. It was the linchpin in a Jew's self-esteem. It lent meaning and purpose to the most difficult and desperate of existences. It illuminated life. It ennobled, inspired, redeemed. It admitted even the humblest Jew to the company of sages, prophets, scholars, saints.
—LEO ROSTEN

The pursuit of knowledge for its own sake, an almost fanatical love of justice, and the desire for personal independence—these are the features of Jewish tradition which make me thank my stars that I belong to it. —ALBERT EINSTEIN

Yes. I am a Jew, and when the ancestors of the right honorable gentleman were brutal savages in an unknown island, mine were priests in the Temple of Solomon.
—BENJAMIN DISRAELI, IN HOUSE OF COMMONS
(ANSWERING DANIEL O'CONNELL)

Yiddish is steeped in sentiment and sluiced with sarcasm. . . . It adores irony because the only way the Jews could retain their sanity was to view a dreadful world with sardonic eyes. —LEO ROSTEN

The Jews are a frightened people. Nineteen centuries of Christian love have broken down their nerves. —ISRAEL ZANGWILL

Calamity may be blind, but it has a remarkable talent for locating Jews. —LEO ROSTEN

I know the Lord will help us—but help us, Lord, *until* you help us.
—JEWISH SAYING

These same Jews, from time immemorial, have been the chief dreamers of the human race and beyond all comparisons its greatest poets; no heritage of modern man is richer; and none has made a more brilliant mark on human thought, not even the legacy of the Greeks.
—H. L. MENCKEN

* * *

I have come to the conclusion that Americans treat "neurotic" as a synonym for "nuts"; that Englishmen think "neurotic" an adjective applicable to foreigners; and that Jews consider "neurotic" a synonym for "human." —LEO ROSTEN

Show me a Jewish boy who doesn't go to medical school and I'll show you a lawyer.   —ANONYMOUS

Journalism

A politician wouldn't dream of being allowed to call a columnist the things a columnist is allowed to call a politician.

—MAX LERNER

*   *   *

Some newspapers are fit only to line the bottom of birdcages.

—SPIRO T. AGNEW

Newspapers don't change tastes. They reflect taste.

—RUPERT MURDOCH

Hitler said that he always knew you could buy the press. What he didn't know was you could get them cheap.   —MORT SAHL

Journalism is a kind of profession, or craft, or racket, for people who never wanted to grow up and go out into the real world. If you're a good journalist, what you do is live a lot of things vicariously, and report them for other people who want to live vicariously.

—HARRY REASONER

Were it left to me to decide whether we should have a government without newspapers or newspapers without a government, I should not hesitate for a moment to prefer the latter.

—THOMAS JEFFERSON

*   *   *

Some statements you make in public . . . are reported as "an unnamed source." . . . Nobody believes the official spokesman, but everyone trusts an unidentified source.
—RON NESSEN, WHITE HOUSE PRESS SECRETARY

Print is the sharpest and the strongest weapon of our party.
—JOSEPH STALIN

I do not take a single newspaper, nor read one a month, and I feel myself infinitely the happier for it.
—THOMAS JEFFERSON

*   *   *

There are honest journalists like there are honest politicians they stay bought.
—BILL MOYERS

There are just two people entitled to refer to themselves as "we"; one is the editor and the other is the fellow with a tapeworm.
—EDGAR WILSON ("BILL") NYE

Our [*New York Times*] composing room has an unlimited supply of periods available to terminate short, simple sentences.
—TURNER CATLEDGE, MANAGING EDITOR, *NEW YORK TIMES*

The freedom of the press works in such a way that there is not much freedom from it.   —PRINCESS GRACE OF MONACO

The real news is bad news.   —MARSHALL McLUHAN

A free press is not a privilege, but an organic necessity in a great society. . . . A great society is simply a big, complicated urban society.
—WALTER LIPPMANN

Freedom of the press is limited to those who own one.
—A. J. LIEBLING

Without criticism and intelligent reporting, a government cannot govern. —WALTER LIPPMANN

News is the first rough draft of history.
—BENJAMIN BRADLEE

The gallery in which the reporters sit has become the Fourth Estate of the realm. —LORD MACAULAY

Our liberty depends on the freedom of the press, and that cannot be limited without being lost. —THOMAS JEFFERSON

I have been reading the morning paper. I do it every morning—well knowing that I shall find in it the usual depravities and baseness and hypocrisies and cruelties that make up civilization, and cause me to put in the rest of the day pleading for the damnation of the human race. —MARK TWAIN

I always turn to the sports pages first, which record people's accomplishments. The front page has nothing but man's failures.
—EARL WARREN

Journalism is organized gossip. —EDWARD EGGLESTON

Journalism: A profession whose business it is to explain to others what it personally does not understand. —LORD NORTHCLIFFE

Most rock journalism is people who can't write interviewing people who can't talk for people who can't read. —FRANK ZAPPA

No government ought to be without censors; and where the press is free, none ever will.
—THOMAS JEFFERSON

✳   ✳   ✳

There is much to be said in favor of modern journalism. By giving us the opinions of the uneducated, it keeps us in touch with the ignorance of the community.   —OSCAR WILDE

Like officials in Washington, we suffer from Afghanistanism. If it's far away, it's news, but if it's close at home, it's sociology.
                                                    —JAMES RESTON

Bad manners make a journalist.   —OSCAR WILDE

News is anything that makes a woman say "For heaven's sake!"
                                      —EDGAR WATSON ("ED") HOWE

The price of freedom of religion, or of speech, or of the press, is that we must put up with a good deal of rubbish.
                                                  —ROBERT JACKSON

                        *   *   *

All newspaper editorial writers ever do is come down from the hills after the battle is over and shoot the wounded.   —ANONYMOUS

Journalists write because they have nothing to say, and have something to say because they write.   —KARL KRAUS

Judges/Justice

The hungry judges soon the sentence sign
And wretches hang that jurymen may dine.
                                                —ALEXANDER POPE

Justice is truth in action.   —BENJAMIN DISRAELI

Injustice is relatively easy to bear; what stings is justice.
                                                —H. L. MENCKEN

                        *   *   *

If there be no officer to enforce the law, what power do judges have?
—MIDRASH

The rabbis said about capital cases: "We decide by a majority of one for acquittal, but only by a majority of at least *two* for conviction."
—RASHI

A judge who has drunk a quart of wine may not sit in judgment; He will condemn the innocent and acquit the guilty.   —MIDRASH

Judges are apt to be naive, simpleminded men.
—OLIVER WENDELL HOLMES, JR.

Don't blame the judge for the law.   —ANONYMOUS

Two scholars who dislike each other may not sit together as judges.
—TALMUD

Juries

The beginning and the end [of Torah] is the performance of loving kindness.   —TALMUD

Jury: Twelve men of average ignorance.
—HERBERT SPENCER

A jury consists of twelve persons chosen to decide who has the better lawyer.   —ROBERT FROST

We have a criminal jury system which is superior to any in the world; and its efficiency is only marred by the difficulty of finding twelve men every day who don't know anything and can't read. —MARK TWAIN

The penalty for laughing in a courtroom is six months in jail; if it were not for this penalty, the jury would never hear the evidence.
—H. L. MENCKEN

A jury too often has at least one member more ready to hang the panel than to hang the traitor. —ABRAHAM LINCOLN

Just Funny

If I could get my membership fee back, I'd resign from the human race. —FRED ALLEN

There is a lot to say in her favor, but the other is more interesting. —MARK TWAIN

Of all men, Adam was the happiest; he had no mother-in-law. —SHOLEM ALEICHEM/MARK TWAIN

We ought never to do wrong when people are looking. —MARK TWAIN

I was gratified to be able to answer promptly. I said I don't know. —MARK TWAIN

My wife is a light eater; as soon as it's light, she starts eating. —HENNY YOUNGMAN

His hair is getting thin—still, who wants fat hair? —MILTON BERLE

A gentleman never strikes a lady with his hat on. —FRED ALLEN

Military justice is to justice what military music is to music. —GEORGES CLEMENCEAU

During the garbage strike here's how I got rid of my garbage: I gift-wrapped it, left it in my car, and they stole it. —HENNY YOUNGMAN

If you can keep your head when all about you are losing theirs, it's just possible you haven't grasped the situation.   —JEAN KERR

Down in Miami I worked in a place called the Deauville Hotel—very exclusive. Room service had an unlisted number.
                                        —HENNY YOUNGMAN

Burt Reynolds once asked me out. I was in his room.
                                        —PHYLLIS DILLER

America has been discovered before, but it has always been hushed up.   —OSCAR WILDE

If this is coffee, please bring me some tea; but if this is tea, please bring me some coffee.
                        —ABRAHAM LINCOLN

*   *   *

A guy walked up to me on Broadway. He said, "Psst, buddy! Wanna see a clean movie?"   —HENNY YOUNGMAN

Statistics show that every four seconds a woman gives birth to a baby. Our problem is to find this woman and stop her.
        —HENNY YOUNGMAN/GEORGE JESSEL/RED SKELTON

One day she drove up the side of a building and there was another woman driver coming down! It was a one-way building.

My best punch was a rabbit punch, but they would never let me fight rabbits.

Those bellhops in Miami are tip-happy. I ordered a deck of playing cards and the bellboy made fifty-two trips to my room.

A drunk walks into an elevator shaft, falls down ten floors. He's lying there bleeding and says, "I said *up*!"
                                        —HENNY YOUNGMAN

Horsepower was a wonderful thing when only horses had it.
—ANONYMOUS

Do you know what it means to come home at night to a woman who'll give you a little love, a little affection, a little tenderness? It means you're in the wrong house, that's what it means. —GEORGE BURNS

The most dangerous thing in the world is to leap a chasm in two jumps. —DAVID LLOYD GEORGE

By a sudden and adroit movement I placed my left eye against his fist. —ARTEMUS WARD/MARK TWAIN

Bad weather always looks worse through a window.
—JOHN KIERAN

I know a guy who reads mystery novels backward. He knows who did it, but he doesn't know what they did. —SHERLOCK VON TSIMMIS

I have already given two cousins to the war and I stand ready to sacrifice my wife's brother. —ARTEMUS WARD

One day my father took me aside and left me there.
—JACKIE VERNON

Knowledge

We don't know half of one millionth of 1 percent about anything.
—THOMAS ALVA EDISON

If a little knowledge is dangerous, where is a man who has so much as to be out of danger?
—THOMAS H. HUXLEY

It is what we think we know already that often prevents us from learning.
—CLAUDE BERNARD

You must know a great deal about a subject to know how little is known about it.
—LEO ROSTEN

The world is governed more by appearances than by realities, so that it is fully as necessary to seem to know something as to know it.
—DANIEL WEBSTER

The man who is too old to learn was probably always too old to learn.
—CARYL HASKINS

Between us, we cover all knowledge; he knows all that can be known, and I know the rest.
—MARK TWAIN (REFERRING TO RUDYARD KIPLING)

To the small part of ignorance that we arrange and classify we give the name knowledge.   —AMBROSE BIERCE

We must view with profound respect the infinite capacity of the human mind to resist the introduction of useful knowledge.
—THOMAS R. LOUNSBURY

We know too much for one man to know much.
—ROBERT OPPENHEIMER

[After eight thousand unsuccessful trials on a nickel-iron storage battery] Well, at least we know eight thousand things that won't work.
—THOMAS ALVA EDISON

Research is a blind date with knowledge.   —ANONYMOUS

The charm of an encyclopedia is that it knows—and I needn't.
—FRANCIS YEATS BROWN

I see men ordinarily more eager to discover a reason for things than to find out whether the things are so.
—MONTAIGNE

✳   ✳   ✳

Everything I know I learned after I was thirty.
                                        —GEORGES CLEMENCEAU

Some men are just as firmly convinced of what they think as others
are of what they know.   —ARISTOTLE

*We are here and it is now. Further than that
all human knowledge is moonshine.*
                                        —H. L. MENCKEN

        *   *   *

Language

We are the slaves of language, not its masters. . . . Language is the most significant and colossal work that the human spirit has evolved.

—EDWARD SAPIR

*   *   *

Political language . . . is designed to make lies sound truthful and murder respectable and to give an appearance of solidarity to pure wind.   —GEORGE ORWELL

My philological studies have satisfied me that a gifted person ought to learn English (barring spelling and pronouncing) in thirty hours, French in thirty days, and German in thirty years. —MARK TWAIN

Yiddish is a tongue that never takes its tongue out of its cheek.

—LEO ROSTEN

Preposition: *An enormously versatile part of grammar, as in "What made you choose this book I didn't want to be read to out of up for?"*
—WINSTON CHURCHILL

*　*　*

The word "good" has many meanings. For example, if a man were to shoot his grandmother at a range of five hundred yards, I should call him a good shot, but not necessarily a good man.
—G. K. CHESTERTON

Slang is language that takes off its coat, spits on its hands, and goes to work. —CARL SANDBURG

A language is a dialect that has an army and a navy.
—MAX WEINREICH

Yiddish is the Robin Hood of languages. —LEO ROSTEN

The two most beautiful words in the English language are "cheque enclosed." —DOROTHY PARKER

"Not guilty:" The best two words in any language.
—ERICH MARIA REMARQUE

The pestilent cosmetic, rhetoric. —THOMAS HENRY HUXLEY

If thought corrupts language, language can also corrupt thought.
—GEORGE ORWELL

I don't give a damn for a man that can spell a word only one way.
—MARK TWAIN

The Japanese . . . have numbers that mean good luck, wealth, bankruptcy, and death. This fact complicates the Japanese telephone system.
—EDWARD T. HALL

They spell it *Vinci* and pronounce it "Vinchy"; foreigners always spell better than they pronounce.
—MARK TWAIN

The linguistic system shapes ideas; it does not merely mirror it.
—BENJAMIN LEE WHORF

What is idiomatic in one tongue is idiotic in another. Think of what happens if a translator of English does not realize that "Tell it to Sweeney" is a rebuff, not a request; that "a Northern Spy" may have been an undercover agent for Ulysses S. Grant—or only a variety of apple; that Occam never used his razor for shaving, any more than Cleopatra used her needle for sewing. . . . Russian physicists believe that the first nuclear atomic pile in history was constructed in a pumpkin field—that being their natural translation of "squash court," the site in the concrete bowels of the stadium of the University of Chicago.
—LEO ROSTEN

Heinrich Heine so loosened the corsets of the German language that today every little salesman can fondle her breasts. —KARL KRAUS

I told [the Frenchman] in French. . . . He said he could not understand me. I repeated. Still, he did not understand. He appeared to be very ignorant of French.
—MARK TWAIN

Japanese has fewer sounds than any other language, and therefore has to ascribe a lot of meanings to the few it does have. . . . Seikan can mean a sexual feeling, naval construction, can manufacturing, or serene contemplation.
—ROBERT CHRISTOPHER

✳   ✳   ✳

Laughter

Men have been wise in many different modes;
but they have always laughed the same way.
—SAMUEL JOHNSON

*　　*　　*

If you want to make people weep, you must weep yourself. If you want to make people laugh, your face must remain serious.
—CASANOVA

Life does not cease to be funny when people die any more than it ceases to be serious when people laugh. —GEORGE BERNARD SHAW

An onion can make people cry, but there has never been a vegetable invented to make them laugh. —WILL ROGERS

We must laugh at man to avoid crying for him.
—NAPOLEON BONAPARTE

Laughter is nothing else but sudden glory arising from some sudden conception of some eminency in ourselves, by comparison with the infirmity of others, or with our own formerly. —THOMAS HOBBES

Laughter is heard farther than weeping. —JEWISH SAYING

The finest satire is that in which ridicule is combined with so little malice and so much conviction that it even rouses laughter in those who are hit. —GEORG CHRISTOPH LICHTENBERG

Laughing is the sensation of feeling good all
over, and showing it principally in one spot.
—JOSH BILLINGS

*　　*　　*

Several have defined man as "an animal that laughs." They might equally well have defined him as an animal that is laughed at.

—Henri Bergson

She laughs at everything you say. Why? Because she has fine teeth.

—Benjamin Franklin

Nobody ever died of laughter.   —Max Beerbohm

We are a nation that has always gone in for the loud laugh, the wow, the belly laugh, and the dozen other labels for the roll-'em-in-the-aisles gagerissimo. This is the kind of laugh that delights actors, directors, and producers, but dismays writers of comedy because it is the laugh that often dies in the lobby. The appreciative smile, the chuckle, the soundless mirth, so important to the success of comedy, cannot be understood unless one sits among the audience and feels the warmth created by the quality of laughter that the audience takes home with it.   —James Thurber

Perhaps I know best why it is man alone who laughs: He alone suffers so deeply that he had to invent laughter.

—Friedrich Wilhelm Nietzsche

Men show their character in nothing more clearly than by what they find laughable.   —Anonymous

Incongruity is the mainspring of laughter.   —Max Beerbohm

Every man is funny if he loses his hat and has to run after it.

—G. K. Chesterton

He who laughs, lasts.   —Leo Rosten

Law

What is hateful to you, do not to your fellow; that is the whole Law; all the rest is interpretation.   —TALMUD

In university they don't tell you that the greater part of the law is learning to tolerate fools.   —DORIS LESSING

When I hear any man talk of an unalterable law, I am convinced that he is an unalterable fool.   —SYDNEY SMITH

When a court has pronounced a sentence of death, its members (judges) should taste nothing for the rest of the day.   —TALMUD

In law, nothing is certain but the expense.   —SAMUEL BUTLER

It is not desirable to cultivate a respect for law so much as a respect for right.   —HENRY THOREAU

I would uphold the law if for no other reason but to protect myself.   —THOMAS MOORE

Lawyer: The only man in whom ignorance of the law is not punished.
—ELBERT HUBBARD/JEREMY BENTHAM

The law, in its majestic equality, forbids the rich as well as the poor to sleep under bridges, to beg in the streets, and to steal bread.
—ANATOLE FRANCE

Little money, little law.   —ENGLISH PROVERB

It is a feature of nearly every Utopia that there has been no place in it for lawyers.   —BENJAMIN N. CARDOZO

In a thousand pounds of law there's not an ounce of love.
—ENGLISH PROVERB

Lawsuit: A machine which you go into as a pig and come out of as a sausage. —AMBROSE BIERCE

I was never ruined but twice: once when I lost a lawsuit, and once when I won one. —VOLTAIRE

A successful lawsuit is the one worn by a policeman.
—ROBERT FROST

Only such decrees should be issued which the majority of a community can endure. —MIDRASH

It would be better to have no laws at all than it is to have too many.
—MONTAIGNE

Every law is an infraction of liberty. —JEREMY BENTHAM

The framers knew that nonangelic societies need laws, have law-breakers, and must punish them to enforce the laws. They worked out principles of checking both law-breaking and law-making.
—ERNEST VAN DEN HAAG

Fish die when they are out of water, and people die without law and order. —TALMUD

The law is reason free from passion. —ARISTOTLE

This is a court of law, young man, not a court of justice.
—OLIVER WENDELL HOLMES, JR.

I think we may class the lawyer in the natural history of monsters.   —JOHN KEATS

Lawyers spend a great deal of their time shoveling smoke.
                                —OLIVER WENDELL HOLMES, JR.

Lawyers are men who hire out their words and anger.
                                                —MARTIAL

I cannot exactly tell you, sir, who he is, and I would be loath to speak ill of any person who I do not know deserves it, but I am afraid he is an attorney.   —SAMUEL JOHNSON

Necessity hath no law.   —OLIVER CROMWELL

When men are pure, laws are useless; when men are corrupt, laws are broken.   —BENJAMIN DISRAELI

Government implies the power of making laws. It is essential to the idea of law that it be attended with the sanction . . . of punishment for disobedience.   —ALEXANDER HAMILTON

Laws are spider webs through which the big flies pass and the little ones get caught.   —HONORÉ DE BALZAC

People who deserve it always believe in capital punishment.
                                        —LINCOLN STEFFENS

Customs are more powerful than laws.   —TALMUD

Government can easily exist without laws, but law cannot exist without government.   —BERTRAND RUSSELL

Liars/Lies

Any fool can tell the truth, but it requires a man of some sense to know how to lie well.　　　　　　　　　—SAMUEL BUTLER

It is always the best policy to tell the truth, unless, of course, you are an exceptionally good liar.
　　　　　　　　　　　—JEROME K. JEROME

✳　　✳　　✳

What he says he doesn't mean, and what he means he doesn't say.
　　　　　　　　　　　—JEWISH SAYING

If you wish to strengthen a lie, mix a little truth in with it.
　　　　　　　　　　　—ZOHAR

To some men, lying is a profession.　　—MOSES HAYYIM LUZZATTO

He only lies twice a year: in summer and in winter.
　　　　　　　　　　　—SHOLEM ALEICHEM

I do not mind lying, but I hate inaccuracy.
　　　　　　　　　　　—SAMUEL BUTLER

✳　　✳　　✳

When liars speak the truth they are not believed.　　—ARISTOTLE

The liar's punishment is not in the least that he is not believed but that he cannot believe anyone else.　　—GEORGE BERNARD SHAW

A half-truth is a whole lie.　　　　　　　　　—ANONYMOUS

I have a higher and grander standard of principle than George Washington. He could not lie; I can, but I won't.   —MARK TWAIN

Truth may walk about naked; but lies should be clothed.
                                        —JEWISH SAYING

No man has a good enough memory to make a successful liar.
                                        —ABRAHAM LINCOLN

No one lies so boldly as the man who is indignant.
                              —FRIEDRICH WILHELM NIETZSCHE

It is hard to believe that a man is telling the truth when you know that you would lie if you were in his place.
                                        —H. L. MENCKEN

                    ✳   ✳   ✳

A lie can run around the world six times while the truth is still trying to put on its pants.   —MARK TWAIN

There are people so addicted to exaggeration that they can't tell the truth without lying.   —JOSH BILLINGS

He who is not very strong in memory should not meddle with lying.
                                        —MONTAIGNE

You don't tell deliberate lies, but sometimes you have to be evasive.
                                        —MARGARET THATCHER

A lie is an abomination unto the Lord and a very present help in time of trouble.   —ANONYMOUS

Liberalism

Liberal: A power-worshiper without power.   —GEORGE ORWELL

The function of Liberalism in the past was that of putting a limit to the powers of kings. The function of true Liberalism in the future will be that of putting a limit to the powers of Parliaments.
                                                    —HERBERT SPENCER

> *I believe in liberalism, but find it hard to believe in liberals.*
>   —G. K. CHESTERTON

                    *   *   *

Liberty

Liberty don't work as good in practice as it does in speeches.
                                                    —WILL ROGERS

Show me the country that has no strikes and I'll show you the country in which there is no liberty.   —SAMUEL GOMPERS

Experience teaches us to be most on our guard to protect liberty when the government's purposes are beneficent.   —LOUIS D. BRANDEIS

Liberty is so much latitude as the powerful choose to accord to the weak.   —LEARNED HAND

Man has to earn his security and his liberty as he has to earn his living. . . . no nation can or will pay *any* price for liberty *anywhere* except, at the most heroic, for its homeland.   —WALTER LIPPMANN

The people have no need for liberty. Liberty is one of the forms of the bourgeois dictatorship. In a state worthy of a name there is no liberty.   —V. I. LENIN

> They who give up essential liberty to obtain a little temporary safety deserve neither liberty nor safety.
>   —BENJAMIN FRANKLIN
>
> Liberty is always dangerous, but it is the safest thing we have.
>   —HARRY EMERSON FOSDICK

Liberty is liberty, not equality or fairness or justice or human happiness or a quiet conscience.   —ISAIAH BERLIN

Liberty, in the lowest rank of every nation, is little more than the choice of working or starving.   —SAMUEL JOHNSON

Liberty is the one thing you can't have unless you give it to others.
                                          —WILLIAM ALLEN WHITE

Give me the liberty to know, to utter, and to argue freely according to conscience, above all liberties.   —JOHN MILTON

The spirit of liberty . . . is the spirit which is not too sure it is always right.   —LEARNED HAND

If none were to have liberty but those who understand what it is, there would not be many freed men in the world. —LORD HALIFAX

The only dependable foundation of personal liberty is the personal economic security of private property.   —WALTER LIPPMANN

Liberty, too, can corrupt, and absolute liberty can corrupt absolutely.
                                          —GERTRUDE HIMMELFARB

Life

It is not reason which is the guide of life, but custom.
—DAVID HUME

People say that life is the thing, but I prefer reading.
—LOGAN PEARSALL SMITH

*The optimist proclaims that we live in the best
of all possible worlds, and the pessimist fears
this is true.*
—JAMES BRANCH CABELL

*　　*　　*

If we were not all so excessively interested in ourselves, life would
be so uninteresting that none of us would be able to endure it.
—ARTHUR SCHOPENHAUER

Cannot we let people be themselves, and enjoy life in their own way?
You are trying to make that man another *you*. One's enough.
—RALPH WALDO EMERSON

Life is a goddamned, stinking, treacherous game, and nine hundred
and ninety-nine men out of a thousand are bastards.
—THEODORE DREISER

We are all on a spaceship, and that spaceship is Earth. Four billion
passengers—and no skippers.　　　—WERNHER VON BRAUN

"Master, I marvel how the fishes live in the sea."
"Why, as men do on land: The great ones eat up the little ones."
—PERICLES

The three most important events of human life are equally devoid of
reason: birth, marriage, and death.　　　—AUSTIN O'MALLEY

We are always getting ready to live, but never living.
                                        —RALPH WALDO EMERSON

The human situation is always desperate. —LEWIS MUMFORD

The basic fact about human existence is not that it is a tragedy,
but that it is a bore.   —H. L. MENCKEN

Life does not begin at the moment of conception or the moment of
birth. It begins when the kids leave home and the dog dies.
                                        —ANONYMOUS

*Is life worth living? The question does not
make any sense.*
                                        —ERICH FROMM

                    *   *   *

The living are the dead on holiday.   —MAURICE MAETERLINCK

We should live our lives as though Christ was coming this afternoon.
                                        —JIMMY CARTER

Life would be infinitely happier if we could only be born at the age of
eighty and gradually approach eighteen.   —MARK TWAIN

Youth is a blunder, manhood a struggle, old age a regret.
                                        —BENJAMIN DISRAELI

Happy or not, life is the only treasure a man possesses; those who do
not love life do not deserve it.   —GIOVANNI CASANOVA

The meaning of life is that it stops.   —FRANZ KAFKA

Life is a dream—but please don't wake me.   —FOLK SAYING

Life: It's full of such suffering and sorrow, sometimes I think it's better not to be born at all. . . . But how many people do you meet in a lifetime who were that lucky? —YIDDISH SAYING

Life is much too important a thing to talk seriously about it.
—OSCAR WILDE

There is more to life than increasing its speed.
—MOHANDAS K. GANDHI

That life is meaningless may be a lie, so far as the whole of life is concerned. But it is the truth at any given instant.
—ALDOUS HUXLEY

A man should go on living—if only to satisfy his curiosity.
—YIDDISH SAYING

Life is not a spectacle or a feast; it is a predicament.
—GEORGE SANTAYANA

That life is worth living is the most necessary of assumptions and, were it not assumed, the most impossible of conclusions.
—GEORGE SANTAYANA

Life is one long process of getting tired. —SAMUEL BUTLER

Threescore years and ten is enough; if a man can't suffer all the misery he wants in that time, he must be numb. —JOSH BILLINGS

Life is not a problem to be solved, but a reality to be experienced.
—SOREN KIERKEGAARD

The longer I live the more beautiful life becomes.
—FRANK LLOYD WRIGHT

Life is a blister on top of a tumor, and a boil on top of that.
—SHOLEM ALEICHEM

There is no cure for birth and death, save to enjoy the interval.
—GEORGE SANTAYANA

How can one deny that all our lives hang by threads of nothing more than luck? A vagrant microbe or an oil slick on the road, an open door, the leak in a gas line, a madman encountered by chance—against these what matters all our painful accumulations of virtue, knowledge, nobility, sacrifice?   —LEO ROSTEN

Life is like an onion: You peel off layer after layer and then you find there is nothing in it.   —JAMES GIBBONS HUNEKER

Life is a dream for the wise, a game for the fool, a comedy for the rich, a tragedy for the poor.   —SHOLEM ALEICHEM

It is not true that we have only one life to live;
if we can read, we can live as many more lives
and as many kinds of lives as we wish.
                        —S. I. HAYAKAWA

✳   ✳   ✳

The time we waste in yawning never can be regained. —STENDHAL

Grief can take care of itself; but to get the full value of a joy you must have somebody to divide it with.   —MARK TWAIN

All life ends in weeping.   —VARIOUS FOLK SAYINGS

Life is too short to be small.   —BENJAMIN DISRAELI

Life is a dream . . . we waking sleep and sleeping wake.
                        —MONTAIGNE

> The unexamined life is not worth living.   —SOCRATES
>
> The good life is one inspired by love and guided by knowledge.
>   —BERTRAND RUSSELL
>
> Life can only be understood backward, but it must be lived for-
> ward.   —SOREN KIERKEGAARD

There are two tragedies in life. One is not to get your heart's desire.
The other is to get it.   —GEORGE BERNARD SHAW

The trouble with life is that there are so many beautiful women and
so little time.   —JOHN BARRYMORE

❦ Limericks ❦

I have no use for people who do not love limericks, which are a
delicious genre of wit. Every good limerick I have ever heard or read
ends with a climax—of pure, unadulterated wit.

No matter how clever the first four lines, it is the last line that is
decisive—and if that line is static or innocuous or fumblefisted, the
limerick is doomed. A limerick that does not close with a triumphant
detonation of wit is a pointless contrivance of rhyming.

I could cite fifty or so limericks that would make you explode with
laughter. I give you my favorite nine. "Why nine, and not ten?" you
(naturally) ask.

That is a good question.

Good limericks are very complex
And chiefly harp upon sex.
They burgeon with virgins
And masculine urgins
And bust with erotic effects.

There's a girl I shall not embarrass,
Who has a super-superlative ass;
Not soft, round, and pink,

As you shamelessly think:
It is brown, has long ears, and eats grass.

A dowager visiting Florida
Broke her leg in the Fontainebleau Corridor
A busboy from Maine
To remove all her pain
Shot her. Could anything be horrider?

She cried, "No, no; stop, Mr.!"
As soon as the sly cad had kissed her
And so out of spite
On the very same night
This Mr. kissed her sister

A beautiful gal named Stella
Fell in love with a bowlegged fella.
This foolhardy chap
Let her sit on his lap
And she flopped way down to the cella.

There was a young beauty from Delaware
Who surely was quite well aware
That to dress for a ball
Was just nothing at all
But wondered what-in-hell would her fellah wear

This immortal statue by Phidias
That outraged Athens' phastidious,
Made a committee of sorts
Cover her crotch with shorts.
So Aphrodite looked hermaphroditious.

A glamorous maid named McCall
Wore a newspaper dress to the ball.
The costume caught fire
And burned up her entire
Front page, sports section, et al.

A fly and a flea in a flue,
Were imprisoned there: What could they do?
Said the flea, "Let us fly,"
Said the fly, "Let us flee,"
So they flew through a flaw in the flue.

A dashing young man in the choir
Had a voice that went hoir and hoir,

Till one memorable night
It soared clear out of sight
And they heard it, in time, in the spoir.

Logic

One often hears the complimentary phrase "flawless logic"; and it is hard to realize that this discipline, so long considered the one kind of thinking or reasoning beyond criticism, should have this mysterious inner flaw, which consists of the fact that you can never discover whether or not it really has a flaw.　　　—WARREN WEAVER

"It's the exception that proves the rule" is idiotic: Is no rule proved until you can find an exception to it?

　　　　　　　　　　　　　　—L. R.

*　　*　　*

Lust is the enemy of logic.　　　　　　　—ANONYMOUS

Logic is a poor guide compared with custom.
　　　　　　　　　　　　　—WINSTON CHURCHILL

Logic: A game invented by a race of beings who cannot define love, explain hate, or replace prejudice with distaste.　　— LEO ROSTEN

Loneliness

Everyone is lonely, at bottom, and cries to be understood; but we can never entirely understand someone else, no matter how much we try or want to.　　　　　　　　　　—LEO ROSTEN

Columbus discovered no isle or key so lonely as himself.
                                    —RALPH WALDO EMERSON

The dread of loneliness is greater than the fear of bondage, so we get
married.   —CYRIL CONNOLLY

> *Loneliness breaks the spirit.*
>   —JEWISH SAYING

* * *

Love

I wonder what fool it was that first invented kissing.
                                    —JONATHAN SWIFT

> *Love is what happens to a man and woman
> who don't know each other.*
>   —W. SOMERSET MAUGHAM

* * *

Love is the wisdom of the fool and the folly of the wise.
                                    —SAMUEL JOHNSON

A false enchantment can last a lifetime.   —W. H. AUDEN

There's always something ridiculous about the passions of people
whom one has ceased to love.   —OSCAR WILDE

Immature love says, "I love you because I need you." Mature love
says, "I need you because I love you."   —ERICH FROMM

*The story of a love is not important—what is
important is that one is capable of love.*
                                    —HELEN HAYES

                    *   *   *

Well-ordered self-love is right and natural.   —THOMAS AQUINAS

First love is only a little foolishness and a lot of curiosity.
                                    —GEORGE BERNARD SHAW

Love is sentimental measles.   —CHARLES KINGSLEY

Safeguarding a girl in love is harder than guarding a sackful of
fleas.   —JEWISH FOLK SAYING

One can find women who have never had one love affair, but it
is rare indeed to find any who have had only one.
                    —FRANÇOIS DE LA ROCHEFOUCAULD

It is better to have loved and lost than never to have lost at all.
                                    —SAMUEL BUTLER

Love is like the measles: We all have to go through it.
                                    —JEROME K. JEROME

Oh, what lies there are in kisses.   —HEINRICH HEINE

Loving you is like loving a red-hot poker: Every caress brings on
agony.   —BERTRAND RUSSELL (TO OTTOLINE MORRELL)

Make love to every woman you meet; if you get 5 percent on your
outlay it's a good investment.   —ARNOLD BENNETT

Love: *A temporary insanity curable by mar-riage.*

                                    —AMBROSE BIERCE

                          *   *   *

Love consists in this, that two solitudes protect and touch and greet each other.   —RAINER MARIA RILKE

All loves but one's own have an element of the tiresome.
                                    —C. P. SNOW

The love game is never called off on account of darkness.
                                    —ANONYMOUS

The magic of first love is our ignorance that it can ever end.   —BENJAMIN DISRAELI

                          *   *   *

Nine tenths of the letters in which people speak unreservedly of their inmost feelings are written after ten at night.   —THOMAS HARDY

Of what use is love if you have no one to love?
                                    —IMMANUEL OF ROME

There are few people who are not ashamed of their love affairs when the infatuation is over.   —FRANÇOIS DE LA ROCHEFOUCAULD

Where love is, no room is too small.   —FOLK SAYING

Love: The only fire for which there is no insurance.   —ANONYMOUS

It is easier to love humanity . . . than to love one's neighbor.
—ERIC HOFFER

Love may be blind, but jealousy sees too much.   —FOLK SAYING

Adultery: Democracy applied to love.   —H. L. MENCKEN

A man can be happy with any woman as long as he does not love her.
—OSCAR WILDE

Take away love and our earth is a tomb.   —ROBERT BROWNING

People who are not in love fail to understand how an intelligent man can suffer because of a very ordinary woman. This is like being surprised that anyone should be stricken with cholera because of a creature so insignificant as the common vacillus.
—MARCEL PROUST

Many a man has fallen in love with a girl in a light so dim he would not have chosen a suit by it.   —MAURICE CHEVALIER

Love is the delusion that one woman differs from another.
—H. L. MENCKEN

There are people who would never have fallen in love if they had never heard of love.   —FRANÇOIS DE LA ROCHEFOUCAULD

The ability to make love frivolously is the chief characteristic that distinguishes human beings from the beasts.   —HEYWOOD BROUN

Religion has done love a great service by making it a sin.
—ANATOLE FRANCE

The ideal love affair is one conducted by post.
—GEORGE BERNARD SHAW

Love takes up where knowledge leaves off.   —THOMAS AQUINAS

Three things can't be hidden: coughing, poverty, and love.
                                        —FOLK SAYING

Love is the form, mover, and root of the virtues.
                                        —THOMAS AQUINAS

Every little girl knows about love. It is only her capacity to suffer
because of it that increases.   —FRANÇOISE SAGAN

Love is a serious mental disease.   —PLATO

Love is the triumph of imagination over intelligence.
                                        —H. L. MENCKEN

One is very crazy when in love.   —SIGMUND FREUD

Luck

Success is just a matter of luck. Ask any failure.   —ANONYMOUS

When a man has luck, even his ox calves.   —JEWISH SAYING

If a *shlimazl* (luckless one) sold umbrellas, it would stop raining; if he
sold candles, the sun would never set; and if he made coffins, people
would stop dying.   —YIDDISH SAYING

Let us be of good cheer, remembering that the misfortunes hardest
to bear are those that never come.   —JAMES RUSSELL LOWELL

We must believe in luck. For how else can we explain the success of those we don't like?
                    —JEAN COCTEAU

*   *   *

My luck is getting worse and worse. Last night, for instance, I was mugged by a Quaker.   —WOODY ALLEN

He is so unlucky that he runs into accidents that started out to happen to somebody else.   —DON MARQUIS

I am a great believer in luck, and I find the harder I work the more I have of it.   —STEPHEN LEACOCK

Even the unlucky need luck.   —YIDDISH SAYING

A shlemiel *(foolish person) is always spilling hot soup—down the neck of a* shlimazl.
                    —YIDDISH SAYING

*   *   *

Need makes people better; luck makes them worse.
                    —HASIDIC SAYING

A *shlimazl* buys a suit with two pair of pants and promptly burns a hole in the jacket.   —YIDDISH SAYING

Whenever you can, hang around the lucky.   —JEWISH SAYING

Lust

The difference between love and lust is like the difference between strolling and skiing. —LEO ROSTEN

Lust should be stifled, for it cannot lead to truth.
—MOSES IBN EZRA

Mankind

I love mankind; it's people I can't stand.
—CHARLES ("PEANUTS") SCHULZ

It is not from the benevolence of the butcher, the brewer, or the baker that we expect our dinner, but from their regard to their own interest. We address ourselves not to their self-love, one never talks to them of our own necessities, but of their advantages. —ADAM SMITH

If man had created man, he would be ashamed of his performance.
—MARK TWAIN

Man is the only animal that eats when he is not hungry, drinks when he is not thirsty, and makes love during all seasons.
—ANONYMOUS

* * *

Ceremony is the invention of wise men to keep fools at a distance.
—RICHARD STEELE

We can easily learn to endure adversity; another man's, I mean.
—MARK TWAIN

Adam was only human. He did not want the apple for the apple's sake; he wanted it only because it was forbidden. —MARK TWAIN

Man is the only animal that can be a fool. —HOLBROOK JACKSON

I sometimes think that God, in creating man, somewhat overestimated his ability. —OSCAR WILDE

Man is the only animal that laughs and weeps, for he is the only animal that is struck by the difference between what things are and what they might have been. —WILLIAM HAZLITT

Man is the only animal that can remain on friendly terms with the victims he intends to eat until he eats them. —SAMUEL BUTLER

Manners

The test of good manners is to be patient with bad ones.
—IBN GABIROL

Good breeding is an expedient to make fools and wise men equals.
—RICHARD STEELE

Marriage

Marriage has many pains, but celibacy has no pleasures.
—SAMUEL JOHNSON

As to marriage or celibacy, let a man take
which course he will. He will be sure to repent.
                                        —SOCRATES

*   *   *

Marriage is a great institution, but I'm not ready for an institution.
                                        —MAE WEST

If we take matrimony at its lowest, we regard it as a sort of friendship
recognized by the police.   —ROBERT LOUIS STEVENSON

Marriage: A word that should be pronounced "mirage."
                                        —HERBERT SPENCER

Marriage is only a relative good, and it would be better if all men
were to refrain from it.   —ST. AUGUSTINE

When a young man marries, he divorces his
mother.
                                        —TALMUD

*   *   *

Marriage is the only adventure open to the cowardly.   —VOLTAIRE

Bigamy is having one wife too many. Monog-
amy is the same.
                                        —OSCAR WILDE

*   *   *

One should always be in love; that is the reason one should never
marry.   —OSCAR WILDE

Marriage is neither heaven nor hell, it is simply purgatory.
                                        —ABRAHAM LINCOLN

Marriage: A master, a mistress, and two slaves, making in all, two.
                                        —AMBROSE BIERCE

Monks are allowed to fornicate but not to marry.   —ERASMUS

By all means, marry. If you get a good wife, you'll become happy; if
you get a bad one, you'll become a philosopher.   —SOCRATES

> *Men marry because they are tired, women be-*
> *cause they are curious; both are disappointed.*
>   —OSCAR WILDE

                    *   *   *

Every woman should marry—and no man.   —BENJAMIN DISRAELI

The only time some fellows are ever seen with their wives is after
they've been indicted.   —FRANK MCKINNEY ("KIN") HUBBARD

Marriage is popular because it combines the maximum of temptation
with the maximum of opportunity.   —GEORGE BERNARD SHAW

> Second marriage: *the triumph of hope over*
> *experience.*
>   —SAMUEL JOHNSON

                    *   *   *

Marriage is a very good thing, but I think it's a mistake to make a
habit of it.   —W. SOMERSET MAUGHAM

Jacqueline Onassis had a very clear understanding of marriage. I have
a lot of respect for women who win the game with rules given you by
the enemy.   —GLORIA STEINEM

When a scholar seeks a bride, he should take an ignoramus along to
advise him.   —JEWISH SAYING

Marriage is the alliance of two people, one of whom never remembers birthdays and the other never forgets them.   —OGDEN NASH

What God hath joined together no man shall ever put asunder; God will take care of that.   —GEORGE BERNARD SHAW

When a woman marries again it is because she detested her first husband; when a man marries again it is because he adored his first wife.   —OSCAR WILDE

Marriage is the price men pay for sex. Sex is the price women pay for marriage.   —ANONYMOUS

I think it can be stated without denial that no man ever saw a man he would be willing to marry if he were a woman. —GEORGE GIBBS

There are some good marriages, but practically no delightful ones.
     —FRANÇOIS DE LA ROCHEFOUCAULD

Remember: It's as easy to marry a rich woman as a poor woman.
     —WILLIAM MAKEPEACE THACKERAY

Young man, if she asks you if you like her hair that way, beware; the woman has already committed matrimony in her heart.
     —DON MARQUIS

Politics doesn't make strange bedfellows—marriage does.
     —GROUCHO MARX

No man should marry until he has studied anatomy and dissected at least one woman.
     —HONORÉ DE BALZAC

*   *   *

The trouble with marriage is that while every woman is at heart a mother, every man is at heart a bachelor.   —E. V. LUCAS

Even in civilized mankind faint traces of a monogamic instinct can sometimes be perceived.   —BERTRAND RUSSELL

When two people are under the influence of the most violent, most insane, most delusive, and most transient of passions, they are required to swear that they will remain in that excited, abnormal, and exhausting condition until death do them part.
          —GEORGE BERNARD SHAW

No man is regular in his attendance at the House of Commons until he is married.   —BENJAMIN DISRAELI

A man in love is incomplete until he is married. Then he is finished.
          —ZSA ZSA GABOR

*   *   *

Marriage is Heaven and Hell.   —GERMAN PROVERB

An archaeologist is the best husband a woman can have; the older she gets, the more interested he is in her.
          —AGATHA CHRISTIE (WHO MARRIED ONE)

A happy marriage is a long conversation that seems all too short.
          —ANDRÉ MAUROIS

Marriage: Anyone who thinks marriage is a fifty-fifty proposition doesn't understand women, or fractions.   —DANNY THOMAS

The man who marries for money earns it.   —JEWISH SAYING

When a man brings his wife a gift for no reason, there's a reason.   —MOLLY MCGEE

American women expect to find in their husbands a perfection that English women only hope to find in their butlers.
                                          —W. SOMERSET MAUGHAM

By day they fight, but they bed at night.   —JEWISH SAYING

Woman begins by resisting a man's advances and ends by blocking his retreat.   —OSCAR WILDE

A successful marriage is not a gift; it is an achievement.
                                          —ANN LANDERS

When you see what some girls marry, you realize how they must hate to work for a living.   —HELEN ROWLAND

We sleep in separate rooms, we have dinner apart, we take separate vacations—we're doing everything we can to keep our marriage together.
                                          —RODNEY DANGERFIELD

*   *   *

Grecian ladies counted their age from their marriage, not from their birth.   —HOMER

Some people ask the secret of our long marriage. We take time to go to a restaurant two times a week. A little candlelight, dinner, soft music, and dancing. She goes Tuesdays, I go Fridays.
                                          —HENNY YOUNGMAN

The husband who wants a happy marriage should learn to keep his mouth shut and his checkbook open. —GROUCHO MARX

Advice to persons about to marry: Don't. —MARCEL PROUST

Marriage is a result of the longing for the deep, deep peace of the double bed after the hurly-burly of the chaise longue.
—MRS. PATRICK CAMPBELL

Martyrs

Martyrdom is the only way in which a man can become famous without ability. —GEORGE BERNARD SHAW

The disciples of a martyr suffer much more than the martyr.
—FRIEDRICH WILHELM NIETZSCHE

Martyrdom covers a multitude of sins. —MARK TWAIN

Although prepared for martyrdom, I prefer that it be postponed. —WINSTON CHURCHILL

I cannot risk my life for the truth. Not all men have the strength [needed] for martyrdom. —ERASMUS

For some not to be martyrs is martyrdom indeed. —LEO ROSTEN

It is the cause, not the death, that makes the martyr.
—NAPOLEON BONAPARTE

✗ Groucho Marx ✗

When Aristotle described wit as "educated insolence" he might have been defining the unique form of mordant ridicule, delivered with affected indignation, that became the hallmark of Julius "Groucho" Marx.

A gushy dowager once stopped at our restaurant table to coo, "Are you Groucho Marx?" The sardonic owl replied, "No. Are you?"

When a drunken oaf flung his arm across Groucho's shoulder, braying, "Groucho! You probably don't remember me," Groucho replied, "I never forget a face, but in your case I'll be glad to make an exception."

Groucho turned any aspect of living into a laugh. "When I came into my hotel room last night I found a strange blonde in my bed. I would stand for none of that nonsense! . . . I gave her exactly twenty-four hours to get out."

He was the darling of intellectuals throughout the English-speaking world. He lent a kind of logic to lunacy. He also championed the lunacy that lurks just beneath the structured solemnities of logic.

On the stage he was the Voltaire of vaudeville. In person he was the undisputed master of insult, which he tossed about with the most brazen gravity. His effrontery remains unique because it was so *confounding:* His flights of calculated derangement expressed what the rest of us simply have not the wit, much less the audacity, to utter.

I once asked George S. Kaufman about the demented dialogue in which the Marx Brothers excelled. He said with a scowl, "I used to go backstage, after the boys were settled into a play, and listen. And every so often I'd say, 'Ah, *that* line is mine.'"

Marx detested the obligatory banalities of etiquette. Once, at his door after dinner, I paused to say, "I'd like to say good-bye to your wife."

Groucho, walleyed, said, "Who wouldn't?" (They were divorced soon after.)

Nothing intimidated him. Consider his now famous rejection of an invitation to join a certain club: "I do not wish to belong to the kind of club that accepts people like me as members." Logicians call such a mind-boggler a "set paradox."

One day Groucho, driving near the ocean with a friend, spied a beach club with a row of pretty cabanas. "That would be a good club for me and my family," Groucho said.

"Um—forget it, Grouch. They don't admit Jews."

To which Groucho, whose wife was Gentile, replied, "Well, my son is only half Jewish. Do you think they'd let him go into the water up to his *knees*?" I know no wit sharper than that.

A Marxian ad-lib that I hope to propel down the ages is this one: Hollywood was all agog over the powers of a spiritualist who was cashing in on large and lucrative séances with awed movie folk. This sorcerer might still be plying his supernatural wiles had not some friends challenged Groucho, who listened to their rapture with dour skepticism, to appraise the psychic's wizardry for himself. Groucho went to a séance.

He sat through an eerie demonstration in which the spiritualist answered the most arcane questions, and elicited answers from loved ones beyond the grave. After an hour of exhausting occult omniscience, the clairvoyant intoned, "And now . . . my spirit grows weary. . . . There is time for only one more question."

Marx asked it: "What's the capital of South Dakota?"

He once offered to write a blurb for a book I was about to publish. Here was his comment, verbatim:

Dear Junior:
From the moment I picked your book up until the moment I put it down, I could not stop laughing. Someday I hope to read it.
—Groucho

Of all his personal lampoonery, the one I most admire is this:

Dear Junior:
Excuse me for not answering your letter sooner. I have been so busy not answering letters lately that I couldn't get around to not answering yours in time.
—Groucho

I stand in awe before so original and anarchic a mind.

Masses/Mass Media

The media, far from being a conspiracy to dull the political sense of the people, could be seen as a conspiracy to disguise the extent of political indifference.　　　　　　　　—DAVID RIESMAN

The American mass media are often superficial, inadequate, incomplete, and unclarifying. They cannot help it: They are produced by human beings. But they are also uncensored, and show an independent and refreshing disdain for demagogues, bureaucrats, drum-beaters, and even presidents.　　　　　　　　—LEO ROSTEN

The masses aren't asses.　　　　　　　　—JEWISH SAYING

The masses will more easily fall victim to a big lie than to a small one.　　　　　　　　—ADOLF HITLER

My work is being destroyed almost as soon as it is printed. One day it is being read; the next day someone's wrapping fish in it.　　　　　　　　—AL CAPP

Mathematics

A straight line is the simplest and most trivial example of a curve.

—ALBERT EINSTEIN/LEOPOLD INFELD

*　　*　　*

Mathematics . . . possesses not only truth, but supreme beauty—a beauty cold and austere, like that of sculpture.

—BERTRAND RUSSELL

The odds against getting a perfect hand in bridge are 1 out of 365 billion. These odds are also the odds for getting the worst possible hand. —Leo Rosten

Mathematics: The subject in which we never know what we are talking about, nor whether what we are saying is true. —Bertrand Russell

---

Few persons invent algebra on their own. —Frederick Mosteller

There are no sects in geometry. —Voltaire

I don't believe in mathematics. —Albert Einstein

Even in the valley of the shadow of death, two and two do not make six. —Bertrand Russell

I maintain that two and two would continue to make four, in spite of the whine of the amateur for three, or the cry of the critic for five. —James McNeill Whistler

A mathematical web of some kind can be woven about any universe containing several objects. The fact that our universe lends itself to mathematical treatment is not a fact of any great philosophical significance. —Bertrand Russell

Medicine

One of the first duties of the physician is to educate the masses not to take medicine. —William Osler

He's a devout believer in the department of witchcraft called medical science. —George Bernard Shaw

Vaccination is the medical sacrament corresponding to baptism.
—SAMUEL BUTLER

Mediocrity

Perseverance: A lowly virtue whereby mediocrity achieves an inglorious success.   —AMBROSE BIERCE

Memory

You never know how much a man can't remember until he is called as a witness.   —ATTRIBUTED TO WILL ROGERS

Memory is the one paradise out of which we cannot be driven.
—SACHA GUITRY

* * *

It's a poor sort of memory that only works backward.
—LEWIS CARROLL

Everyone complains of his memory, no one of his judgment.
—FRANÇOIS DE LA ROCHEFOUCAULD

You can close your eyes to reality but not to memories.
—STANISLAW J. LEC

Lending money to friends causes them to lose their memories.
—LAURENCE J. PETER

* * *

My memory is the thing I forget with.   —A CHILD

Creditors have better memories than debtors.
                                        —BENJAMIN FRANKLIN

People with good memories seldom remember anything worth remembering.   —ANONYMOUS

Cherish all your happy moments; they make a fine cushion for old age.
                                        —BOOTH TARKINGTON

God gave us our memories so that we might have roses in December.
                    —JAMES MATTHEW BARRIE

*   *   *

We do not remember days, we remember moments.
                                        —CESARE PAVESE

The things that are hardest to bear are sweetest to remember.
                                        —SENECA

Memory and teeth grow weaker with time.   —ANONYMOUS

Memory is the diary we all carry about with us.   —OSCAR WILDE

A good memory is one trained to forget the trivial.
                                        —CLIFTON FADIMAN

"I have done this," says memory; "I can't have done this," says pride.
In the end, memory yields.   —FRIEDRICH WILHELM NIETZSCHE

I've a grand memory for forgetting.   —ROBERT LOUIS STEVENSON

Nothing so deeply imprints anything on our memory as the desire to forget it. —MONTAIGNE

The advantage of a bad memory is that one enjoys several times the same good things for the first time.
—FRIEDRICH WILHELM NIETZSCHE

*   *   *

The best qualification of a prophet is to have a good memory.
—GEORGE SAVILE HALIFAX

Men (and Women)

Nothing confuses a man more than driving behind a woman who does everything right. —ANONYMOUS

I only like two kinds of men—domestic and imported. —MAE WEST

Men are creatures with two legs and eight hands.
—JAYNE MANSFIELD

*   *   *

Nine hundred and ninety-nine men out of a thousand are bastards.
—THEODORE DREISER

Women represent the triumph of matter over mind, just as men represent the triumph of mind over morals. —OSCAR WILDE

A woman is no sooner ours than we are no longer hers.
—MONTAIGNE

Men have as exaggerated an idea of their rights as women have of their wrongs. —EDGAR WATSON ("ED") HOWE

Men are never so tired and harassed as when they have to deal with a woman who wants a raise. —MICHAEL KORDA

Shaw has pleased all the bohemians by saying that women are equal to men; but he has infuriated them by suggesting that men are equal to women.

—G. K. CHESTERTON

* * *

The ideal man has the strength of a man and the compassion of a woman. —ZOHAR

Man is always looking for someone to boast to; woman is always looking for a shoulder to put her head on. —H. L. MENCKEN

Men who do not make advances to women are apt to become victims to women who make advances to them. —WALTER BAGEHOT

Man is a clever animal who behaves like an imbecile.
—ALBERT SCHWEITZER

Behind every successful man you'll find a woman who has nothing to wear.

—JAMES STEWART

* * *

Women in love are less ashamed than men. They have less to be ashamed of. —AMBROSE BIERCE

Women lie about their age; men lie about their income.

—WILLIAM FEATHER

*　*　*

Gentlemen prefer blondes, but take what they can get.

—DON HEROLD

Men aren't attracted to me by my mind. They're attracted by what I don't mind.

—GYPSY ROSE LEE

*　*　*

A woman's mind is cleaner than a man's: She changes it more often.

—OLIVER HERFORD

A man chases a woman until she catches him.　　—ANONYMOUS

I like men who have a future and women who have a past.

—OSCAR WILDE

A clever, ugly man every now and then is successful with the ladies, but a handsome fool is irresistible.

—WILLIAM MAKEPEACE THACKERAY

Man weeps to think that he will die so soon; woman, that she was born so long ago.　　—H. L. MENCKEN

Men always want to be a woman's first love. Women have a more subtle instinct: What they like is to be a man's last romance.　　—OSCAR WILDE

Women still remember the first kiss after men have forgotten the last.　　—RÉMY DE GOURMONT

What passes for woman's intuition is often nothing more than man's transparency.   —GEORGE JEAN NATHAN

Until Eve arrived, this was a man's world.   —RICHARD ARMOUR

A man without a wife is not complete.   —TALMUD

All heiresses are beautiful.   —JOHN DRYDEN

Nowadays most women grow old gracefully; most men, disgracefully.
                    —HELEN ROWLAND

Whether women are better than men I cannot say, but I can say they certainly are no worse.
                    —GOLDA MEIR

*   *   *

The average man is more interested in a woman who is interested in him than he is in a woman with beautiful legs.
                    —MARLENE DIETRICH

A woman without a man is like a fish without a bicycle.
                    —GLORIA STEINEM

Men mourn for what they have lost; women for what they ain't got.
                    —JOSH BILLINGS

I like men to behave like men—strong and childish.
                    —FRANÇOISE SAGAN

Human being: *An ingenious assembly of portable plumbing.*

—CHRISTOPHER MORLEY

* * *

A woman's preaching is like a dog's walking on his hind legs: It is not done well, but you are surprised to find it done at all.

—SAMUEL JOHNSON

The main difference between men and women is that men are lunatics and women are idiots.

—REBECCA WEST

* * *

Sometimes I wonder if men and women really suit each other. Perhaps they should live next door and just visit now and then.

—KATHARINE HEPBURN

As I grow older and older
And totter toward the tomb
I find that I care less and less
Who goes to bed with whom.

—DOROTHY PARKER

What men desire is a virgin who is a whore. —EDWARD DAHLBERG

Behind every great man is a nag. —LEO ROSTEN

∽ H. L. Mencken ∽

H. L. Mencken was one of America's greatest editors, critics, and writers. A master of rollicking prose and withering wit, Mencken was a libertarian par excellence. He was a cynic, an erudite agnostic, an ebullient pessimist, and one of the funniest writers America ever turned out.

He had no equal as a defender of freedom. He detested prudes and the self-righteous. He excoriated pomposity. He mocked hypocrisy with deadly sense. He loathed moralists of all persuasions and censors of any ilk. He used the English language as a club, a rapier, a scalpel, a trumpet. He lived with endless gusto and rowdy delights. He was not so much a wit as an epigrammatist.

Among his countless blistering animadversions, I treasure these:

Idealist: One who upon observing that a rose smells better than a cabbage, concludes that it will also make better soup.

∞

Operas in English are about as sensible as baseball in Italian.

∞

News: Anything that makes a woman say, "For heaven's sake!"

∞

Injustice is not hard to bear; it is justice that really hurts.

∞

Morals: He had the morals of a Baptist Sunday school superintendent in Paris for the first time.

∞

Demagogue: A man who preaches doctrines he knows to be untrue to men he knows to be idiots.

∞

Lies: It is hard to believe that a man is telling the truth when you know that you would lie if you were in his place.

∞

Love: The triumph of imagination over intelligence.

∞

Conscience: The inner voice that tells you that someone may be watching.

Miracles

The most astonishing thing about miracles is that they happen.

—G. K. CHESTERTON

*　*　*

It would have approached nearer to the idea of miracle if Jonah had swallowed the whale. —THOMAS PAINE

Mysteries are not necessarily miracles. —GOETHE

It's a miracle if miracles don't happen. —ANDREW LANG

A miracle: *An event described by those to whom it was told by men who did not see it.*

—ELBERT HUBBARD

*　*　*

Miracles do occur, but they rarely provide food. —TALMUD

Though a good deal is too strange to be believed, nothing is too strange to have happened. —THOMAS HARDY

A miracle cannot prove what is impossible; it is only useful to confirm what is possible. —MAIMONIDES

Every desire bears its death in its very gratification. Curiosity languishes under repeated stimulants, and novelties cease to excite surprise, until at length we do not wonder even at a miracle.

—WASHINGTON IRVING

Apparently there is nothing that cannot happen. —MARK TWAIN

An act of reason is a miracle.
       —MONTAIGNE/BERTRAND RUSSELL

*   *   *

Mob

A mob is a society of bodies voluntarily bereaving themselves of reason. . . . A mob is man voluntarily descending to the nature of the beast.   —RALPH WALDO EMERSON

Only one more indispensable massacre of Capitalists or Communists or Fascists or Christians or Heretics, and there we are in the Golden Future.   —ALDOUS HUXLEY

Why babble about brutality and be indignant about tortures? The masses want that. They need something that will give them a thrill of horror.   —ADOLF HITLER

It's a characteristic of all movements and crusades that the psychopathic element rises to the top.
       —ROBERT LINDNER

*   *   *

A riot is the language of the unheard. —MARTIN LUTHER KING, JR.

Those who try to lead the people can only do so by following the mob.
       —OSCAR WILDE

The multitude . . . is a beast of many heads.   —ERASMUS

Modesty

The man who is ostentatious of his modesty is twin to the statue that wears a fig leaf. —MARK TWAIN

Modesty: The gentle art of enhancing your charm by pretending not to be aware of it. —OLIVER HERFORD

Money

Lack of money is the root of all evil. —GEORGE BERNARD SHAW

Money is the most egalitarian force in society. It confers power on whoever holds it. —ROGER STARR

There is only one class in the community that thinks more about money than the rich, and that is the poor.

—OSCAR WILDE

* * *

If you want him to mourn, you had best leave him nothing.

—MARTIAL

No one would remember the Good Samaritan if he had only had good intentions. He had money as well. —MARGARET THATCHER

Money doesn't always bring happiness. A man with ten million dollars is no happier than a man with nine million dollars. —ANONYMOUS

The most valuable of all human possessions, next to a superior and disdainful air, is the reputation of being well-to-do.

—H. L. MENCKEN

*I haven't got as much money as some folks, but
I've got as much impudence as any of them,
and that's the next thing to money.*
                              —JOSH BILLINGS

                    *   *   *

Whoever said money can't buy happiness didn't know where to shop.
                              —GITTEL HUDNICK

Money, which represents the prose of life, and which is hardly spoken
of in parlors without an apology, is, in its effects and laws, as beautiful
as roses.   —RALPH WALDO EMERSON

The greatest miser with money is the biggest spendthrift with desires.
                              —MOSES IBN EZRA

Money-getters are the benefactors of our race. To them . . . are we
indebted for our institutions of learning, and of art, our academies,
colleges and churches.   —P. T. BARNUM

His money is twice tainted: 'Tain't yours and 'tain't mine.
                              —MARK TWAIN

Borrowing, like scratching, is only good for a while.
                              —JEWISH SAYING

A fool and her money are soon courted.   —HELEN ROWLAND

When I was young I used to think that money was the most important
thing in life; now that I am old, I know it is.   —OSCAR WILDE

To have money is not always so *ai-yi-yi*, but not to have it is *oy-oy-
oy*!   —MY TANTE YETTA

I have enough money to last me the rest of my life, unless I buy something.   —JACKIE MASON

Never invest your money in anything that eats or needs repainting.
                                                               —BILLY ROSE

Why is there so much month left at the end of the money?
        —MAURICE CHEVALIER/JOHN BARRYMORE

                    ✳   ✳   ✳

It is a kind of spiritual snobbery that makes people think they can be happy without money.   —ALBERT CAMUS

He was subject to a kind of disease, which at that time they called lack of money.   —FRANÇOIS RABELAIS

If you would know the value of money, go try to borrow some; for he that goes a-borrowing goes a-sorrowing.   —BENJAMIN FRANKLIN

It is surprising how many spots on the character are removed by a solution of gold.   —ANONYMOUS

I cannot afford to waste my time making money.
                                                        —LOUIS R.J. AGASSIZ

I don't like money actually, but it quiets my nerves.
                                                        —JOE E. LEWIS

It doesn't matter whether you are rich or poor—as long as you've got money.   —JOE E. LEWIS

If you lend someone money and he avoids you, you've gotten off cheap.
                                                        —YIDDISH SAYING

The money men make lives after them. —SAMUEL BUTLER

Money can't buy happiness, but neither can poverty. —LEO ROSTEN

The chief value of money lies in the fact that one lives in a world in which it is overestimated. —H. L. MENCKEN

To be clever enough to get a great deal of money, one must be stupid enough to want it. —G. K. CHESTERTON

When a man says money can do anything, that settles it: He hasn't any. —EDGAR WATSON ("ED") HOWE

I've been rich and I've been poor—and believe me, rich is better. —JOE E. LEWIS/SOPHIE TUCKER

It is better to have a permanent income than to be fascinating. —OSCAR WILDE

A dollar saved is a quarter earned. —O. O. MCINTIRE/OSCAR LEVANT

Morals/Morality

The problem is how to construct a world in which immoral people can do the least harm; not how to enable moral people to do the most good. —MILTON FRIEDMAN

*A Puritan is a person who pours righteous in-
dignation into the wrong things.*
                    —G. K. CHESTERTON

                    *   *   *

The middle class is the moral guardian of society; the elite are worried
not by immorality, but by scandal.   —LEO ROSTEN

[Morality rests] on the inescapable exigencies of human cohabitation.
                                                —SIGMUND FREUD

Any preoccupation with ideas of what is right or wrong in conduct
shows an arrested intellectual development.   —OSCAR WILDE

Ours is a world of nuclear giants and ethical infants.
                                                —OMAR BRADLEY

I never came across anyone in whom the moral sense was dominant
who was not heartless, cruel, vindictive, log-stupid, and entirely lack-
ing in the smallest sense of humanity.   —OSCAR WILDE

The objection to Puritans is not that they try to make us think as
they do, but that they try to make us do as they think.
                                                —H. L. MENCKEN

A heathen wrote this to a heathen, and yet his moral principles contain
justice, sanctity, and truth. . . . I can hardly refrain from crying, "St.
Socrates, pray for me!"   —ERASMUS

We must learn to distinguish morality from moralizing.
                                                —HENRY KISSINGER

The more things a man is ashamed of, the more respectable he is.
                                                —GEORGE BERNARD SHAW

We have, in fact, two kinds of morality, side by side: one that we preach but do not practice, and another that we practice but seldom preach.   —BERTRAND RUSSELL

What is moral is what you feel good after, and what is immoral is what you feel bad after.   —ERNEST HEMINGWAY

Men are more moral than they think and far more immoral than they can imagine.   —SIGMUND FREUD

Moral indignation is jealousy with a halo.   —H. G. WELLS

The hottest places in Hell are reserved for those who, in a time of great moral crisis, maintain their neutrality.   —DANTE

Morality is the theory that every human act must either be right or wrong and that 99 percent of them are wrong.   —H. L. MENCKEN

Neither the individuals nor the ages most distinguished for intellectual achievements have been distinguished for moral excellence.
                    —W.E.H. LECKY

*   *   *

The difference between a moral man and a man of honor is that the latter regrets a discreditable act even when it has worked.
                    —H. L. MENCKEN

Mothers

God could not be everywhere, so he invented mothers.
                    —JEWISH SAYING

A mother understands what a child does not say. —JEWISH SAYING

*I've never struck a woman in my life, not even
my own mother.*

— W. C. FIELDS

*   *   *

My mother didn't breast-feed me. She said she liked me as a friend.
— RODNEY DANGERFIELD

The warmest bed of all is Mother's.   — ANONYMOUS

All women become like their mothers—that is their tragedy; no man
does—that's his.   — OSCAR WILDE

The most remarkable thing about my mother is that for thirty years
she served the family nothing but leftovers. The original meal has
never been found.   — CALVIN TRILLIN

*My mother had a great deal of trouble with me,
but I think she enjoyed it.*

— MARK TWAIN

*   *   *

Movies

That movie? Terrible! Don't fail to miss it if you can!
— BRONX SAYING

Through the movies, a Frenchman remarked, the United States has
effected a "cultural colonization" of the world.   — LEO ROSTEN

Movies: The wide screen will only make bad films twice as bad.

They didn't *release* that movie; it escaped.
—SAMUEL GOLDWYN

It is often said that the movies are an escape for the masses; it is rarely suggested that they are also an escape for the movie-makers.
—LEO ROSTEN

American motion pictures are written by the half educated for the halfwitted. —ST. JOHN ERVINE

When the U.S. cavalry won, it was a great victory; when the Indians won, it was a massacre.
—DICK GREGORY

* * *

Movie business: You'll get along fine in this business as long as you don't bite the hand that lays the golden eggs.
—ATTRIBUTED TO SAMUEL GOLDWYN

The first producers combined the talents of craftsmen, impresarios, and circus barkers. They did not cater to small, cultivated circles. They were sensitive to mass desires, for they were of the masses themselves. They had the virtues and the failings of pioneers. They were accused of being vulgar, and with justice, yet it was their very unrefinement that fitted them so perfectly for their function.
—LEO ROSTEN

What is a writer but a *shmuck* with a typewriter! —JACK WARNER

"Forget it, Looey. No Civil War picture ever made a nickel."
—IRVING THALBERG (TO LOUIS B. MAYER
REGARDING THE FILM RIGHTS TO
GONE WITH THE WIND)

Movies are a fad. Audiences really want to see live actors on a stage. —CHARLIE CHAPLIN

The cinema, like the detective story, makes it possible to experience without danger all the excitement, passion, and desirousness that must be suppressed in a humanitarian ordering of society.
—C. G. JUNG

A "woman's movie" is one where the woman commits adultery all through the picture, and, at the end, her husband begs her to forgive him. —OSCAR LEVANT

What I am waiting for is a movie about beautiful quintuplets who love the same man. —HARRY KURNITZ

Sneak preview: A place where four or five men, making four or five thousand a week, go to watch a pimply-faced kid write "It stinks" on a card. —NUNNALLY JOHNSON

Associate producer: About the only guy in Hollywood who will associate with a producer. —FRED ALLEN

Music

A musicologist is a man who can read music but cannot hear it.
—SIR THOMAS BEECHAM

Without music, life would be a mistake.
                    —FRIEDRICH WILHELM NIETZSCHE

If I were to begin life again, I would devote it to music. It is the only
cheap and unpunished rapture on earth.   —SYDNEY SMITH

Rock 'n' roll is the most brutal, ugly, degenerate, vicious form of expression it has been my displeasure to hear. . . . It fosters almost
totally negative and destructive reactions in young people. . . . It is
sung, played, and written for the most part by cretinous goons, and
by means of its almost imbecilic reiterations and sly, lewd—in plain
fact—filthy lyrics, it manages to be the martial music of every side-
burned delinquent on the face of the earth.   —FRANK SINATRA

Classical music is the kind we keep thinking will turn into a
tune.   —FRANK MCKINNEY ("KIN") HUBBARD

Rock music: Hear today, deaf tomorrow.   —LEO ROSTEN

Nothing is capable of being well set to music that is not nonsense.
                              —JOSEPH ADDISON

[George Bernard Shaw] persisted in regarding the fortissimos of Pa-
derewski . . . as brutal contests between the piano and the pianist to
settle the question of survival of the fittest.
                              —ARCHIBALD HENDERSON

Wagner has beautiful moments but awful quarter hours.   —ROSSINI

If one hears bad music, it is one's duty to drown it by one's conversation.   —OSCAR WILDE

A carpenter's hammer, in a warm summer noon, will fret me into more
than midsummer madness. But those unconnected, unset wounds are
nothing to the measured malice of music.   —CHARLES LAMB

A good composer does not imitate; he steals.
—IGOR STRAVINSKY

Give me a laundry list and I'll set it to music.
—GIOACCHINO ANTONIO ROSSINI

A love song is just a caress set to music.   —SIGMUND ROMBERG

Rock 'n' roll might best be summed up as monotony tinged with hysteria.   —VANCE PACKARD

Music is essentially useless—as life is.   —GEORGE SANTAYANA

Composers shouldn't think too much—it interferes with their plagiarism.   —HOWARD DIETZ

Jazz will endure just as long as people hear it through their feet instead of their brains.   —JOHN PHILIP SOUSA

Youth has many glories, but judgment is not one of them, and no amount of electronic amplification can turn a belch into an aria.
—ALAN JAY LERNER

What I want to write is songs without words—or music.
—SAMUEL BUTLER

Swans sing before they die—'twere no bad thing did certain persons die before they sing.   —SAMUEL TAYLOR COLERIDGE

Berlioz says nothing in his music, but he says it magnificently.
—JAMES GIBBONS HUNEKER

Who hears music, feels his solitude peopled at once.
                                    —ROBERT BROWNING

The easiest kind of relationship for me is with ten thousand
people. The hardest is with one.   —JOAN BAEZ

Musical people always want one to be perfectly dumb at the very
moment when one is longing to be absolutely deaf. —OSCAR WILDE

Difficult do you call it, sir? I wish it were impossible.
                        —SAMUEL JOHNSON (COMMENT ABOUT A
                                    VIOLINIST'S PLAYING)

National Character

An Englishman thinks seated; a Frenchman, standing; an American, pacing; an Irishman, afterward. —Austin O'Malley

Macedonia is where Yugoslavian territorial and linguistic disputes dissolve into utter formlessness. . . . Bulgarians doubt the existence of the Macedonian language, claiming it is really a western Bulgarian dialect. Macedonians claim parts of Bulgaria, Greece, and Albania, too. Everyone's map is different from everybody else's. No region of Europe has the abstract potential for violent anarchy and redrawing of borders as does Macedonia. For Rebecca West, Macedonia is the ultimate metaphor for the Balkans. We shall see.
—Robert D. Kaplan

They ask me for an epitaph for dead Belgium. In vain I rack my brains; I can find only one phrase: "at last!" —Baudelaire

I know of no existing nation that deserves to live, and I know of very few individuals. —H. L. Mencken

AMERICA AND AMERICANS

America: A country whose youth is one of her oldest and most hallowed traditions.   —OSCAR WILDE

America is a mistake—a giant mistake!   —SIGMUND FREUD

The American people, taking one with another, constitute the most timorous, sniveling, poltroonish, ignominious mob of serfs and goose-steppers ever gathered under one flag in Christendom since the end of the Middle Ages.   —H. L. MENCKEN

In America, the young are always ready to give to those who are older than themselves the full benefit of their inexperience.   —OSCAR WILDE

America is the only nation in history that miraculously has gone directly from barbarism to degeneration without the usual interval of civilization.   —GEORGES CLEMENCEAU

Q: If you find so much that is unworthy of reverence in the United States, why do you live here?
A: Why do men go to zoos?   —H. L. MENCKEN

I find that the Americans have no passions, they have appetites.   —RALPH WALDO EMERSON

Americans are like a rich father who wishes he knew how to give his son the hardships that made him rich.   —ROBERT FROST

The Arabs never miss an opportunity to miss an opportunity.   —ABBA EBAN

ENGLAND AND THE ENGLISH

The English think that incompetence is the same thing as sincerity.   —QUENTIN CRISP

Men and nations behave wisely once they have exhausted all other alternatives. —WILL ROGERS

A nation may be said to consist of its territory, its people, and its laws. The territory is the only part which is of certain durability. —ABRAHAM LINCOLN

A nation is a society united by a delusion about its ancestry and by a common hatred of its neighbors.
—ATTRIBUTED TO WILLIAM RALPH INGE

An Englishwoman's shoes look as if they were made by someone who had heard shoes described but had never actually seen any.
—MARGARET HALSEY

I know why the sun never sets on the British Empire: God wouldn't trust an Englishman in the dark. —DUNCAN SPAETH

The Englishman has all the qualities of a poker except its occasional warmth. —DANIEL O'CONNELL

It is the unshakable sincerity of the Englishman's belief in his own superiority which is at once the strength and weakness of his race.
—NICOLAS BENTLEY

You should study the *Peerage*. . . . It is the best in fiction the English have ever done. —OSCAR WILDE

In dealing with Englishmen you can be sure of one thing only: that is, the logical solution will not be adopted. —WILLIAM RALPH INGE

We have no amusements in England but vice and religion.
—SYDNEY SMITH

The English have an extraordinary ability for flying into a calm.
—ALEXANDER WOOLLCOTT/WINSTON CHURCHILL

Nearly all people in England are of the superior sort, superiority being an English ailment.   —D. H. LAWRENCE

The government of England is a limited mockery.
—LOUIS UNTERMEYER

The English instinctively admire any man who has no talent and is modest about it.   —JAMES AGATE

Of all nations on earth, the British require to be treated with the most *hauteur*. They require to be kicked into common manners.
—THOMAS JEFFERSON

I know not where any personal eccentricity is so freely allowed. . . . An Englishman walks in the pouring rain, swinging his closed umbrella like a walking stick; wears a wig, or a shawl, or a saddle or stands on his head, and no remark is made. . . . Every one of these islanders is an island himself, safe, tranquil, incommunicable.
—RALPH WALDO EMERSON

My father and I had one of those English friendships that begin by avoiding intimacies and eventually eliminate speech altogether.
—JORGE LUIS BORGES

Those comfortably padded lunatic asylums, which are known, euphemistically, as the stately homes of England.   —VIRGINIA WOOLF

It is not that the Englishman can't feel—it is that he is afraid to feel. He has been taught at his public school that feeling is bad form. He must not express great joy or sorrow, or even open his mouth too wide when he talks—his pipe might fall out if he did.
—E. M. FORSTER

Don't trust any Englishman who speaks French with a correct accent.
—FRENCH PROVERB

The world is inhabited by two species of human beings: mankind and the English.   —G. J. RENIER

Other nations use "force"; we Britons alone use "might."
                                          —EVELYN WAUGH

That silly, sanguine notion . . . that one Englishman can best three Frenchmen, encourages, and has sometimes enabled, one Englishman, in reality, to best two.   —LORD CHESTERFIELD

The people of England are never so happy as when you tell them they are ruined.   —ANONYMOUS

Those things which the English public never forgives: youth, power, and enthusiasm.   —OSCAR WILDE

The English have better sense than any other nation—and they are fools.   —METTERNICH

The earth is a place on which England is found.
                                          —G. K. CHESTERTON

The English have a miraculous power of turning wine into water.
                                          —OSCAR WILDE

England seems to me full of people doing things they don't want to do, because other people expect it of them.
                                          —W. SOMERSET MAUGHAM

An Englishman is a man who has never been able to tell a lie about others and who is never willing to face the truth about himself.
                                          —MICHAEL ARLEN

England and America are two countries separated by the same language.   —GEORGE BERNARD SHAW

A foggy, dead-alive city like a dying ant-heap. London was created for rich young men to shop in, dine in, ride in, get married in, go to theaters in, and die in as respected householders. It is a city for the unmarried upper class, not for the poor.   —CYRIL CONNOLLY

Englishmen never will be slaves; they are free to do whatever the government and public opinion allow them to do.
                                        —GEORGE BERNARD SHAW

No one can be as calculatedly rude as the British, which amazes Americans, who do not understand studied insult and can only offer abuse as a substitute.   —PAUL GALLICO

The English country gentleman galloping after a fox—the unspeakable in full pursuit of the uneatable.   —OSCAR WILDE

The English—"What a sweet house you have" means what a small house. "What an interesting house" is an ugly house. "What a splendid house" describes an ostentatious house. All three are terms used by the upper class, who imagine (wrongly, but it doesn't matter) that the lower class is as obsessed as they by architecture and interior decoration.   —DAVID FROST/ANTHONY JAY

FRANCE AND THE FRENCH

France was long a despotism tempered by epigrams.
                                        —THOMAS CARLYLE

Everything is on such a clear financial basis in France. It is the simplest country to live in. No one makes things complicated by becoming your friend for any obscure reason. If you want people to like you, you have only to spend a little money.   —ERNEST HEMINGWAY

What I gained by being in France was learning to be better satisfied with my own country. —SAMUEL JOHNSON

French political thought is either nostalgic or utopian. —RAYMOND ARON

In Paris, great ideas perish, done to death by a witticism. —HONORÉ DE BALZAC

France is the only country where the money falls apart and you can't tear the toilet paper. —BILLY WILDER

The French are wiser than they seem, and the Spaniards seem wiser than they are. —FRANCIS BACON

The French probably invented the very notion of discretion. . . . To the French, lying is simply talking. —FRAN LEBOWITZ

GERMANY AND THE GERMANS

Everything that is ponderous, viscous and pompously clumsy, all long-winded and wearying kinds of style, are developed in great variety among Germans. —FRIEDRICH WILHELM NIETZSCHE

The Germans are very seldom troubled with any extraordinary . . . effervescences of wit, and it is not prudent to try it upon them. —LORD CHESTERFIELD

IRELAND AND THE IRISH

The Irish are a fair people: They never speak well of one another. —SAMUEL JOHNSON

An Irishman is never at his best except when fighting. —IRISH PROVERB

In Ireland there is so little sense of compromise that a girl has to choose between perpetual adoration and perpetual pregnancy.

—GEORGE MOORE

I showed my appreciation of my native land in the usual Irish way: by getting out of it as soon as I possibly could.

—GEORGE BERNARD SHAW

An Irishman is the only man in the world who will step over the bodies of a dozen naked women to get to a bottle of stout.   —ANONYMOUS

Put an Irishman on the spit and you can always get another Irishman to turn him.   —GEORGE BERNARD SHAW

The Irish people do not gladly suffer common sense.
        —OLIVER ST. JOHN GOGARTY

The Irish ignore anything they can't drink or punch.
        —OLD SAYING

The Irish didn't even know what a snake was until St. Patrick told them the story of the Garden of Eden, for there have *never* been any snakes in Ireland.   —ANONYMOUS

ISRAEL

A tent cannot stand without pegs and cord, and Israel cannot stand without scholars.   —*SEDER ELIYAHU RABBAH*

In Israel, in order to be a realist you must believe in miracles.

—DAVID BEN-GURION

＊ ＊ ＊

There are two Italies. . . . The one is the most sublime and lovely contemplation than can be conceived by the imagination of man; the other is the most degraded, disgusting, and odious. What do you think? Young women of rank actually eat—you will never guess what—garlic!   —PERCY BYSSHE SHELLEY

The Creator made Italy from designs by Michelangelo.
                                                —MARK TWAIN

A Japanese will beckon you by pushing his or her arm out, turning the hand *down*, and fluttering the fingers. (To Anglo-Saxons that is a gesture of dismissal, not invitation.)
    To symbolize money, Japanese make a circle of thumb and index finger. (We make that gesture to signify "perfect!" or "beautiful girl!")
    They point the little finger upward to mean sexual intercourse.
    They cross and uncross the forearms in front of their chests to signify "The decision is negative," or "The one you came to visit is not in."
    They turn their eyes away from you to show respect—not, as with us, embarrassment.   —LEO ROSTEN

Japanese describe themselves as "wheat-colored" rather than yellow.
                                          —ROBERT CHRISTOPHER

Poor Mexico, so far from God and so near to the United States.
                                              —PORFIRIO DIAZ

Any Pole who can read and write is a nobleman.   —ANONYMOUS

The noblest prospects which a Scotchman ever sees is the high road that leads him to England.   —SAMUEL JOHNSON

Scotsman: A man who, before sending his pajamas to the laundry, stuffs a sock in each pocket.   —AMBROSE BIERCE

Switzerland: Beautiful but dumb.   —EDNA FERBER

Switzerland is a curst, selfish, swinish country of brutes, placed in the most romantic region of the world.   —LORD BYRON

In Switzerland they had brotherly love, five hundred years of democracy and peace, and what did they produce? The cuckoo clock!
                          —ORSON WELLES

Switzerland is simply a large, humpy, solid rock with a thin skin of grass stretched over it.   —MARK TWAIN

The only interesting thing that can happen in a Swiss bedroom is suffocation by a feather pillow.   —NUNNALLY JOHNSON

Turkey is the sick man of Europe.   —LORD PALMERSTON

Turkey is most famous for its goblets.   —A CHILD

When in Turkey, do as the turkeys do.   —HONORÉ DE BALZAC

There are still parts of Wales where the only concession to gaiety is a striped shroud.   —GWYN THOMAS

Nature

Man is nature's sole mistake.   —W. S. GILBERT

I can see nature only as an enemy; a highly respected enemy, but an enemy.   —ALBERT JAY NOCK

Nature does not care whether the hunter slays the beast or the beast the hunter. She will make good compost of them both.
                          —JOHN BURROUGHS

While man the scientist was developing his first aerial bomb—a bomb that would one day be charged with enough explosives to wipe out a hundred thousand people—the tiny flea wiped out ten million in India alone. —JAMES CLARK

I do not understand where the "beauty" and "harmony" of nature are supposed to be found. . . . For my part, I am unable to see any very great beauty or harmony in the tapeworm. —BERTRAND RUSSELL (TO L. R.)

Nature does not bestow virtue; to be good is an art. —SENECA

Nature has no principles. She . . . makes no distinction between good and evil. —ANATOLE FRANCE

I like trees because they seem more resigned to the way they have to live than other things do. —WILLA CATHER

In nature there are neither rewards nor punishments, there are consequences.
—ROBERT G. INGERSOLL

* * *

Let Nature have her way; she understands her business better than we do. —MONTAIGNE

The whole of nature . . . is a conjunction of the verb to eat, in the active and passive. —WILLIAM RALPH INGE

At twilight, nature is not without loveliness, though perhaps its chief use is to illustrate quotations from the poets. —OSCAR WILDE

News

News is what a chap who doesn't care much about anything wants to read. And it's only news until he's read it. After that, it's dead.

—EVELYN WAUGH

Noise

The amount of noise that anyone can bear undisturbed stands in inverse proportion to his mental capacity.

—ARTHUR SCHOPENHAUER

Noise proves nothing. Often a hen who has merely laid an egg cackles as if she's laid an asteroid. —MARK TWAIN

Obituary

After I depart this vale, if you remember me and have thought to please my ghost, forgive some sinner and wink your eye at a homely girl. —H. L. MENCKEN

Obscenity

Obscenity is whatever gives a judge an erection. —ANONYMOUS

Observations

An ape's an ape, though clad in scarlet. —ERASMUS

The eyes are more exact witnesses than the ears. —HERACLITUS

One never dives into the water to save a drowning man more eagerly than when there are others present who dare not take the risk.
—FRIEDRICH WILHELM NIETZSCHE

The winds and the waves are always on the side of the ablest navigators.
—EDWARD GIBBON

* * *

He that is good for making excuses is seldom good for anything else.
—BENJAMIN FRANKLIN

When you have to kill a man it costs nothing to be polite.
—WINSTON CHURCHILL

Nobuddy ever fergits where he buried the hatchet.
—FRANK MCKINNEY ("KIN") HUBBARD

* * *

You can't fall off the floor.   —ANONYMOUS

Few great men could pass Personnel.   —PAUL GOODMAN

Gifts are like fishhooks.   —MARTIAL

Some folks can keep so busy doing nothin' that they seem indispensable.
—FRANK MCKINNEY ("KIN") HUBBARD

Thanks to the interstate highway system, it is now possible to travel across the country from coast to coast without seeing anything.
—CHARLES KURALT

* * *

He who hesitates is a damned fool. —MAE WEST

One's eyes are what one is; one's mouth, what one becomes.
—GALSWORTHY

Three things matter in a speech—who says it, how he says it, and what he says—and of the three, the last matters the least.
—JOHN MORLEY

To a chemist nothing on earth is unclean. —ANTON CHEKHOV

Elephants are always drawn smaller in life, but a flea always larger.
— JONATHAN SWIFT

Aristotle maintained that women have fewer teeth than men, although he was twice married, it never occurred to him to verify this statement by examining his wives' mouths. He said also that children would be healthier if conceived when the wind is in the north. One gathers that the two Mrs. Aristotles both had to run out and look at the weathercock every evening before going to bed.
—BERTRAND RUSSELL

* * *

You are noticed more if you stand on your head than you are if you are the right way up. —GEORGE ORWELL

The average man's judgment is so poor, he runs a risk every time he uses it. —Edgar Watson ("Ed") Howe

No one can feel as helpless as the owner of a sick goldfish. —Frank McKinney ("Kin") Hubbard

Better an insincere "Good morning" than a sincere "Go to hell." —My Cousin

A sign of a celebrity is that his name is often worth more than his services.
—Daniel J. Boorstin

* * *

Every time I paint a portrait I lose a friend. —John Singer Sargent

Entrances are wide, but exits are narrow. —Jewish saying

The young have aspirations that never come to pass; the old have reminiscences of what never happened. —H. H. Munro ("Saki")

The moon is a dream of the sun.
—Paul Klee

* * *

He is not only dull himself, but the cause of dullness in others. —Samuel Johnson

The only thing that is ridiculous about collective security is that we have not got it. There is not much collective security in a flock of sheep on the way to the butcher. —Winston Churchill

The most anxious man in a prison is the warden. —George Bernard Shaw

The race is not always to the swift, nor the battle to the strong—but that's the way to bet.   —DAMON RUNYON

When a habit begins to cost money, it's called a hobby.
                                                —JEWISH SAYING

The one thing curiosity can*not* be is idle.   —LEO ROSTEN

When I was fourteen, my father was so ignorant I could hardly stand to have him around. When I got to be twenty-one, I was astonished at how much he had learned in seven years.   —MARK TWAIN

A loafer always has the correct time.
                          —FRANK MCKINNEY ("KIN") HUBBARD

The higher a monkey climbs, the more you see of his ass.
                                        —"VINEGAR JOE" STILWELL

Too often the strong, silent man is silent only because he does not know what to say, and is reputed strong only because he has remained silent.
                                            —WINSTON CHURCHILL

                           ✳   ✳   ✳

A man's worst difficulties begin when he is able to do as he likes.
                                          —THOMAS H. HUXLEY

Why was I born with such contemporaries?!
                                      —GEORGE BERNARD SHAW

It makes all the difference whether you hear an insect in the bedroom or in the garden.   —ROBERT LYND

Man: A creature made at the end of the week's work when God was tired.   —MARK TWAIN

Opposites attract—almost as often as they repel.

—L. R.

* * *

The nose of the bulldog has been slanted backward so that he can breathe without letting go.   —WINSTON CHURCHILL

There is just one thing I can promise you about the outer-space program: Your tax dollar will go farther.   —WERNHER VON BRAUN

A good servant should be faithful, fierce, and ugly.

—ERASMUS

* * *

It is amazing how nice people are to you when they know you are going away.   —MICHAEL ARLEN

Man: An ape with possibilities.   —ROY CHAPMAN ANDREWS

A hick town is the one where even a haircut changes the appearance of the whole community.   —FRANK MCKINNEY ("KIN") HUBBARD

Man: The inventor of stupidity.   —RÉMY DE GOURMONT

Most people would die sooner than think; in fact, they do.

—BERTRAND RUSSELL

* * *

God shows his contempt for wealth by the kind of person he selects to receive it.   —AUSTIN O'MALLEY

The only antidote to mental suffering is physical pain.—KARL MARX

Adam and Eve had many advantages, but the principal one was that they escaped teething.   —MARK TWAIN

Why was man created on the last day? So that he can be told when pride takes hold of him, "God created the gnat before thee."
—TALMUD

The greatest animal in creation [man], the animal who cooks.
—DOUGLAS JERROLD

The young man who has not wept is a savage, and the old man who will not laugh is a fool.
—GEORGE SANTAYANA

*   *   *

Once the toothpaste is out of the tube, it's hard to get it back in.
—H. R. HALDEMAN

The man who believes he can live without others is mistaken; and the man who thinks others can't live without him is more mistaken.
—HASIDIC SAYING

The earth has a skin, and that skin has diseases; one of its diseases is called man.   —FRIEDRICH WILHELM NIETZSCHE

The question "Who ought to be boss?" is like asking "Who ought to be the tenor in the quartet?" Obviously the man who can sing tenor.
—HENRY FORD

Our Heavenly Father invented man because he was disappointed in the monkey.   —MARK TWAIN

The brotherhood of man is not a mere poet's dream; it is a most depressing and humiliating reality.

—OSCAR WILDE

*　*　*

Wild animals never kill for sport. Man is the only one to whom the torture and death of his fellow creatures is amusing in itself.

—JAMES A. FROUDE

Human beings are the only animals of which I am thoroughly and cravenly afraid.　　　—GEORGE BERNARD SHAW

No living creature is subject to absurdity—except man.　—HOBBES

Man is either a beast or a god.　　　—ARISTOTLE

Man: Of all created creatures man is the most detestable. Of the entire brood he is the only one . . . that possesses malice.

—MARK TWAIN

I have found little that is good about human beings. In my experience, most of them are trash.　　　—SIGMUND FREUD

Man is a two-legged animal without feathers.　　　—PLATO

Do what we can, summer will have its flies. If we walk in the woods, we must feed mosquitoes.　　　—RALPH WALDO EMERSON

By the way, did you ever realize that if Moses would have turned right instead of left, we'd have had the oil, the Arabs would have had the sand?　　　—GOLDA MEIR

A committee is a cul-de-sac from which ideas are lured and then quietly strangled.   —BARNETT COCKS

In every American town with five thousand or more people, there is at least one man qualified to serve on the Supreme Court.
                                —WILLIAM HOWARD TAFT

And so we plough along, the fly said to the ox.
                                —HENRY WADSWORTH LONGFELLOW

Don't trust first impulses—they are always good.   —TALLEYRAND

The world gets better every day—then worse again in the evening.
        —FRANK McKINNEY ("KIN") HUBBARD

*   *   *

Too good is bad for you.   —JEWISH SAYING

I trust you completely, but please send cash.   —FOLK SAYING

Hindsight is always 20/20.   —BILLY WILDER

No good deed goes unpunished.   —CLARE BOOTHE LUCE

It's hard to beat a day in which you are permitted the luxury of four sunsets.   —JOHN GLENN

All the legislation in the world wouldn't abolish kissing.
                                —ELINOR GLYN

Man is the only creature who has a nasty mind.   —MARK TWAIN

Mankind: *The most pernicious race of little odious vermin that nature ever suffered to crawl on the face of the earth.*
—JONATHAN SWIFT

*   *   *

No matter what happens, there is someone who knew it would.
—ANONYMOUS

Apart from man, no being wonders at its own existence.
—ARTHUR SCHOPENHAUER

Nowhere probably is there more true feeling, and worse taste, than in a churchyard.   —BENJAMIN JOWETT

Never ascribe to an opponent motives meaner than your own.
—JAMES MATTHEW BARRIE

The Puritan hated bear-baiting, not because it gave pain to the bear, but because it gave pleasure to the spectators.
—THOMAS BABINGTON MACAULAY

Gardner's Law: Eighty-seven percent of all people in all professions are incompetent.   —JOHN GARDNER

A man of sixty has spent twenty years in bed and over three years in eating.
—ARNOLD BENNETT

*   *   *

In America there are two classes of travel—first class, and with children.   —ROBERT BENCHLEY

Nothing will ever be attempted if all possible objections must be first overcome.   —SAMUEL JOHNSON

A man should look for what is, and not for what he thinks should be.
—ALBERT EINSTEIN

Simple pleasures are the last refuge of the complex.
—OSCAR WILDE

People who work sitting down get paid more than people who work standing up. —OGDEN NASH

We always like those who admire us, but we do not always like those whom we admire. —FRANÇOIS DE LA ROCHEFOUCAULD

Don't overestimate the decency of the human race.

—H. L. MENCKEN

* * *

We have long passed the Victorian era, when asterisks were followed after a certain interval by a baby. —W. SOMERSET MAUGHAM

Onomatopoeia

The notion that onomatopoeia crosses the frontiers of language rests on the misconception that verbal allusions accurately mirror "real" sounds. *They do not; they record . . . those sounds our culture has instructed us to hear, or predisposed us not to hear.* A German child is taught to hear the buzzing of a bee not as *bzz-bzz* . . . but as *sum-sum*. If you will repeat *sum-sum* for a while, you may come to prefer it to *bzz-bzz*.

Do you think dogs go *woof-woof, bow-wow,* or *arrf-arf?* In English prose, they bark that way. But in German, dogs go *wau-wau,* in Chinese *wang-wang,* in Russian *gav-gav,* in Vietnamese *gau-gau,* in Japanese *wan-wan,* and in Yiddish, dogs go *how-how.*

In German *frogs* are said to croak *quak-quak,* and in Russian ducks go *kriak-kriak.* In French novels roosters do not go *cock-a-doodle-*

doo—but *cocorico*. Arabic donkeys, Arabic writers tell us, go *ham-ham*, but in Romania it is *dogs* that go *ham-ham*!

In English, the human heartbeat sounds like this: *thump-thump, thump-thump*. But in German the human heart is more martial: "*bum-bum, bum-bum. . . .*" In English, horses whinny "*ne-e-eigh*"—but not in, say, Russian, where children's stories have horses fleering *Ee-go-go*.

Any American will tell you that scissors go *snip-snip*, or *snap-snap*. But to a Greek, scissors go *kritz-kritz*. And to a Chinese, scissors hiss *su-su*. As for Spaniards, Italians, and Portuguese, their scissors retain as marked a national identity as any other, being written respectively as *ri-ri, kri-kri*, and *terre-terre*.

Verbal allusions do not mirror "real" sounds; they record and reflect those *sounds our culture has instructed us to hear*, or predisposed us *not* to hear.   —LEO ROSTEN

Opera

How wonderful opera would be if there were no singers.
                                    —GIACCHINO ANTONIO ROSSINI

*The opera . . . is to music what a bawdyhouse
is to a cathedral.*
                                    —H. L. MENCKEN

*   *   *

Opera in English is, in the main, just about as sensible as baseball in
Italian.   —H. L. MENCKEN

People are wrong when they say that the opera isn't what it used to
be. It *is* what it used to be. That's what's wrong with it.
                                    —NOËL COWARD

Opera: A play representing life in another world, whose inhabitants
have no speech but song, no motions but gestures, and no postures
but attitudes.   —AMBROSE BIERCE

The banging and slamming and booming and crashing were something beyond belief. The racking and pitiless pain of it remain stored up in my memory alongside the memory of the time that I had my teeth fixed.   —MARK TWAIN

Opinion

The average man's opinions are much less foolish than they would be if he thought for himself.   —BERTRAND RUSSELL

There is no process of amalgamation by which opinions, wrong individually, can become right merely by their multitude.
                                                —JOHN RUSKIN

Those who begin coercive elimination of dissent soon find themselves exterminating dissenters. Compulsory unification of opinion achieves only the unanimity of the graveyard.
                                                —ROBERT JACKSON

We can never be sure that the opinion we are endeavoring to stifle is a false opinion; and if we were sure, stifling it would be an evil still.
                                                —JOHN STUART MILL

He never chooses an opinion; he just wears whatever happens to be in style.   —TOLSTOY

It is not the facts which guide the conduct of men, but their opinions about facts.
                                                —NORMAN ANGELL

*   *   *

A universal feeling, whether ill or well formed, cannot be safely disregarded.   —ABRAHAM LINCOLN

If all mankind minus one were of one opinion, and only one person were of the contrary opinion, mankind would be no more justified in silencing that one person, than he, if he had the power, would be justified in silencing mankind.   —JOHN STUART MILL

Optimists/Optimism

Optimism: The doctrine or belief that everything is beautiful, including what is ugly.   —AMBROSE BIERCE

The place where optimism flourishes most is the lunatic asylum.   —HAVELOCK ELLIS

The man who is a pessimist before forty-eight knows too much; the man who is an optimist after forty-eight knows too little.
          —MARK TWAIN

Optimist: A proponent of the doctrine that black is white.
          —AMBROSE BIERCE

The basis of optimism is sheer terror.   —OSCAR WILDE

Pessimism, when you get used to it, is just as agreeable as optimism.
          —ARNOLD BENNETT

There is no sadder sight than a young pessimist, except an old optimist.   —MARK TWAIN

An optimist is a man who has never had much experience.
          —DON MARQUIS

*   *   *

I believe that man will not merely endure; he will prevail.
—WILLIAM FAULKNER

A pessimist is a man who thinks all women are bad. An optimist is one who hopes they are.   —CHAUNCEY DEPEW

Oratory

Blessed are they that have nothing to say, and who cannot be per-suaded to say it.   —JAMES RUSSELL LOWELL

The aim of the sculptor is to convince us that he is a sculptor; the aim of the orator is to convince us that he is not an orator.
—G. K. CHESTERTON

✳   ✳   ✳

P

✎ Dorothy Parker ✎

She was the wittiest woman of her time—and one of the most tragic. During the 1920s and 1930s she was the reigning queen of wit at the Algonquin Round Table. She wrote remarkable short stories, drenched in intensely personal feelings, bristling with irony and rich in insight, and volumes of poetry—cynical, lovelorn, bittersweet, celebrating drinking (she drank much too much), flapperdom, necking, a girl's right to be unfaithful. Above all, her verses wept with despair, touted suicide, and glorified death.

She was tiny, a waif with large, mournful dark eyes, bobbed hair, a deadly gift for repartee, and the swiftest, most acidulous wisecracks.

She was born Dorothy Rothschild, married a man named Parker, divorced him to marry the elegant, very handsome (and bisexual) Alan Campbell, who was, as she was, half Scottish, half Jewish. (Neither she nor Campbell felt the slightest relation to Judaism.) She divorced Campbell—and remarried him three years later. She ran through such a long list of doomed, miserable love affairs that Alexander Woollcott once snapped, "She must know eighteen languages and can't say 'no' in any one of them." Her wrists bore the scars of many razors.

But how she could write! Her book reviews for *Vanity Fair*, *The New Yorker*, and *Esquire* created a sensation, so original were they in form, so sharp and independent in judgment, so personal and funny

354

and unorthodox. ("This novel brings back all my faith in terror and death. I can offer no higher praise.") Miss Parker wrote many book reviews for *The New Yorker*, under the pen name Constant Reader. In reviewing the latest A. A. Milne tearjerker, this one-liner deserves amber: "At this point, Tonstant Weader frowed up."

Her short stories were unlike anyone else's: sad, drenched in a sense of doom, brilliant in a wholly original style, bittersweet in tone, steeped in introversion, scornful, despondent, startling in the digressions to the reader about herself. (Some of her stories were really monologues, wrapped in misery and lacerating emotion.)

And whether a poem, a book review, a short story, a letter, a conversation, the dialogue for a movie, over lunch or dinner or at any one of a thousand Park Avenue parties, Mrs. Parker (she always kept that name) played the irrepressible wit—a wit punctured with irony, gorgeous puns, dazzling wordplay, banter, farce, drollery, and wisecrack after wisecrack. Tears trembled on the edges of that tormenting depression that never left her. No wonder Alexander Woollcott called her "a cross between Little Nell and Lady Macbeth." Her tongue was a rapier, I thought, her style a stiletto. (Describing one novel, she wrote, "He had a child by her—I imagine he swam over her.") But she worshiped Hemingway and Hammett and Edna St. Vincent Millay—and Robert Benchley.

Parker and Benchley were fast friends. They greatly admired each other's work. He once said, "At one time Dottie and I decided to share an office. She found a small, inexpensive place." They sat in the empty office. She said, "What will we put on the door?"

"Why do we have to put anything on the door?" asked Benchley.

"Well, we'll get awfully lonely sitting here all day, day after day, just the two of us; we should put *something* on the door."

Benchley nodded gravely. "Okay, what would *you* put on the door?"

Parker said, "MEN."

Benchley chuckled. "You certainly won't get lonely, ma'am, but you'll never get any work done."

Two of the greatest wits in the world now spent the next half hour trying to decide on the most dull and uninviting of names. What they came up with was masterful:

UTICA
DROP FORGE COMPANY

I wish they had added, BY APPOINTMENT ONLY.

Here is a Parkerism I'll wager you never heard. She and Alan and I were at a session of the Screen Writers' Guild in Hollywood. Later we repaired to Dave Chasen's Restaurant. Over drinks we discussed the meeting, and especially complained about the lawyer for the guild. Alan said, "God, he goes on and on, uses technical jargon, hasn't a shred of—"

"Wait a minute," Mrs. Parker said. "Give the man his due. Sure, he has a mind that's slow"—she leered like a homicidal Kewpie doll —"but it's *dull*."

❧

Here is the skimpiest garland of her wit: "This book should not be tossed aside lightly; it should be flung with great force."

❧

". . . the assisted gold of her hair . . ." (I could never forget, or fail to smile at that.)

❧

"The *Home Beautiful* . . . is the play lousy."

❧

"If all the girls who attended the Yale Prom were laid end to end, I wouldn't be a bit surprised."

❧

A telegram to Robert Sherwood's wife, on giving birth: "Good work! We all knew you had it in you!"

❧

After she underwent an abortion, she mourned, "I should never have put all my eggs in that bastard."

❧

In a word game, upon being asked to use "horticulture" in a sentence: "You can lead a horticulture, but you can't make her think."

❧

Upon being told President Coolidge had died: "How can they tell?"

❧

"The affair between Margot Asquith and Margot Asquith will go down as one of the prettiest love stories in all literature."

❧

"One more drink and I would have been under my host."

During opening night of *The Lake:* "Katharine Hepburn runs the gamut of emotions from A to B."

And, of course, the inspired, "Men seldom make passes at girls who wear glasses."

Or this unforgettable quote: "She wore a low but futile décolletage."

Hail to thee, sad, sad spirit. Racked by merciless despair, you made millions laugh and laugh and laugh.

Dorothy Parker died at seventy-six. She became a heavy drinker and a headstrong leftist in her later years. She left her entire estate to The National Association for the Advancement of Colored People.

Passion

Our passions are like travelers: At first they make a brief stay; then they are like guests who visit often; and then they turn into tyrants who hold us in their power.   —TALMUD

Natural man has only two primal passions: to get and to beget.

—WILLIAM OSLER

*   *   *

In how many lives does love really play a dominant part? The average taxpayer is no more capable of a "grand passion" than of a grand opera.   —ISRAEL ZANGWILL

A man of any age can persuade himself that a woman's thighs are altar rails and that her passion is the hosanna of virtuous love rather than the wanton tumult of nerve endings.   —BEN HECHT

Passions are fashions.
—CLIFTON FADIMAN

*   *   *

Past

The past always looks better than it was; it's only pleasant because it isn't here.
—FINLEY PETER DUNNE ("MR. DOOLEY")

*   *   *

Of only eighty-two fables attributed to Aesop, only one can safely be called original.
—ARISTOTLE

An original writer is not one who imitates nobody but one whom nobody can imitate.
—CHATEAUBRIAND

Patriotism

Patriotism is a pernicious, psychopathic form of idiocy.
—GEORGE BERNARD SHAW

Patriotism is the willingness to kill and be killed for trivial reasons.
—BERTRAND RUSSELL

Patriotism is often an arbitrary veneration of real estate above principles.
—GEORGE JEAN NATHAN

Patriotism, what humbug it is; it is a word which always commemorates a robbery. There isn't a foot of land in the world which doesn't represent the ousting and reousting of a long line of successive owners.
—MARK TWAIN

Patriots always talk of dying for their country, but never of killing for their country.　　　　　　　　　　—BERTRAND RUSSELL

"My country, right or wrong" is a thing that no patriot would think of saying except in a desperate case. It is like saying, "My mother, drunk or sober."

　　　　　　　　　—G. K. CHESTERTON

　　　　＊　　＊　　＊

If you want a symbolic gesture, don't burn the flag, wash it.

　　　　　　　　　—NORMAN THOMAS

Though I love my country, I do not love my countrymen.

　　　　　　　　　—LORD BYRON

Patriotism is the last refuge of a scoundrel.　　—SAMUEL JOHNSON

In Dr. Johnson's famous dictionary, patriotism is defined as the last resort of a scoundrel. With all due respect to an enlightened but inferior lexicographer, I beg to submit that it is the first.

　　　　　　　　　—AMBROSE BIERCE

Patriotism varies from a noble devotion to a moral lunacy.

　　　　　　　　　—WILLIAM RALPH INGE

　　　　＊　　＊　　＊

Peace

Peace: Time out.　　　　　　　　　　　—LEO ROSTEN

To be enduring, a peace should be endurable.　　　—EVAN ESAR

I do not want the peace which passeth understanding, I want the understanding which bringeth peace. —HELEN KELLER

Peace: In international affairs, a period of cheating between two periods of fighting. —AMBROSE BIERCE

Pax Romana: Where they make a desolation, they call it a peace. What absolute nonsense! It was a nasty, vulgar sort of civilization, only dignified by being hidden under a lot of declensions.
—ANTHONY BURGESS

It is madness for sheep to talk peace with a wolf.

—THOMAS FULLER

* * *

If the history of the past fifty years teaches us anything, it is that peace does not follow disarmament—disarmament follows peace.
—BERNARD BARUCH

Peace is poor reading. —THOMAS HARDY

For the sake of peace one may lie, but peace itself should never be a lie. —TALMUD

Even on the threshold of war, we [Jews] are bidden to begin in no other way than with peace, for it is written: "When you draw near a city to fight, first offer it peace." —MIDRASH

Whenever a treaty of peace is signed, God is present.
—NACHMAN OF BRATSLAV

Performing

I resent performing for fricking idiots who don't know anything.
—JOHN LENNON

Persecution

It is better to be persecuted than to persecute others.
—JEWISH SAYING

Pessimists

A pessimist thinks everybody is as nasty as himself, and hates them for it. —GEORGE BERNARD SHAW

If it weren't for the optimist, the pessimist would never know how happy he isn't.
—ANONYMOUS

* * *

A pessimist is a person who has had to listen to too many optimists.
—DON MARQUIS

Philosophy

While wading through the whimsies, the puerilities, and unintelligible jargon of this work [Plato's *Republic*], I laid it down often to ask myself how it could have been that the world should have so long consented to give reputation to such nonsense as this?
—THOMAS JEFFERSON

*Existentialism means that no one else can take
a bath for you.*
                        —DELMORE SCHWARTZ

                    *   *   *

Wonder is what the philosopher endures most; for there is no other
beginning of philosophy than this.   —PLATO

O physics! Preserve me from metaphysics!   —ISAAC NEWTON

Philosophy triumphs easily over past and future misfortunes, but
present misfortunes triumph over philosophy.
                    —FRANÇOIS DE LA ROCHEFOUCAULD

*A serious and good philosophical work could
be written consisting entirely of jokes.*
                        —LUDWIG WITTGENSTEIN

                    *   *   *

Philosophy teaches us to bear with equanimity the misfortunes of others.   —OSCAR WILDE

All are lunatics, but he who can analyze his delusion is called a philosopher.   —AMBROSE BIERCE

To be a real philosopher one must be able to laugh at philosophy.
                            —BLAISE PASCAL

The value of a principle is the number of things it will explain.
                            —RALPH WALDO EMERSON

Those who lack the courage will always find a philosophy to justify it.
                            —ALBERT CAMUS

The society which scorns excellence in plumbing because plumbing is a humble activity, and tolerates shoddiness in philosophy because it is an exalted activity, will have neither good plumbing nor good philosophy. Neither its pipes nor its theories will hold water.
                                        —JOHN W. GARDNER

*   *   *

All philosophies, if you ride them home, are nonsense, but some are greater nonsense than others.   —SAMUEL BUTLER

There was never yet a philosopher that could endure the toothache patiently.   —SHAKESPEARE

A clash of doctrines is not a disaster—it is an opportunity.
                    —ALFRED NORTH WHITEHEAD

*   *   *

Unintelligible answers to insoluble problems.
                    —HENRY ADAMS (OF PHILOSOPHY)

There is no opinion so absurd but that some philosopher will express it.   —CICERO

There are nowadays professors of philosophy, but not philosophers.
                    —HENRY DAVID THOREAU

The theological problems of original sin, origin of evil, predestination, and the like are the soul's mumps, and measles, and whooping coughs.
                    —RALPH WALDO EMERSON

Among philosophers anxious to establish the religious significance of God, an unfortunate habit has prevailed of paying him metaphysical compliments.   —ALFRED NORTH WHITEHEAD

*Bad philosophers may have a certain influence;
good philosophers, never.*
　　　　　　　　　　　—BERTRAND RUSSELL

*　*　*

I have a new philosophy: I'm only going to dread one day at a time.
　　　　　　　　　　　—CHARLES SCHULZ

The "silly" question is the first intimation of some totally new development.
　　　　　　　　　　　—ALFRED NORTH WHITEHEAD

What is mind? No matter. What is matter? Never mind.
　　　　　　　　　　　—BISHOP BERKELEY

The philosopher has to be the bad conscience of his age.
　　　　　　　　　　　—FRIEDRICH WILHELM NIETZSCHE

Nothing is more rewarding than the effort a man makes to *matter*—
to count, to stand for something, to have it make some difference that
he lived at all.　　　　　　　　　—LEO ROSTEN

If I am not for myself, who will be for me? And if I am only for myself,
what am I? And if not now—when?　　　　　　　　—HILLEL

What sort of philosophers are we, who know absolutely nothing about
the origin and destiny of cats?　　　—HENRY DAVID THOREAU

Philosophy is to the real world as masturbation is to sex.
　　　　　　　　　　　—KARL MARX

Philosophy is an unusually ingenious attempt to think fallaciously.　　　　　　　　—BERTRAND RUSSELL

To poke fun at philosophy is to be a philosopher.　—PASCAL

Because philosophy arises from awe, a philosopher is bound in his way to be a lover of myths and poetic fables. Poets and philosophers are alike in being big with wonder.   —THOMAS AQUINAS

I have tried in my time to be a philosopher; but I don't know how, cheerfulness was always breaking in.   —OLIVER EDWARDS

It is a great advantage for a system of philosophy to be substantially true.   —GEORGE SANTAYANA

Philosophy is doubt.   —MONTAIGNE

Men of action are, after all, only the unconscious instruments of the men of thought.   —HEINRICH HEINE

Believe everything you hear about the world; nothing is too impossibly bad.   —HONORÉ DE BALZAC

The fruits of philosophy are the important thing, not the philosophy itself. When we ask the time, we don't want to know how watches are made.   —GEORG CHRISTOPH LICHTENBERG

There is no record in human history of a happy philosophy.
                    —H. L. MENCKEN

Metaphysics is almost always an attempt to prove the incredible by an appeal to the unintelligible.

—H. L. MENCKEN

* * *

Phrasings

I knew a man scared by the rustle of his own hatband.
                                        —RALPH WALDO EMERSON

He flung himself upon his horse and rode madly off in all directions.   —STEPHEN LEACOCK

His style has the desperate jauntiness of an orchestra fiddling away for dear life on a sinking ship.
                                        —EDMUND WILSON (ON EVELYN WAUGH)

It is not worthwhile to go round the world to count the cats in Zanzibar.   —HENRY DAVID THOREAU

Thrifty! Man, she'd skin a flea for his hide.   —JAMES DUFFY

He might have brought an action against his countenance for libel and recovered heavy damages.   —CHARLES DICKENS

She is a very fascinating woman, and he is very fond of fascinating with her.   —SAMUEL BUTLER

Thunder is good, thunder is impressive; but it is lightning that does the work.   —MARK TWAIN

Wrinkles should merely indicate where smiles have been.
                                        —MARK TWAIN

The girl had as many curves as a scenic railway.

—P. G. Wodehouse

＊　　＊　　＊

No more privacy than a goldfish.　　　　—H. H. Munro ("Saki")

I get my exercise acting as a pallbearer to my friends who exercise.
—attributed to Chauncey Depew/
Mark Twain/Robert Hutchins

Nye was born old and died young.
—Jennie Lee (on her husband, Aneurin Bevan)

Fred Allen's voice has the sound of teeth chewing on slate pencils.
—O. O. McIntyre

When I walk with you I feel as if I had a flower in my buttonhole.
—William Makepeace Thackeray

Leave only three wasps alive in the whole of Europe and the air of Europe will still be more crowded with wasps than space with stars.
—James Jeans

He's such an insomniac that when he falls asleep he dreams he's awake.　　　　　　　　　　　　　　　—Anonymous

He gradually wormed his way out of my confidence.

—Nunnally Johnson

＊　　＊　　＊

And thrice he routed all his foes, and thrice he slew the slain.
—John Dryden

Going round the country stirring up complacency.
— WILLIAM WHITELAW

*   *   *

Mr. [Joseph] Chamberlain has one power which is the soul of melodrama—the power of pretending, even when backed up by a huge majority, that he has his back to the wall.   —G. K. CHESTERTON

Picturesque Language

Language (which is the formal attire of thinking) is so often funny, laugh-provoking, original *(even if mischievous), and plain colorful, that I cannot allow myself the lazy luxury of omitting the following, which defy categories:*

Our laundry has just sent back some buttons with no shirt on them.
— ANONYMOUS

I was underwhelmed.   — GEORGE S. KAUFMAN (OF A PLAY)

"Shut up!" he explained.

He looked at me as if I was a side dish he hadn't ordered.
— RING LARDNER

He thinks he can hear a flea cough.   — YIDDISH SAYING

If not actually disgruntled, he was far from being gruntled.
— P. G. WODEHOUSE

It's no longer a question of staying healthy. It's a question of finding a sickness you like.
                                   —JACKIE MASON

*   *   *

Publishing a volume of verse is like dropping a rose petal down the Grand Canyon and waiting for the echo.   —DON MARQUIS

She is a peacock in everything but beauty.   —OSCAR WILDE

Drawing on my fine command of language, I said nothing.
                    —ROBERT BENCHLEY/MARK TWAIN

When you smoke cigarettes you're likely to burn yourself to death; with chewing tobacco the worst thing you can do is drown a midget.
                                   —FRED ALLEN

Secret, and self-contained, and solitary as an oyster.
                                   —CHARLES DICKENS

*   *   *

Her cooking suggested she had attended the *Cordon Noir*.
                                   —LEO ROSTEN

Writing free verse is like playing tennis with the net down.
                                   —ROBERT FROST

*   *   *

Like telling a man going to the electric chair that he has a choice of AC or DC.   —GOODMAN ACE

He has more kinfolk than a microbe.   —IRVIN S. COBB

To give an accurate and exhaustive account of that period would need a far less brilliant pen than mine. —MAX BEERBOHM

His reason is as thin as the homeopathic soup that was made by boiling the shadow of a pigeon that had been starved to death.
—ABRAHAM LINCOLN (ON STEPHEN DOUGLAS)

My dwelling was so small I could hardly entertain an echo in it.
—HENRY DAVID THOREAU

She wears her clothes as if they were thrown on her with a pitchfork. —JONATHAN SWIFT

She looked as if she had been poured into her clothes and had forgotten to say "when." —P. G. WODEHOUSE

If the ends don't justify the means, what can?
—JOHN MAYNARD KEYNES

He fell down a great deal during his boyhood because of a trick he had of walking into himself. —JAMES THURBER

What's on your mind?—if you'll forgive the overstatement.
—FRED ALLEN

Occasionally she looked at the witness with scorn. Her mother looked at him with several scorns. —DAMON RUNYON

The body is but a pair of pincers set over a bellows and a stewpan, and the whole fixed upon stilts. —SAMUEL BUTLER

She looked as respectable as a pair of rubbers.
—FRANCIS BRONSON

Extracting sunbeams out of cucumbers. —JONATHAN SWIFT

Two minds without a single thought. —PHILIP BARRY

Melancholy is the pleasure of being sad. —VICTOR HUGO

When a man knows he is to be hanged in a fortnight, it concentrates his mind wonderfully.
—SAMUEL JOHNSON

* * *

The man was so small, he was a waste of skin. —FRED ALLEN

I spent a year in that town, one Sunday. —WARWICK DEEPING

Why is this true? What is the reason for this thusness?
—ARTEMUS WARD

His huff arrived and he departed in it. —ALEXANDER WOOLLCOTT

His family were the largest dandruff manufacturers in France.
—ARTHUR ("BUGS") BAER

"Whom are you?" said he, for he had been to night school.
—GEORGE ADE

His hobby is collecting old echoes. —FRED ALLEN

There's nothing in Christianity or Buddhism that quite matches the sympathetic unselfishness of an oyster.
—H. H. MUNRO ("SAKI")

* * *

He was capable of bringing out an expurgated edition of Wordsworth.
—SAMUEL BUTLER

The worst sensation I know of is getting up at night and stepping on a toy train of cars. —FRANK MCKINNEY ("KIN") HUBBARD

You have the manners of a perfect gentleman: Whose are they?
—HENNY YOUNGMAN

If a thing is worth doing, it is worth doing badly.
—G. K. CHESTERTON

If a thing is worth doing, it is worth doing slowly . . . very slowly.
—GYPSY ROSE LEE

He was the mildest-manner'd man that ever scuttled ship or cut a throat. —LORD BYRON

Every line in her face is the line of least resistance.—IRVIN S. COBB

Her interest in natural history was confined to observation of the crow's-feet gathering around her eyes. —NICOLAS BENTLEY

There's so much to say, but your eyes keep interrupting me.
—CHRISTOPHER MORLEY

Piety

Better be good than pious. —FOLK SAYING

All corpses look pious. —TALMUD/SAMUEL BUTLER

Pity

Pity was invented by the weak.   —MENDELE MOCHER SERFORIM

Places

Boston is a moral and intellectual nursery always busy applying first principles to trifles.   —GEORGE SANTAYANA

Alaska: Nothing but miles and miles of miles and miles of land.
                                                        —ANONYMOUS

The situation in Germany is serious but not hopeless; the situation in Austria is hopeless but not serious.   —VIENNESE SAYING

California: The west coast of Iowa.   —JOAN DIDION

*In Boston they ask, "How much does he know?"
In New York, "How much is he worth?" In
Philadelphia, "Who were his parents?"*
                                —MARK TWAIN

*   *   *

I have just returned from Boston. It is the only thing to do if you find yourself up there.   —FRED ALLEN

Los Angeles: I mean, who would want to live in a place where the only cultural advantage is that you can turn right on a red light?
                                                        —WOODY ALLEN

There's nothing wrong with Southern California that a rise in the ocean level wouldn't cure.   —ROSS MACDONALD

Everything in Los Angeles is too large, too loud, and usually banal in concept. . . . The plastic asshole of the world.

—WILLIAM FAULKNER

If you don't like the weather in New England, just wait a few minutes.

—RING LARDNER

New York: Where everyone mutinies but no one deserts.

—HARRY HERSHFIELD

I have no relish for the country; it is a kind of healthy grave.

—SYDNEY SMITH

Whenever a massacre of Armenians is reported from Asia Minor, everyone assumes that it has been carried out "under orders" from somewhere or another; no one seems to think that there are people who might *like* to kill their neighbors now and then.

—H. H. MUNRO ("SAKI")

The trouble with Oakland is that when you get there, there isn't any there there.   —GERTRUDE STEIN

The trouble with Oakland is that when you get there, it's there.

—HERB CAEN

Platonism

Of course a platonic relationship is possible—but only between husband and wife.   —ANONYMOUS

Pleasure

All pleasures contain an element of sadness.

—Jonathan Eibeschutz

Illusion is the first of all pleasures.

—Voltaire

Perpetual pleasure is no pleasure.

—Folk saying

Poets/Poetry

Homer has taught all other poets the art of telling lies skillfully.

—Aristotle

It is easier to write a mediocre poem than to understand a good one.

—Montaigne

Poetry ennobles the heart and the eyes . . . and restores to us forgotten paradises.

—Edith Sitwell

I've read some of your modern free verse and wonder who set it free.

—John Barrymore

米   米   米

All bad poetry springs from genuine feeling.

—Oscar Wilde

Poetry is the bill and coo of sex.

—Elbert Hubbard

A poet more than thirty years old is simply an overgrown child.

—H. L. Mencken

It is a great fault, in poetry, to describe everything.
—ALEXANDER POPE

Poetry is to prose as dancing is to walking. —JOHN WAIN

Poets have been mysteriously silent on the subject of cheese.
—G. K. CHESTERTON

Free verse is like free love: It is a contradiction in terms.
—G. K. CHESTERTON

* * *

There is a great deal of prose license in Walt Whitman's poetry.
—MARY WILSON LITTLE

Politics

Politics is perhaps the only profession for which no preparation is thought necessary.
—ROBERT LOUIS STEVENSON

* * *

All Congresses and Parliaments have a kindly feeling for idiots and a compassion for them, on account of personal experience and heredity.
—MARK TWAIN

Kings are not born; they are made by universal hallucination.
—GEORGE BERNARD SHAW

Politics is the art of the next best. —BISMARCK

My deepest feeling about politicians is that they are dangerous lunatics to be avoided when possible and carefully humored; people, above all, to whom one must never tell the truth. —W. H. AUDEN

There is no act of treachery or meanness of which a political party is not capable; for in politics there is no honor.
—BENJAMIN DISRAELI

In order to become the master, the politician poses as the servant. —CHARLES DE GAULLE

Men are marked from the moment of birth to rule or be ruled.
—ARISTOTLE

The folly and presumption of that insidious and crafty animal . . . a politician. —ADAM SMITH

When there is no middle class, and the poor greatly exceed in number, troubles arise, and the state soon comes to an end. —ARISTOTLE

Too bad all the people who know how to run the country are busy driving taxicabs and cutting hair. —GEORGE BURNS

No party is as bad as its leaders. —WILL ROGERS

Sometimes in politics one must duel with skunks, but no one should be fool enough to allow the skunks to choose the weapons.
—JOE CANNON

*   *   *

A radical is a man with both feet firmly planted in the air.
—FRANKLIN D. ROOSEVELT

Politics, when I am in it, makes me sick. —WILLIAM HOWARD TAFT

Politics: Who gets what, when, how.   —HAROLD D. LASSWELL

The only way a reporter should look at a politician is down.
—FRANK KENT

All politics are based on the indifference of the majority.
—JAMES RESTON

To rule is easy, to govern difficult.   —GOETHE

A ruler needs only obedience from those he rules, whereas a leader needs their enthusiasm as well. Leadership is a good deal more strenuous than rulership.   —KENNETH MINOGUE

> *They will all promise every man, woman, and child in the country whatever he, she, or it wants. They'll all be roving the land looking for chances to make the rich poor, to remedy the irremediable, to succor the unsuccorable, to unscramble the unscrambleable, to dephlogisticate the undephlogisticable. They will all be curing warts by saying words over them, and paying off the national debt with money that no one will have to earn. . . . In brief, they will divest themselves of their character as sensible, candid, and truthful men, and become simply candidates for office.*
>
> —H. L. MENCKEN

*   *   *

Politics and the fate of mankind are shaped by men without ideals and without greatness. Men who have greatness within them don't go in for politics.   —ALBERT CAMUS

Political language . . . is designed to make lies sound truthful and murder respectable, and to give an appearance of solidarity to pure wind.   —GEORGE ORWELL

A politician is a man who can be verbose in fewer words than anyone else.   —PETER DE VRIES

We must not mistake anger for argument, good goals for good sense. For passion, like politics, makes very strange bedfellows; it even leads the young to mistake gripes for principles. Hate makes more rebels than Hegel.   —LEO ROSTEN

Politics is not the art of the possible. It consists in choosing between the disastrous and the unpalatable.   —JOHN KENNETH GALBRAITH

A memorandum is written not to inform the reader but to protect the writer.   —DEAN ACHESON

Now and then an innocent man is sent to the legislature.
                              —FRANK MCKINNEY ("KIN") HUBBARD

In Germany they came first for the Communists, and I didn't speak up because I wasn't a Communist. Then they came for the Jews, and I didn't speak up because I wasn't a Jew. Then they came for the trade unionists, and I didn't speak up because I wasn't a trade unionist. Then they came for the Catholics, and I didn't speak up because I was a Protestant. Then they came for me, and by that time no one was left to speak up.

—MARTIN NIEMOLLER

✳   ✳   ✳

I must follow the people. Am I not their leader?
                              —BENJAMIN DISRAELI

A virtuous king is a king who has shirked his proper function to embody for his subjects an idea of illustrious misbehavior beyond their reach.   —LOGAN PEARSALL SMITH

In politics, nothing is contemptible.   —BENJAMIN DISRAELI

Never take a nickel; just hand them your business card.
                         —REPORTEDLY SAID BY RICHARD M. DALEY,
    MAYOR OF CHICAGO, WHEN MAKING A POLITICAL APPOINTMENT

The best political community is formed by citizens of the middle class, and those states are likely to be well administered in which the middle class is large, and larger if possible than both the other classes . . . or at any rate than either singly.   —ARISTOTLE

In politics . . . never retreat, never retract . . . never admit a mistake.
                                          —NAPOLEON BONAPARTE

A very considerable part of human effort and energy must always be expended in preventing things from getting worse.   —R. J. WHITE

Church and State are a loathsome combination.
                                          —THOMAS JEFFERSON

It is a curious fact that when we get sick we want an uncommon doctor. If we have a construction job, we want an uncommon engineer. When we get into a war, we want an uncommon admiral and an uncommon general. Only when we get into politics are we content with the common man.   —HERBERT HOOVER

The political pyramid of power: income, deference, and safety.
                         —HAROLD D. LASSWELL/WALTER LIPPMANN

Honest statesmanship is the wise employment of individual meanness for the public good. —ABRAHAM LINCOLN

Politicians are the same all over. They promise to build a bridge even where there is no river. —NIKITA KHRUSHCHEV

It is frequently a misfortune to have very brilliant men in charge of affairs; they expect too much of ordinary men.
—THUCYDIDES

The more you read and observe about this politics thing, the more you've got to admit that each party's worse than the other. The one that's out always looks the best. —WILL ROGERS

Politics: That which makes strange postmasters.
—FRANK MCKINNEY ("KIN") HUBBARD

It doesn't matter what I say as long as I sound different from other politicians. —JERRY BROWN

Conservative: A statesman who is enamored of existing evils, as distinguished from the liberal, who wishes to replace them with others.
—AMBROSE BIERCE

The first basis of government is justice, not pity.
—WOODROW WILSON

Successful democratic politicians are insecure and intimidated men. They advance politically only as they placate, appease, bribe, seduce, bamboozle, or otherwise manage to manipulate the demanding and threatening elements in their constituencies. —WALTER LIPPMANN

Since a politician never believes what he says, he is surprised when others believe him. —CHARLES DE GAULLE

Politics: Organized hatred, that is unity.
                                    —JOHN JAY CHAPMAN

Politics, as a practice . . . has always been the systematic organization of hatreds.   —HENRY BROOKS ADAMS

The only political system that can endure is one that prevents the rich from impoverishing the poor (by talent or shrewdness) and the poor from robbing the rich—by votes or through violence. —ARISTOTLE

It takes a politician to run a government. A statesman is a politician who's been dead for fifteen years.   —HARRY S TRUMAN

Politics: A strife of interests masquerading as a contest of principles.
                                    —AMBROSE BIERCE

The professional politician is one of the mysteries of American life, a bundle of paradoxes, shrewd as a fox, naive as a schoolboy. He has great respect for the people yet treats them like boobs, and is constitutionally unable to keep his mouth shut.   —JAMES RESTON

A liberal is a man who leaves a room when the fight begins.
                                    —HEYWOOD BROUN

Political ability: *The ability to foretell what is going to happen tomorrow, next week, next month, and next year. And to have the ability afterward to explain why it didn't happen.*
                                    —WINSTON CHURCHILL

*   *   *

If I was forced to choose between the penitentiary and the White House for four years, I would say the penitentiary, thank you.
                                    —WILLIAM TECUMSEH SHERMAN

If you ever live in a country run by a committee, be on the committee.
—WILLIAM GRAHAM SUMNER

The first mistake in public business is going into it.
—BENJAMIN FRANKLIN

In politics, an absurdity is not a handicap.
—NAPOLEON BONAPARTE

Politics is far more complicated than physics.
—ALBERT EINSTEIN

A political leader must keep looking over his shoulder all the time to see if the boys are still there. If they aren't still there, he's no longer a political leader.
—BERNARD BARUCH

An empty stomach is not a good political adviser.
—ALBERT EINSTEIN

Nowhere are prejudices more mistaken for truth, passion for reason, and invective for documentation, than in politics. That is a realm, peopled only by villains or heroes, in which everything is black or white, and gray is a forbidden color.
—JOHN MASON BROWN

One is a lie, two are lies, but three lies become politics.
—ANONYMOUS

I never said all Democrats were saloonkeepers; what I said was all saloonkeepers are Democrats.
—HORACE GREELEY

A political convention is not a place where you can come away with any trace of faith in human nature.
— MURRAY KEMPTON

*   *   *

Ignorance makes most men go into a political party, and shame keeps them from getting out of it.   — LORD HALIFAX

Kings govern by means of popular assemblies only when they cannot do without them.   — CHARLES JAMES FOX

It's a great country, where anybody can grow up to be president . . . except me.   — BARRY GOLDWATER

Politicians who wish to succeed must be prepared to dissemble, at times to lie. All deceit is bad. In politics some deceit or moral dishonesty is the oil without which the machinery would not work.
— WOODROW WYATT

Poor/Poverty

The real tragedy of the poor is that they can afford nothing but self-denial.   — OSCAR WILDE

I am a poor man, but I have this consolation: I am poor by accident, not by design.   — JOSH BILLINGS

Poverty, of course, is no disgrace, but it is damned annoying.
— WILLIAM PITT

*If the rich could hire the poor to die for them,
the poor would make a very good living.*
— JEWISH SAYING

*   *   *

A decent provision for the poor is the true test of civilization.
— SAMUEL JOHNSON

Honor the sons of the poor, for they give science its splendor.
— TALMUD

God has always been hard on the poor.   — JEAN-PAUL MARAT

Our rabbi is so poor that if he didn't fast every Monday and Thursday,
he'd starve to death.   — YIDDISH SAYING

If a poor man asks for alms and you have nothing to give, console him
with words; for it is forbidden to chastise a poor man, or raise your
voice against him, since his heart is broken.   — MAIMONIDES

One of the advantages of being poor is that it necessitates the culti-
vation of the virtues.   — JEROME K. JEROME

Poverty is an anomaly to rich people; it is very difficult to make
out why people who want dinner do not ring the bell.
— WALTER BAGEHOT

I've never been poor, only broke. Being poor is a frame of mind.
Being broke is only a temporary situation.   — MIKE TODD

The greatest charity is to enable the poor to earn a living.
— TALMUD

About the only thing we have left that actually discriminates in favor
of the plain people is the stork.

—FRANK McKINNEY ("KIN") HUBBARD

One of the strangest things about life is that the poor, who need
money the most, are the very ones who never have it.

—FINLEY PETER DUNNE ("MR. DOOLEY")

The poor have it hard only twice a year: in the summer and in the
winter.   —SHOLEM ALEICHEM

*It's no disgrace to be poor, but it might as well
be.*

—FRANK McKINNEY ("KIN") HUBBARD

* * *

The surest way to remain poor is to be an honest man.

—NAPOLEON BONAPARTE

Take care of the children of the poor, for they will be the ones who
advance knowledge.   —TALMUD

You can often hide poverty with a needle and a brush.

—ANONYMOUS

The sages would sometimes tie money in a cloth bag and throw it
behind their backs for poor men to pick up, so that the poor should
not feel shame.   —MAIMONIDES

It isn't that a full purse is so good; it's that an empty one is so bad.

—JEWISH SAYING

Those who are sated don't believe those who are hungry.

—JEWISH SAYING

It would be nice if the poor got a fifth of the money we spend in studying them.
—ANONYMOUS

* * *

Popularity

He liked to like people, therefore people liked him.   —MARK TWAIN

Woe to the one nobody likes, but beware of the one everyone likes.
—JEWISH SAYING

If you make people think they're thinking, they'll love you; but if you really make them think, they'll hate you.   —DON MARQUIS

Anyone who is popular is bound to be disliked.
—YOGI BERRA

* * *

If you want to be popular, ask people for advice; don't do anything about it—just ask.   —LEO ROSTEN

Pornography

I don't think pornography is very harmful, but it is terribly, terribly boring.   —NOËL COWARD

They are doing things on the screen these days that the French don't even put on postcards.
—BOB HOPE

* * *

My reaction to porno films is as follows: After the first ten minutes, I want to go home and screw. After the first twenty minutes, I never want to screw again as long as I live.   —ERICA JONG

A sodomite got very excited looking at a zoology text. Does that make it pornography?   —STANISLAW J. LEC

Power

Power is not a means, it is an end.   —GEORGE ORWELL

Except by saints, the problem of power is finally insoluble.
            —ALDOUS HUXLEY

Experience shows us that every man who is invested with power is likely to abuse it. . . . Is it not strange . . . to say that virtue itself has need of limits?   —MONTESQUIEU

The displacement of infantile . . . affects upon symbols of ambiguous reference has led to the creation of remarkable monuments to human vanity.   —H. D. LASSWELL

Power corrupts the few, while weakness corrupts the many.
            —ERIC HOFFER

Power is the ultimate aphrodisiac.   —HENRY KISSINGER

Power is my mistress. I have worked too hard at her conquest to allow anyone to take her away from me.
            —NAPOLEON BONAPARTE

In a hierarchy every employee tends to rise to his level of incompetence.   —LAURENCE J. PETER

A general inclination of all mankind is a perpetual and restless desire of power that ceases only in death.　　　　　—Thomas Hobbes

No one is fit to be trusted with power. . . . Any man who has lived at all knows the follies and wickedness he's capable of. If he does not know it, he is not fit to govern others. And if he does know it, he knows also that neither he nor any man ought to be allowed to decide a single human fate.　　　　　—C. P. Snow

Concentrated power is not rendered harmless by the good intentions of those who create it.　　　　　—Milton Friedman

I am more and more convinced that man is a dangerous creature and that power, whether vested in many or a few, is ever grasping.
　　　　　—Abigail Adams

The urge to save humanity is almost always a false front for the urge to rule.
　　　　　—H. L. Mencken

✳　　✳　　✳

A friend in power is a friend lost.　　　　　—Henry Adams

The exercise of power in this century has meant for all of us in the United States not arrogance but agony.　　　　　—Lyndon B. Johnson

Power is so apt to be insolent, and liberty to be saucy, that they are very seldom upon good terms.　　　　　—Lord Halifax

I hold it better for the ruler to be feared than to be loved.
　　　　　—Machiavelli/Aristotle/H. L. Mencken

Power intoxicates men. When a man is intoxicated by alcohol, he can recover, but when intoxicated by power, he seldom recovers.
　　　　　—James F. Byrnes

It is useless for the sheep to pass resolutions in favor of vegetarianism while the wolf remains of a different opinion.
—WILLIAM RALPH INGE

Nearly all men can stand adversity, but if you want to test a man's character, give him power.
—ABRAHAM LINCOLN

＊　　＊　　＊

Power corrupts, but lack of power corrupts absolutely.
—ADLAI STEVENSON

No man, no class, no group, no party is good enough, wise enough, *and* sane enough to be entrusted with too much power. For good men are often silly, competent men are often wicked, and even the combination of virtue and ability does not in the slightest way guarantee reason. . . .

Human history is a tragedy precisely because too often men have seized, or been permitted to enjoy, the power to do what *they* thought best.
—LEO ROSTEN

Men hesitate less to injure a man who makes himself loved than to injure one who makes himself feared.
—MACHIAVELLI

Some paradox of our natures leads us, once we have made our fellow-man the object of our enlightened interest, to go on to make them the objects of our pity, then of our wisdom, [and] ultimately of our coercion.
—LIONEL TRILLING

Men ought either to be well treated or crushed—because they can adjust to lighter injuries [but] not to more serious ones. He who becomes master of a city accustomed to freedom and told not to destroy it, may expect to be destroyed by it.
—MACHIAVELLI

Prayer

Work as if you were to live a hundred years. Pray as if you were to die tomorrow.   —BENJAMIN FRANKLIN

The act of worship, as carried on by Christians, seems to me to be debasing rather than ennobling. It involves groveling before a Being who, if He really exists, deserves to be denounced instead of respected.   —H. L. MENCKEN

The various modes of worship which prevailed in the Roman world were all considered by the people as equally true, by the philosopher as equally false, and by the magistrate as equally useful. And thus toleration produced not only mutual indulgence but even religious concord.
       —EDWARD GIBBON

*   *   *

Common people do not pray; they only beg.
       —GEORGE BERNARD SHAW

Prayer must never be answered; if it is, it ceases to be prayer and becomes a correspondence.   —OSCAR WILDE

Pray that you will never have to bear all that you are able to endure.
       —JEWISH SAYING

My prayer to God is a very short one: "O Lord, make my enemies look ridiculous!" God has granted it.   —VOLTAIRE

Under certain circumstances, profanity provides a relief denied even to prayer.
       —MARK TWAIN

*   *   *

Prayers are to men as dolls are to children. They are not without use and comfort, but it is not easy to take them very seriously.

—SAMUEL BUTLER

What men usually ask of God when they pray is that two and two not make four. —ANONYMOUS

When I pray, I pray quickly, because I am talking to God; but when I read the Torah, I read slowly, because God is talking to me.

—OLD RABBI

Oh, Lord, give me a good excuse! —JEWISH SAYING

The gates of prayer are sometimes open, sometimes closed; but the gates of repentance are open forever.

—MIDRASH

*　*　*

When I hear a man preach, I like to see him act as if he were fighting bees. —ABRAHAM LINCOLN

When someone raises the palms of his hands together, we do not know whether it is to bury himself in prayer or to throw himself into the sea. —ORTEGA Y GASSET

The prayers of the poor are heard by God ahead of all others.

—ZOHAR

You don't have to pray loudly; just direct your heart to heaven.

—RABBI CHIA

If prayer did any good, they'd be hiring men to pray.

—JEWISH SAYING

Prayer is the service of the heart. —TALMUD

Pray only in a room with windows [to remember the world outside].

—TALMUD

* * *

He who prays for his neighbor will be heard for himself. —TALMUD

Prayer: Dear Lord, make me chaste and continent, but not yet.
—ST. AUGUSTINE

Pray: To ask that the rules of the universe be annulled in behalf of a single petitioner, confessedly unworthy. —AMBROSE BIERCE

There is not the least use preaching to anyone unless you chance to catch them ill. —SYDNEY SMITH

Prejudice

Prejudice not being founded on reason cannot be removed by argument. —SAMUEL JOHNSON

Humanity is in the highest degree irrational, so that there is no prospect of influencing it by reasonable arguments. . . . Against prejudice one can do nothing. —SIGMUND FREUD

A prejudice is a vagrant opinion without visible means of support.
—AMBROSE BIERCE

Two things reduce prejudice: education and laughter.
—LAURENCE J. PETER

I am free of all prejudices. I hate everyone equally.
—W. C. FIELDS

For those who do not think, it is best at least to rearrange their prejudices once in a while. —LUTHER BURBANK

The collection of prejudices called political philosophy is useful—provided it is not called philosophy. —BERTRAND RUSSELL

Many [of the Americans] polled showed a marked disapproval of the Wallonians, Danerians, and Pirenians. The fact that these minorities were invented by the pollster did not diminish the hostility.
—LEO ROSTEN

Pride

While you're saving your face you're losing your ass.
—LYNDON B. JOHNSON

If ever man becomes proud, let him remember that a flea preceded him in the divine order of creation.

—TALMUD

*　*　*

Pride is the reservoir of sin. —OLD TESTAMENT

If you harden your heart with pride, you will soften your brain with it, too. —ANONYMOUS

Principles

Principles have no real force except when one is well fed.
—MARK TWAIN

It is easier to fight for one's principles than to live up to them.
—ALFRED ADLER

When you say that you agree to a thing in principle, you mean that you have not the slightest intention of carrying it out in practice.
—OTTO VON BISMARCK

* * *

Progress

Is it progress if a cannibal uses a fork? —STANISLAW J. LEC

Propaganda

Propaganda is that branch of lying which often deceives your friends without ever deceiving your enemies. —WALTER LIPPMANN

All propaganda is lies—even when it is telling the truth.
—GEORGE ORWELL

Property

But above all, a prince must refrain from taking property, for men forget the death of a father more quickly than the loss of their patrimony.   —MACHIAVELLI/H. L. MENCKEN

The preservation of the rights of private property was the very keystone of the arch upon which all civilized governments rest.
                     —JOSEPH H. CHOATE

The only dependable foundation of personal liberty is the personal economic security of private property.   —WALTER LIPPMANN

Private property is the natural bulwark of liberty because it ensures that economic power is not entirely in the hands of the state.
                     —QUENTIN HOGG

*   *   *

The system of private property is the most important guaranty of freedom, not only for those who own property, but for those who do not. It is only because the control of the means of production is divided among many people acting independently that nobody has complete power over us, that we as individuals can decide what to do with ourselves.   —FRIEDRICH A. HAYEK

Prophecy

There is no likelihood man can ever tap the power of the atom.
                     —ROBERT MILLIKEN

Don't ever prophesy—unless you know. —JAMES RUSSELL LOWELL

Don't ever prophesy; for if you prophesy wrong, nobody will forget it; and if you prophesy right, nobody will remember it.

—JOSH BILLINGS

The prediction, as is usual, contributed to its own accomplishment.

—EDWARD GIBBON

*   *   *

Armed prophets succeed, but unarmed prophets come to ruin.

—MACHIAVELLI

Proverbs

A proverb is a short sentence based on long experience.

—CERVANTES

Proverbs are the primers we inherit from the past.   —LEO ROSTEN

The tortoise falls and says there is a curse on haste.

MALTESE PROVERB

Though boys throw stones at frogs in sport, the frogs die in earnest.

—PLUTARCH

Proverbs are the portable wisdom of a people.   —LEO ROSTEN

A man in love mistakes a pimple for a dimple.

—JAPANESE PROVERB

The man who is surrounded by dwarfs looks like a giant.

—JEWISH SAYING

The fish sees the bait but not the hook.   —CHINESE PROVERB

After shaking hands with a Greek, count your fingers.

—ALBANIAN PROVERB

If you want to succeed you must not be too good.

—ITALIAN PROVERB

Do not use a hatchet to remove a fly from your friend's forehead. —CHINESE PROVERB

The reverse side also has a reverse side.

—JAPANESE PROVERB

It is better to be a coward for a minute than dead for the rest of your life. —IRISH PROVERB

Fools build houses, and wise men buy them. —ENGLISH PROVERB

The wise make proverbs, and fools repeat them. —ISAAC D'ISRAELI

Trust in Allah, but tie your camel. —ARABIAN PROVERB

The best way to get praise is to die. —ITALIAN PROVERB

The girl who can't dance says the band can't keep time.

—YIDDISH PROVERB

*   *   *

If you scatter thorns, don't go barefoot. —ITALIAN PROVERB

Beat your child once a day. If you don't know why, the child does.

—CHINESE PROVERB/MANY OTHERS

Even the lion has to defend himself against flies.

—GERMAN PROVERB

To be cheated once is understandable; to be cheated thrice is inexcusable.   —YIDDISH SAYING

A nation's treasure is its scholars.   —YIDDISH/CHINESE PROVERB

Don't open a shop unless you like to smile.
—CHINESE PROVERB

*   *   *

With virtue you can't be entirely poor; without virtue you can't really be rich.   —CHINESE PROVERB

Deep doubts, deep wisdom; small doubts, little wisdom.
—CHINESE PROVERB

If you give people nuts, you'll get shells thrown at you.
—YEMENITE PROVERB

What's cheap is expensive.   —JEWISH SAYING

The eye is small but devours all.   —JEWISH SAYING

Good luck beats early rising.   —IRISH PROVERB

A rat who gnaws at a cat's tail invites destruction.
—CHINESE PROVERB

Of all the thirty-six alternatives, running away is best.

                                        —CHINESE PROVERB

                    *   *   *

Visits always give pleasure—if not the arrival, the departure.

                                        —PORTUGUESE PROVERB

Psychiatry/Psychoanalysis

Everything great in the world comes from neurotics. They alone have founded our religions and composed our masterpieces. Never will the world know all it owes to them, nor all that they have suffered to enrich it.   —MARCEL PROUST

Psychoanalysis is confession without absolution.

                                        —G. K. CHESTERTON

                    *   *   *

Joyous distrust is a sign of health. Everything absolute belongs to pathology.   —FRIEDRICH WILHELM NIETZSCHE

Psychiatry is the care of the id by the odd.   —ANONYMOUS

Psychoanalysis is that form of mental illness for which it regards itself as therapy.   —KARL KRAUS

Psychoanalysis makes quite simple people feel they're complex.

                                        —S. N. BEHRMAN

                    *   *   *

Roses are red, violets are blue,
I'm schizophrenic, and so am I. —OSCAR LEVANT

Depression is melancholy minus its charms. —SUSAN SONTAG

I'm going to give my psychoanalyst one more year, then I'm going to
Lourdes. —WOODY ALLEN

The neurotic builds castles in the air, the psychotic thinks he lives in
them, and the psychoanalyst collects rent from both. —ANONYMOUS

*I don't want an elderly gentleman from Vienna
with an umbrella inflicting his dreams upon
me.*
—VLADIMIR NABOKOV

*   *   *

Psychiatry enables us to correct our faults by confessing our parents'
shortcomings. —LAURENCE J. PETER

Why should I tolerate a perfect stranger at the bedside of my mind?
—VLADIMIR NABOKOV

Neurosis does not deny the existence of reality, it merely tries to
ignore it; psychosis denies it and tries to substitute something else for
it. . . . —SIGMUND FREUD

Everyone is a moon, and has a dark side which he never shows to
anybody. —MARK TWAIN

[Freud] was the Columbus of psychology, which still awaits its Euclid.
—LEO ROSTEN

Anybody who goes to see a psychiatrist ought to have his head ex-
amined. —SAMUEL GOLDWYN

The mind is an iceberg—it floats with only one seventh of its bulk above water. —SIGMUND FREUD

A man should not strive to eliminate his complexes but to get into accord with them; they are legitimately what directs his conduct in the world. —SIGMUND FREUD

To study the abnormal is the best way of understanding the normal. —WILLIAM JAMES

All day long the door of the subconscious remains just ajar; we slip through to the other side, and return again, as easily and secretly as a cat. —WALTER DE LA MARE

I just want to make one brief statement about psychoanalysis: "Fuck Dr. Freud."
—OSCAR LEVANT

* * *

Let the credulous and the vulgar continue to believe that all mental woes can be cured by a daily application of old Greek myths to their private parts. —VLADIMIR NABOKOV

Punishment

Punishment is a sort of medicine. —ARISTOTLE

If life is to be valued and secured, it must be known that anyone who takes the life of another forfeits his own. —ERNEST VAN DEN HAAG

Jail is jail for thieves. . . . For me, it [is] a palace.
—MOHANDAS K. GANDHI

If I wished to punish a province, I would have it governed by philosophers.   —FREDERICK THE GREAT

*We withdraw our wrath from the man who ad-
mits that he is justly punished.*
                                               —ARISTOTLE

                    *   *   *

If you must beat a child, use a string.   —TALMUD

If you strike a child, take care that you strike it in anger, even at the
risk of maiming it for life. A blow in cold blood neither can nor should
be forgiven.   —GEORGE BERNARD SHAW

The worst punishment is a sleepless night.   —JEWISH SAYING

Puns

He's not worth her wiles.   —JOHN GALSWORTHY

A woman is never too old to yearn.   —ADDISON MIZNER

The nation is prosperous on the whole, but how much prosperity is
there in a hole?   —WILL ROGERS

I thought he was a young man of promise, but it appears he is a young
man of promises.   —ARTHUR JAMES BALFOUR

Free verse: The triumph of mind over meter.   —ANONYMOUS

One of those characteristic British faces that, once seen, are never
remembered.   —OSCAR WILDE

Every crowd has a silver lining. —P. T. BARNUM

Ye shall know the truth, and the truth shall make you mad.
—ALDOUS HUXLEY

A kleptomaniac is a person who helps himself because he can't help himself.
—HENRY MORGAN

* * *

To err is human, to forgive supine. —S. J. PERELMAN

Only the young die good. —OLIVER HERFORD

Religion: The prophet system. —ANONYMOUS

Population explosion: When people take leave of their census.
—ANONYMOUS

* * *

Chaste makes waste.

Where there's a will there's a wail. —LEO ROSTEN

Better to be *nouveau* than never to have been *riche* at all.
—ANONYMOUS

The plural of spouse is spice. —CHRISTOPHER MORLEY

A pun is the lowest form of humor—when you didn't think of it first.
—OSCAR LEVANT

To err is human, but it feels divine.

—MAE WEST

*   *   *

Men love in haste, but they detest at leisure.   —LORD BYRON

Greater luck hath no man than this, that he lay down his wife at the right moment.   —SAMUEL BUTLER

Dictator: A self-madman.   —ANONYMOUS

Grave: The last resort.   —ANONYMOUS

She was suffering from fallen archness.

—FRANKLIN PIERCE ADAMS

None but the brave desert the fair.   —WILSON MIZNER

Women should be obscene and not heard.   —GROUCHO MARX

Birth Control. In Prague: canceled Czechs   —ANONYMOUS

Rich relatives are the kin we love to touch.   —EDDIE CANTOR

The Devil finds work for idle glands.   —*PETER'S ALMANAC*

My wife has a whim of iron.   —OLIVER HERFORD

She who hesitates is won.
                                        —OSCAR WILDE

                    *   *   *

When I am dead, I hope it may be said: "His sins were scarlet, but his books were read."   —HILAIRE BELLOC

Birth control: Copulation without population.   —LEO ROSTEN

You can lead a horticulture, but you can't make her think.
                                        —DOROTHY PARKER

Bachelor: A man who tries to avoid issues.   —ANONYMOUS

Hangover: The wrath of grapes.
            —DOROTHY PARKER/OSCAR LEVANT/ROBERT BENCHLEY

Please return this book; I find that though many of my friends are poor arithmeticians, they are nearly all good bookkeepers.
                                        —SIR WALTER SCOTT

It is better to copulate than never.
                                        —ROBERT HEINLEIN

                    *   *   *

Experimental psychologist: A scientist who pulls habits out of rats.
                                        —L. L. LEVINSON

    Genius, cried the commuter,
    As he ran for the 8:13,
    Consists of an infinite capacity
    For catching trains.   —CHRISTOPHER MORLEY

Many good friends have given me asylum, at times when I feared I was ready for one.   —LEO ROSTEN

I kept reading between the lies.   —GOODMAN ACE

Oh, what a tangled web we weave when first we practice to conceive.
—DON HEROLD

In the midst of life we are in debt.   —LEO ROSTEN

A man is as young as the woman he feels. —GROUCHO MARX

He is old enough to know worse.   —OSCAR WILDE

Epitaph: A monumental liar.   —ANONYMOUS

Christmas seasons are alcoholidays.
—SIGMUND FREUD/OSCAR WILDE

Q

Quarrels

The test of a man or woman's breeding is how they behave in a quarrel.   —George Bernard Shaw

People generally quarrel because they cannot argue.
                                                 —G. K. Chesterton

Quarreling is like cutting water with a sword.   —Chinese proverb

When two men quarrel, the one who yields first displays the nobler nature.   —Talmud

When men quarrel, even God's anger does not frighten them.
                                                       —Zohar

The world stands firm because of those who close their lips during a quarrel.   —Nachman of Bratslav

Don't quarrel with a loud man.   —Apocrypha

Quips

When one has never heard a man's name in the course of one's life, it speaks volumes for him; he must be quite respectable.

—OSCAR WILDE

Lady Astor: If I were your wife, I would flavor your coffee with poison!
Winston Churchill: And if I were your husband, madam, I would drink it.

When I was young I looked like Al Capone, but I lacked his compassion. —OSCAR LEVANT

Reagan won because he ran against Jimmy Carter. Had Reagan run unopposed, he would have lost. —MORT SAHL

And where does she find them?
—DOROTHY PARKER (ON HEARING THAT CLARE BOOTHE LUCE
WAS KIND TO HER "SOCIAL INFERIORS")

You don't have to have relatives in St. Louis to be miserable.
—GROUCHO MARX

The honorable gentleman should not generate more indignation than he can conveniently contain.
—WINSTON CHURCHILL (IN A DEBATE IN PARLIAMENT)

The one serious conviction that a man should have is that nothing is to be taken too seriously. —SAMUEL BUTLER

I think there is only one quality worse than hardness of heart and that is softness of head.
—THEODORE ROOSEVELT

*   *   *

I've just learned about his illness; let's hope it's nothing trivial.
—IRVIN S. COBB

If there were many more like her, the stock of halos would give out.
—ARTHUR WING PINERO

I admire him, I freely confess it. And when his time comes I shall buy a piece of the rope for a keepsake.   —MARK TWAIN

If some people got their rights they would complain of being deprived of their wrongs.   —OLIVER HERFORD

She never had a proposal, only propositions.   —ILKA CHASE

He was too bad to be true.   —MICHAEL HOLROYD

I would like to take you seriously, but to do so would affront your intelligence.   —WILLIAM F. BUCKLEY, JR.

Animals, I hope.
—ERIC PHIPPS (TO HERMANN GÖRING, WHO EXPLAINED HIS LATE ARRIVAL AT A DINNER BECAUSE OF HIS ATTENDANCE AT "A SHOOTING PARTY")

Any man who hates dogs and babies can't be all bad.
—LEO ROSTEN (OF W. C. FIELDS)

Leo Rosten "Do you know Doris Day?"
Groucho Marx: "Shucks, I knew her before she was a virgin."

He hasn't been himself lately, let's hope he stays that way.
—IRVIN S. COBB

She is an excellent creature, but she never can remember which came first, the Greeks or the Romans.   —BENJAMIN DISRAELI

One of the best ways to persuade others is with your ears—by listening to them.   —DEAN RUSK

I can't remember your name, but don't tell me.
                    —ALEXANDER WOOLLCOTT

*   *   *

I never forget a face, but in your case I am willing to make an exception.   —GROUCHO MARX

Does the name Pavlov ring a bell?   —ANONYMOUS

Leo Rosten (at Groucho Marx's front door): "I'd like to say good-bye to your wife."
Groucho: "Who wouldn't?"

I'm going to Boston to see my doctor. He's a very sick man.
                                        —FRED ALLEN

To give an accurate and exhaustive account of that period would need a far less brilliant pen than mine.   —MAX BEERBOHM

Now I suppose we'll have to have the Trumans over to *our* house.
                —OSCAR LEVANT (TO HIS WIFE, AFTER DINNER
                                    AT THE WHITE HOUSE)

If I were two-faced, would I be wearing this one?

                    —ABRAHAM LINCOLN

*   *   *

There's absolutely nothing wrong with you that reincarnation won't cure.   —JACK E. LEONARD (TO ED SULLIVAN)

Racism

Racism is the snobbery of the poor. —RAYMOND ARON

Racism is man's gravest threat to man—the maximum of hatred for a minimum of reason. —ABRAHAM JOSHUA HESCHEL

Reality

Reality is for people who can't face drugs.
—LAURENCE J. PETER

* * *

The dignity of man lies in his ability to face reality in all its sense-lessness. —MARTIN ESSLIN

Perched on the loftiest throne in the world, we are still sitting on our
own behind.   —MONTAIGNE

What is reality but a fortuitous play of circumstance, indifferent to
our hopes or our unutterable aspirations?   —LEO ROSTEN

> *Everything is a dangerous drug except reality,*
> *which is unendurable.*
> —CYRIL CONNOLLY

*   *   *

Realism is simply romanticism that has lost its reason.
                                                   —G. K. CHESTERTON

If a man will begin with certainties, he will end in doubts; but if he
will be content to begin with doubts, he will end in certainties.
                                                   —FRANCIS BACON

It requires a very unusual mind to undertake the analysis of the obvious.   —ALFRED NORTH WHITEHEAD

"For instance" is not proof.   —JEWISH SAYING

The only force I fear more than human irrationality is irrationality
armed with passion.   —LEO ROSTEN

Reason

Most of our so-called reasoning consists in finding arguments for going
on believing as we already do.   —JAMES HARVEY ROBINSON

Nothing hath an uglier look to us than reason when it is not on our
side.   —GEORGE SAVILE

*I am sure that, since I have had the full use of
my reason, nobody has ever heard me laugh.*
　　　　　　　　—EARL OF CHESTERFIELD

*　　*　　*

If you follow reason far enough it always leads to conclusions that are
contrary to reason.　　　　　　　　　　　　　—SAMUEL BUTLER

Reasoning draws a conclusion—but does not make the conclusion certain, unless the mind discovers it by the path of experience.
　　　　　　　　　　　　　　　　　　　—ROGER BACON

Delight of mind does not clog the use of reason; on the contrary, we
are more intent on what we more enjoy.　　　　—THOMAS AQUINAS

In this time I find no maxim sounder than Winston Churchill's: "I
cannot remain impartial as between the fire brigade and the fire."
　　　　　　　　　　　　　　　　　　　—LEO ROSTEN

I can stand brute force, but brute reason is quite unbearable. There
is something unfair about its use. It is hitting below the intellect.
　　　　　　　　　　　　　　　　　　　—OSCAR WILDE

Between craft and credulity, the voice of reason is stifled.
　　　　　　　　　　　　　　　　　　　—EDMUND BURKE

When custom and reason are at odds, custom always wins out.
　　　　　　　　　　　　　　　　　—NAPOLEON BONAPARTE

A man has free choice to the extent that he is rational.
　　　　　　　　　　　　　　　　　　　—THOMAS AQUINAS

Error of opinion may be tolerated where reason is left free to combat
it.　　　　　　　　　　　　　　　　　—THOMAS JEFFERSON

Man is a reasonable animal who always loses his temper when he is called upon to act in accordance with the dictates of reason.

—OSCAR WILDE

Reason is a light that God has kindled in the soul. —ARISTOTLE

Reason, however sound, has little weight with ordinary theologians.

—BARUCH SPINOZA

We shall succeed only so far as we continue that most distasteful of all activity, the intolerable labor of thought. —LEARNED HAND

Most men seem to live according to sense rather than reason.

—THOMAS AQUINAS

Your arguments against reasoning are so persuasive that one is almost tempted to get down on all fours.

—VOLTAIRE (TO ROUSSEAU)

* * *

The true triumph of reason is that it enables us to get along with those who do not possess it. —VOLTAIRE

Of all the ways of defining man, the worst is the one that makes him out to be a rational animal. —ANATOLE FRANCE

The madman is not the man who has lost his reason. He is the man who has lost everything except his reason. —G. K. CHESTERTON

Reason is a whore, the greatest enemy that faith has.

—MARTIN LUTHER

*   *   *

Reform

Unless the reformer can invent something that substitutes attractive virtues for attractive vices, he will fail.   —WALTER LIPPMANN

[Melbourne] thought change always ran the risk of disturbing the security of society. . . . Sensational reforms, like parliamentary reform, did positive harm. For by raising hopes that could never be fulfilled, they left people more discontented than ever.

—DAVID CECIL

*   *   *

He who would reform himself must first reform society.

—GEORGE BERNARD SHAW

Nothing so needs reforming as other people's habits.—MARK TWAIN

I am . . . compelled to see that the best-meaning social planners, whether Democrat, Republican, Demo-Republicans . . . have inflicted social and economic disasters on our cities.

They have done so not because they are stupid or malevolent or ill-informed. They have done so because they assumed that humane intentions will produce laudable results.   —GEORGE WEIGEL

A reformer is a guy who rides through a sewer in a glass-bottomed boat.

—JIMMY WALKER

When Dr. Johnson defined patriotism as the last refuge of a scoundrel, he ignored the enormous possibilities of the word "reform."
—ROSCOE CONKLING

The most astounding fact about reformers, driven by the purest of motives and the most spotless goodwill, is that it does not dawn on them that their programs can make things worse.   —LEO ROSTEN

Every reform is only a mask under cover of which a more terrible reform, which dares not yet name itself, advances.
—RALPH WALDO EMERSON

All movements go too far.
—BERTRAND RUSSELL

*   *   *

Every reform, however necessary, will by weak minds be carried to an excess which will itself need reforming.
—SAMUEL TAYLOR COLERIDGE

A reform is a correction of abuses, a revolution is a transfer of power.
—EDWARD BULWER-LYTTON

Religion

Religion is a thing of [our] own contrivance. What kind of truth is it that is true on one side of a mountain and false on the other?
—MONTAIGNE

Religion is the heart in a heartless world.   —KARL MARX

When a man is freed of religion, he has a better chance to live a normal and wholesome life.   —SIGMUND FREUD

The whole religious complexion of the modern world is due to the absence from (ancient) Jerusalem of a lunatic asylum.
—HAVELOCK ELLIS

*　　*　　*

The first priest was the first knave who met the first fool.
—VOLTAIRE

Religion is the masterpiece of the art of animal training, for it trains people as to how they shall think.　　—ARTHUR SCHOPENHAUER

There is no social evil, no form of injustice, whether of the feudal or capitalist order, which has not been sanctified in some way or another by religious sentiment and thereby rendered more impervious to change.　　—REINHOLD NIEBUHR

Religion is what keeps the poor from murdering the rich.
—NAPOLEON BONAPARTE

If men are so wicked with religion, what would they be without it?
—BENJAMIN FRANKLIN

No man with any sense of humor ever founded a religion.
—ROBERT G. INGERSOLL

*　　*　　*

Anything which is rational is always difficult for the lay mind. But the thing which is irrational anyone can understand. That is why religion came so early into the world.　　—G. K. CHESTERTON

Religion: A fantastic faith in gods, angels, and spirits. A faith without any scientific foundations, religion is being supported and maintained

by the reactionary circles. It serves for the subjugation of the working people and increases the power of the exploiting bourgeois class.
—DICTIONARY, USSR, 1951 EDITION

Religion is a monumental chapter in the history of human egotism.
—WILLIAM JAMES

So far as the religion of the day is concerned, it is a damned fake. . . . Religion is all bunk. —THOMAS ALVA EDISON

Religion is a mass obsessional neurosis . . . patently infantile . . . incongruent with reality. —SIGMUND FREUD

Religion: A daughter of Hope and Fear, explaining to Ignorance the nature of the Unknowable. —AMBROSE BIERCE

Man . . . is the only animal that has the true religion—several of them.
—MARK TWAIN

There is something feeble and a little contemptible about a man who cannot face the perils of life without the help of comfortable myths.
—BERTRAND RUSSELL

Theology is the effort to explain the unknowable in terms of the not worth knowing. —II. L. MENCKEN

Religion is excellent stuff for keeping common people quiet.
—NAPOLEON BONAPARTE

Religion is caught, not taught.
—WILLIAM RALPH INGE

*   *   *

Religion is the opiate of the people.
—KARL MARX (BUT HEINRICH HEINE BEFORE HIM)

Religion depends as little upon theology as love upon phrenology.
—ISRAEL ZANGWILL

It is conceivable that religion may be morally useful without being intellectually sustainable. —JOHN STUART MILL

What religion is he of? Why, he is an Anythingarian.
—JONATHAN SWIFT

The great religious waves have a momentum all their own. . . . And this one has the mightiest, holiest roll of all, the beat that goes . . . Me . . . Me . . . Me . . . Me. . . . —TOM WOLFE

The liberality of sentiment toward each other, which marks every political and religious denomination of men in this country, stands unparalleled in the history of nations. —GEORGE WASHINGTON

We must respect the other fellow's religion, but only in the sense and to the extent that we respect his theory that his wife is beautiful and his children smart.

—H. L. MENCKEN

*   *   *

I want nothing to do with any religion concerned with keeping the masses satisfied to live in hunger, filth, and ignorance.
—JAWAHARLAL NEHRU

A man who should act, for one day, on the supposition that all the people about him were influenced by the religion which they professed, would find himself ruined by night.

—THOMAS BABINGTON MACAULAY

*   *   *

Men will wrangle for religion; write for it; fight for it; die for it; anything but live for it. —CHARLES CALEB COLTON

My theology, briefly, is that the universe was dictated but not signed. —CHRISTOPHER MORLEY

A little philosophy inclineth men's minds to atheism; but depth in philosophy bringeth men's minds to religion. —FRANCIS BACON

We have just enough religion to make us hate but not enough to make us love one another. —JONATHAN SWIFT

Theology is an attempt to explain a subject by men who do not understand it. The intent is not to tell the truth but to satisfy the questioner.
—ELBERT HUBBARD

✳ ✳ ✳

No new sect ever had humor; no disciples either, even the disciples of Christ. —ANNE MORROW LINDBERGH

The best theology would need no advocate; it would prove itself. —KARL BARTH

Religion is a noble disease. —HERACLITUS

Religion is the vaccine of the imagination. —NAPOLEON BONAPARTE

There are no sects in geometry. —VOLTAIRE

All religions are founded on the fear of the many and the cleverness of the few. —STENDHAL

The test of a good religion is whether you can joke about it.
                                    —G. K. CHESTERTON

* * *

There seems to be an excess of everything except parking space and religion.   —FRANK McKINNEY ("KIN") HUBBARD

Flying is against his religious principles; he is an Orthodox Coward.
                                    —LEO ROSTEN

Repartee

Somebody once asked me, "Do you like bathing beauties?" I said, "I don't know, I never bathed one."

                                    —MILTON BERLE

* * *

I've only slept with the men I've been married to. How many women can make that claim?   —ELIZABETH TAYLOR

Repartee: What you wish you'd said.   —HEYWOOD BROUN

My father was a Creole, his father a Negro, and his father a monkey; my family, it seems, begins where yours left off.
                                    —ALEXANDRE DUMAS, *PÈRE*

Aristocratic young lord: "By the way, I passed your house last night."
James McNeill Whistler: "Thank you."

Repartee is something we think of twenty-four hours too late.

—MARK TWAIN

A summer-stock producer who had produced a Kaufman play without paying royalties explained, "After all, it's only a small, insignificant theater."

"Then you'll go to a small, insignificant jail," Kaufman answered.

"How could they tell?"

—DOROTHY PARKER (ON BEING TOLD THAT
CALVIN COOLIDGE HAD JUST DIED)

A woman: "I really can't come to your party. I can't bear fools."
Dorothy Parker: "That's strange, your mother could."

Repentance

When the sin is sweet, repentance is not so bitter.   —ANONYMOUS

God will accept repentance for all sins except one: giving another man a bad name.

—ZOHAR

When we are young, God forgives our stumblings; when we mature, He weighs our words; and when we grow old, He waits—for our repentance.

—ANONYMOUS

Never mind the remorse; just don't do what causes it.

—JEWISH SAYING

Reputation

My reputation's terrible, which comforts me a lot.

—NOËL COWARD

Reputation is what men and women think of us; character is what God and the angels know of us. —THOMAS PAINE

Revenge

Revenge is often like biting a dog because the dog bit you.
—AUSTIN O'MALLEY

Forgive your enemies, but never forget their names.
—JOHN F. KENNEDY

If you take revenge, you will regret it; if you forgive, you will rejoice.
—ANONYMOUS

Revolution

Revolutions are always verbose. —LEON TROTSKY

One does not establish a dictatorship in order to safeguard a revolution. One establishes the revolution in order to establish the dictatorship. —GEORGE ORWELL

The revolutionary spirit is mightily convenient in this: that it frees one from all scruples as regards ideas. —JOSEPH CONRAD

All modern revolutions have ended in a reinforcement of the power of the State. —ALBERT CAMUS

There is perhaps in all misfits a powerful secret craving to turn the whole of humanity into misfits. Hence partly their passionate advocacy of a drastically new social order. For we are all misfits when we have to adjust ourselves to the wholly new. —ERIC HOFFER

Revolutions have never lightened the burden of tyranny, they have only shifted it to another shoulder.

—GEORGE BERNARD SHAW

Every revolution evaporates and leaves behind only the slime of a new bureaucracy. —FRANZ KAFKA

We are not to expect to be translated from despotism to liberty in a feather bed. —THOMAS JEFFERSON

The world is always childish, and with each new gewgaw of a revolution or a constitution that it finds, thinks it shall never cry anymore.

RALPH WALDO EMERSON

I'm strong for any revolution that isn't going to happen in my day.
—FINLEY PETER DUNNE ("MR. DOOLEY")

* * *

Every successful revolution puts on in time the robes of the tyrant it has deposed. —BARBARA TUCHMAN

Revolutions are not about trifles, but spring from trifles.

—ARISTOTLE

Those who make peaceful revolution impossible make violent revolution inevitable. —JOHN F. KENNEDY

The saddest illusion of revolutionary socialism is that revolution itself will transform the nature of human beings. —SHIRLEY WILLIAMS

The twentieth century has seen the revolutions of high expectations.

—HAROLD D. LASSWELL

Nothing is clearer in history than the adoption by successful rebels of the methods they were accustomed to condemn in the forces they deposed.　　　　　　　　　　　　—WILL AND ARIEL DURANT

The fight is never about grapes or lettuce. It is always about people.　　　　　　　　　　　　—CESAR CHAVEZ

When the people contend for their liberty, they seldom get anything by their victory but new masters.　　　　　　　—LORD HALIFAX

Revolution: An abrupt change in the form of misgovernment.　　　　　　　　　　　　—AMBROSE BIERCE

If you feed the people just with revolutionary slogans they will listen today, they will listen tomorrow, and they will listen the day after tomorrow, but on the fourth day they will say, "To hell with you!"　　　　　　　—NIKITA KHRUSCHEV

I have never feared that the revolution could be produced at the universities; yet I feel certain that a whole generation of revolutionaries is being bred there.

—METTERNICH

* 　 * 　 *

They who are engrossed in the realization of an extravagant hope tend to view facts as something base and unclean. Facts are counterrevolutionary.　　　　　　　　　　　　—ERIC HOFFER

Those who set out to be their brother's keeper sometimes end up by becoming his jailer. Every emancipation has within it the seeds of a new slavery, and every truth can easily become a lie. —I. F. STONE

With the exception of capitalism, there is nothing so revolting as revolution.   —GEORGE BERNARD SHAW

Revolution is a trivial shift in the emphasis of suffering.
                                                —TOM STOPPARD

Those who give the first shock to a state are the first overwhelmed in its ruin.   —MONTAIGNE

In a revolution, as in a novel, the most difficult part to invent is the end.
                            —ALEXIS DE TOCQUEVILLE

*   *   *

No one can foresee where violence will end. The Robespierres and Madame Rolands die on the guillotine; the Slanskys perish in dungeons; the Trotskys end in exile/murder. Revolutions *do* devour their own.   —LEO ROSTEN

Revolutions are not made by men in spectacles.
                                —OLIVER WENDELL HOLMES

Every revolutionist ends as a heretic—or an oppressor.
                                                —LEO ROSTEN

Rich

Who is rich? He that is content. Who is that? Nobody.
                            —BENJAMIN FRANKLIN

*   *   *

The rich aren't like us; they pay less taxes.   —PETER DE VRIES

The observances of the church concerning feasts and fasts are tolerably well kept, since the rich keep the feasts and the poor the fasts.
—VOLTAIRE

There is no stronger craving in the world than that of the rich for titles, except that of the titled for riches.   —HESKETH PEARSON

The rich swell up with pride, the poor from hunger.
—SHOLEM ALEICHEM

It is the wretchedness of being rich that you have to live with rich people.   —LOGAN PEARSALL SMITH

What is the matter with the poor is poverty; what is the matter with the rich is uselessness.   —GEORGE BERNARD SHAW

The death of the rich is smelled far away.   —JEWISH SAYING

Many speak the truth when they say that they despise riches, but they mean the riches possessed by other men.
—CHARLES CALEB COLTON

* * *

Rich widows: The only secondhand goods that sell at first-class prices.
—BENJAMIN FRANKLIN

It is easier for a camel to go through the eye of a needle than for a rich man to enter heaven—the impossibility is not alleged but the rarity is emphasized.   —THOMAS AQUINAS

If a free society cannot help the many who are
poor, it cannot save the few who are rich.
                              —JOHN F. KENNEDY

*   *   *

Wealthy students often act as if ashamed of their wealth. I have
sometimes been tempted to point out that the rich are a minority and
have rights, too.   —DAVID RIESMAN AND SIDNEY HOOK

The poor profit more from the luxuries of the rich than from their
philanthropy.   —ADAPTED FROM TALMUD

The rich man and his daughter are soon parted.
                      —FRANK McKINNEY ("KIN") HUBBARD

❖ Bertrand Russell ❖

I don't suppose anyone ever wrote clearer, cleaner, more pure and
bracing prose. He was brilliant and profound, a master clarifier and
simplifier of the most complex philosophical, mathematical, scientific,
and social problems. He was a passionate pacifist, a total agnostic, a
reformer and crusader of complete independence and fearless com-
mitment. He detested superstition, mocked prayer, and preached free
love, agnosticism, and nonconformity. An aristocrat (he died an earl),
he lampooned aristocracy and the royal establishment. He was a genius at antiseptic propositions about religion, morals, marriage, war,
and education.

Russell was short and frail, with a huge head (much too large for
his body)—an elf with a crown of puffy white hair that resembled an
aureole. His mouth was singularly expressive—turning sardonic,
ironic, amused, stubborn, or defiant. He always held or smoked or
filled or tamped or reamed a pipe. I am sure he used the time he took
to fiddle with that pipe to think through what he was going to say,
rehearsing it, I mean editing and polishing it—so that when he spoke
out, it was exact, beautifully phrased, not a word too much, breath-
taking in its cool, bracing precision.

As often as not, his conversation was a succession of definitive
conclusions grounded in impeccable logic and crowned by flashes of

mischievous wit. His prose, too, had that commanding authority: seasoned by skepticism, steeped in cynicism, drenched with irony, and redeemed by his total earnestness of stark reasoning.

Many years ago, I spent two afternoons in London at Russell's house on Queen's Road, Richmond. I interviewed him in the hope of persuading him to write a question-and-answer article called "What Is an Agnostic?"

His first response was masterful: "Atheists are not agnostics. They are like Christians; both hold that we *can* know that God exists. The atheist holds that we know that God does *not* exist. But the agnostic holds that we do not know enough either to affirm *or* deny the existence of a Supreme Being. . . . I believe that although the existence of God is not *impossible*, it is improbable. *Quite* improbable."

He answered each question I asked in as careful and unambiguous a formulation.

At one point I asked, "How do you explain the beauty and harmony of nature?"

He cocked his head like a very bright-eyed, amused sparrow. "I fail to see much beauty in a tapeworm. . . . As for the 'harmony' of nature, my dear fellow, animals throughout the kingdom of 'beautiful' nature constantly slaughter each other without mercy. Even the stars, in their 'harmonious' heavens, explode from time to time and simply destroy everything in their vicinity. . . . 'Beauty' is entirely subjective. It exists only in the eye—and mind—of an observer."

Once I asked, "Do you never fear God, or God's judgment?"

He did not take two seconds to reply with a shrug, "*If* there is, in fact, a Supreme Being, which I doubt, I think it unlikely that he would possess so uneasy a vanity [what a phrase!] as to be offended by my views about his existence."

Later I asked, "To an agnostic, what is the meaning of life?"

"What," he said with a sigh, "is the meaning of 'the meaning of life'? I do not believe that life *has* meaning; it just happens."

But the exchange I remember most vividly is this: I said, "Suppose that after you—uh—left this sorry vale, you actually found yourself in Heaven, standing before the throne! And there, radiant in His glory, sat the Lord. God. Himself. The Creator and King of the Universe."

I think Russell winced.

I asked, "*What would you think—or say—then?*"

The luminous pixie wrinkled his nose. "I probably would say, 'But sir, *Why did you not give me better evidence?*'"

No cherub ever looked more saintly, more kind, more considerate of my naïveté and God's presumed inability to answer.

You will find Russell's cleansing, intrepid wit scattered throughout the pages of this book. You may find it stimulating to read (or reread) a few of my favorites:

❖

Boredom is a vital problem for the moralist, since half the sins of mankind are caused by the fear of it.

❖

The infliction of cruelty with a good conscience pleases the moralists—which is why they invented Hell.

❖

Man is a credulous animal, and must believe *something*; in the absence of good grounds for belief, he will accept bad ones.

❖

To conquer fear is the beginning of wisdom.

❖

Aristotle maintained that women have fewer teeth than men. He was married twice, but it never occurred to him to ask either of his wives to open her mouth so he could count her teeth.

❖

Three passions, simple but overwhelmingly strong, have governed my life: the longing for love, the search for knowledge, and unbearable pity for the suffering of mankind.

But in his private life, "Bertie" was often insensitive, juvenile, and selfish vis-à-vis his sexual encounters. His libido seemed (at least to me) too powerful, too aggressive, too complex and insistent to be governed (much less controlled) by his reason or his will.

Sabbath

On the Sabbath, the wicked in Hell, too, rest.   —TALMUD

There are many persons who look on Sunday as a sponge to wipe out
the sins of the week.   —HENRY WARD BEECHER

Millions long for immortality who don't know what to do on a rainy
Sunday afternoon.   —SUSAN ERTZ

Sadism

Sadist: Someone who sends get-well cards to hypochondriacs.
                                      —SHOLEM PINSKY

A sadist is someone who refuses to be mean to a masochist.
                                      —ANONYMOUS

Saints

Nothing makes a man or woman look so saintly as seasickness.
—SAMUEL BUTLER

All snakes who wish to remain in Ireland will please raise their right hands.
—ATTRIBUTED TO ST. PATRICK

The history of the saints is mainly the history of insane people.
—BENITO MUSSOLINI

Only a saint could be quite honest in politics, and saints do not enter politics; but Disraeli was as honest as a man can be who is chiefly devoted to his own interests.   —HESKETH PEARSON

Living with a saint is more grueling than being one.
—ROBERT NEVILLE

Saint: A dead sinner revised and edited. —AMBROSE BIERCE

I am a politician trying . . . to be a saint.   —MOHANDAS K. GANDHI

Saints should always be judged guilty until proved innocent.
—GEORGE ORWELL (ON GANDHI)

The wicked do well in this world; the saints in the next.
—ANONYMOUS

There never was a saint with red hair.   —RUSSIAN PROVERB

Nine saints do not make a minyan [quorum for prayer], but one ordinary man can—by joining them.   —JEWISH SAYING

Sarcasm

Partner, I know that you learned how to play bridge only yesterday. But may I ask: What *time* yesterday?   —GEORGE S. KAUFMAN

I refused to attend his funeral. But I wrote a very nice letter explaining that I approved of it.   —MARK TWAIN

Many thanks; I shall lose no time in reading your book.
        —BENJAMIN DISRAELI (TO AN AUTHOR
            WHO HAD SENT HIM A BOOK)

*   *   *

Don't you realize that missionaries are the divinely provided food for destitute and underfed cannibals? Whenever they are on the brink of starvation, Heaven in its infinite mercy sends them a nice plump missionary.   —OSCAR WILDE

Saturday afternoon, although occurring at regular and well-foreseen intervals, always takes this railway by surprise.   —W. S. GILBERT

Scholars

Some scholars are like donkeys: They only carry a lot of books.
        —BAHYA IBN PAQUDA

Kings may be judges of the earth, but wise men are the judges of kings.   —IBN GABIROL

When a sage dies, all men should mourn, for they are his kinsmen.
        —TALMUD

The table that has fed no scholars is not blessed.
—JEWISH SAYING

A sage takes precedence over a king.
—ADAPTED FROM MISHNAH

Just as a tent cannot stand without pegs and cords, so Israel cannot stand without scholars.
—*SEDER ELIYAHU RABBAH*

The scholar [lost in his thoughts] does not see that borsht is red.
—MY GRANDFATHER

Science

Science without religion is lame, religion without science is blind.
—ALBERT EINSTEIN

I have never met a man yet who understands in the least what Einstein is driving at. . . . I very seriously doubt that Einstein himself really knows what he is driving at. . . . In a word, the outcome of this befogged speculation about time and space is a cloak which hides the ghastly apparition of atheism.
—WILLIAM HENRY CARDINAL O'CONNELL

In the field of observation, chance favors only the prepared minds.
—LOUIS PASTEUR

If I have ever made any valuable discoveries, it has been owing more to patient attention, than to any other talent. —SIR ISAAC NEWTON

Science is the greatest antidote to the poison of enthusiasm and superstition.
—ADAM SMITH

Art is I; science is we.   —CLAUDE BERNARD

I do not fear computers. I fear the lack of them.   —ISAAC ASIMOV

Any sufficiently advanced technology is indistinguishable from
magic.   —ARTHUR C. CLARKE

Although this may seem a paradox, all exact science is domi-
nated by the idea of approximation.   —BERTRAND RUSSELL

If man is but another animal species, why has no other species produced even one Darwin?

                                                     —A RABBI

Science increases our power in proportion as it lowers our pride.
                                          —CLAUDE BERNARD

As long as men are free to ask what they must—free to say what
they think—free to think what they will—freedom can never be lost
and science can never regress.   —J. ROBERT OPPENHEIMER

The realization that our small planet is only one of many worlds gives
mankind the perspective it needs to realize sooner that our own world
belongs to all of its creatures, that the moon landing marks the end
of our childhood as a race and the beginning of a newer and better
civilization.   —ARTHUR C. CLARKE

Never lose a holy curiosity.   —ALBERT EINSTEIN

The attempt to understand the intricacies of our own minds in scientific terms—this is to say, in terms of a well-specified and rigorous
theory on whose workings we can all agree—is surely the most difficult scientific enterprise yet begun.   —N. S. SUTHERLAND

There is a single light of science, and to brighten it anywhere is to brighten it everywhere. —ISAAC ASIMOV

The solar system has no anxiety about its reputation. —RALPH WALDO EMERSON

Somewhere, something incredible is waiting to be known. —CARL SAGAN

A beautiful theory killed by a nasty, ugly little fact. —THOMAS H. HUXLEY

There is no logical way to the discovery of the elementary laws of nature; there is only the way of intuition. —ALBERT EINSTEIN

The radical novelty of modern science lies precisely in the rejection of the belief, which is at the heart of all popular religion, that the forces which move the stars and atoms are contingent upon the preferences of the human heart. —WALTER LIPPMANN

Science commits suicide when it adopts a creed.
—THOMAS H. HUXLEY

* * *

Every sentence I utter must be understood not as an affirmation, but as a question. —NIELS BOHR

The most beautiful thing we can experience is the mysterious. It is the source of all true art and science. —ALBERT EINSTEIN

It is more important that a proposition be interesting than that it be true. This statement is almost a tautology. For the energy of operation of a proposition in an occasion of experience is its interest and is its importance. But of course a true proposition is more apt to be interesting than a false one. —ALFRED NORTH WHITEHEAD

Where it is a duty to worship the sun it is pretty sure to be a crime to examine the laws of heat. —JOHN MORLEY

To a chemist nothing on earth is unclean. —ANONYMOUS

Even when the experts all agree, they may well be mistaken.
—BERTRAND RUSSELL

* * *

The process of scientific discovery is, in effect, a continual flight from wonder. —ALBERT EINSTEIN

It is a mistake to believe that a science consists in nothing but conclusively proved proposition. [This] demand is only made by those who feel a craving for authority . . . to replace the religious catechism by something else, even if it be scientific. —SIGMUND FREUD

The essence of science is to ask an impertinent question, and you are on your way to a pertinent answer. —JACOB BRONOWSKI

We can lick gravity, but sometimes the paperwork is overwhelming. —WERNHER VON BRAUN

Everything should be made as simple as possible, but not simpler. —ALBERT EINSTEIN

Seek simplicity and distrust it.
—ALFRED NORTH WHITEHEAD

Without experiment I am nothing. I was never able to make a fact my own without seeing it; I could trust a fact, and always cross-examined an assertion. —MICHAEL FARADAY

[Einstein] would have been one of the greatest theoreticians of physics even if he had never written a line on relativity. —MAX BORN

The scientific theory I like best is that the rings of Saturn are composed entirely of lost airline baggage. —MARK RUSSELL

Every great advance in natural knowledge has involved the absolute rejection of authority. —THOMAS H. HUXLEY

Basic research is what I am doing when I don't know what I am doing. —WERNHER VON BRAUN

Research is something that tells you that a jackass has two ears. —ATTRIBUTED TO ALBERT LASKER

Secrets

Your friend has a friend; don't tell him. —CHINESE PROVERB

What three know is no longer a secret. —JEWISH SAYING

Your secret is your prisoner; once you reveal it, you become its slave. —IBN GABIROL

Secret: *What we tell everybody to tell nobody.* —AMBROSE BIERCE

✳   ✳   ✳

Every profession has its secrets . . . if it hadn't, it wouldn't be a profession. —H. H. MUNRO ("SAKI")

A woman can keep one secret—the secret of her age. —VOLTAIRE

You can be sincere and still be stupid.   —CHARLES F. KETTERING

> *Three may keep a secret—if two of them are dead.*
> —BENJAMIN FRANKLIN

* * *

Sex

Celibacy is not hereditary.   —ATTRIBUTED TO OSCAR WILDE

Marriage has driven more than one man to sex. —PETER DE VRIES

I can understand companionship. I can understand bought sex in the afternoon. I cannot understand the love affair.   —GORE VIDAL

The act of procreation and the members employed therein are so repulsive, that if it were not for the beauty of the faces, the adornments of the actors, and the pent-up impulse, nature would lose the human species.   —LEONARDO DA VINCI

The pleasure is momentary, the position ridiculous, and the expense damnable.   —ATTRIBUTED TO LORD CHESTERFIELD

One woman I was dating said, "Come on over, there's nobody home." I went over—nobody was home.   —RODNEY DANGERFIELD

Going to bed with a woman never hurt a ballplayer. It's staying up all night looking for them that does you in.   —CASEY STENGEL

Give a man a free hand and he'll run it all over you.   —MAE WEST

Nature abhors a virgin—a frozen asset.   —CLARE BOOTHE LUCE

Sex is the most fun you can have without laughing.
                    —LEO ROSTEN (VARIOUSLY ATTRIBUTED; USED BY
                              WOODY ALLEN IN A MOVIE)

Sexual morality, as society defines it, is contemptible.
                                        —SIGMUND FREUD

The backseat produced the sexual revolution.
                              —JERRY RUBIN

                    *   *   *

Never go to bed with anyone whose emotional problems are greater
than your own.   —SATCHEL PAIGE

In Spain lust is in the air. There is nothing clandestine about the
Spanish appreciation of sex, nothing inhibited or restrained. That is
why there are very few sexual crimes in Spain.
                                  —FERNANDO DIAZ-PLAJA

She was still keeping open bed.   —ALDOUS HUXLEY

Beds are the poor man's opera.   —ITALIAN PROVERB

In America sex is an obsession; in other parts of the world it is a fact.
                                    —MARLENE DIETRICH

That melancholy sexual perversion known as continence.
                                      —ALDOUS HUXLEY

*Vasectomy means never having to say you're
sorry.*
                                        —ANONYMOUS

              *   *   *

There are three sexes: men, women, and clergymen.
                                        —SYDNEY SMITH

Sex: The thing that takes up the least amount of time and causes the
most amount of trouble.   —JOHN BARRYMORE

Sex is one of the nine reasons for reincarnation. . . . The other eight
are unimportant.   —HENRY MILLER

You cannot separate young limbs and lechery.   —SHAKESPEARE

More chorus girls are kept than promises.   —FRED ALLEN

Whoever named it necking was a poor judge of anatomy.
                                        —GROUCHO MARX

I wonder why murder is considered less immoral than fornication in
literature.   —GEORGE MOORE

The only unnatural sex act is that which you cannot perform.
                                        —ALFRED KINSEY

If it weren't for pickpockets I'd have no sex life at all.
                                        —RODNEY DANGERFIELD

The good thing about masturbation is that you don't have to dress up
for it.   —TRUMAN CAPOTE

Why should we take advice on sex from the pope? If he knows anything about it, he shouldn't.   —GEORGE BERNARD SHAW

If God meant us to have group sex, he'd have given us more organs.
                                                —MALCOLM BRADBURY

When a man says he had pleasure with a woman he does not mean conversation.   —SAMUEL JOHNSON

There are really not many jobs that actually require a penis or a vagina, and all other occupations should be open to everyone.
                                                —GLORIA STEINEM

It doesn't matter what you do, as long as you don't do it in public and frighten the horses.
                                —ATTRIBUTED TO
                        MRS. PATRICK CAMPBELL
                        ✳   ✳   ✳

Bisexuality immediately doubles your chances for a date on a Saturday night.   —WOODY ALLEN

When I consider the absurd titillations of [love], the brainless motions it excites, the countenance inflamed with fury and cruelty doing its sweetest effects; the grave, solemn, entranced air in an action downright silly, the supreme moment . . . bathed, like pain, in sighing and fainting—I then believe, with Plato, that the gods made men for their sport.   —MONTAIGNE

Shame

Where there is yet shame, there may in time be virtue.
                                                —SAMUEL JOHNSON

Better be ridiculed than shamed.   —TALMUD

We are ashamed of everything that is real about us. Ashamed of ourselves, of our relations, of our incomes, of our accents, of our opinions, of our experience. The more things a man is ashamed of, the more respectable he is.   —GEORGE BERNARD SHAW

A stranger's folly creates laughter; your own folly produces shame.
                                                              —ANONYMOUS

★ George Bernard Shaw ★

This brilliant, immensely gifted, mockingly immodest Irishman was the greatest wit of our century—and its cleverest self-publicist. He wrote a dozen or more plays that will be performed in the future as they have been in the past (and in as many lands and languages)— and they will be as admired for the cleverness of their humor as they have been for the acuteness of their social observations. I cite the best known: *Pygmalion, Back to Methuselah, Caesar and Cleopatra, Candida, Mrs. Warren's Profession, Man and Superman, Major Barbara, Heartbreak House, The Doctor's Dilemma, The Devil's Disciple, Saint Joan*. But his plays all suffer from being as much debates as drama. He never could leave his soapbox, or restrain his argumentativeness.

He was a superb essayist (the prefaces to his plays are very long, far-ranging, funny, and astute). As a reviewer of plays, his self-assurance was staggering and his analysis pitiless.

He was a commanding figure: tall, thin, very pale, red-haired, with a carefully trimmed forked beard and carefully cultivated Mephistophelean eyebrows. He loved the satanic role. He was a fearless (and widely feared) polemicist: blasphemous, knavish, and incorrigible. And he loved to pour out paradoxes, parodies, and devastating opinions.

He pilloried the English, the Irish, the class system, the church, morality, royalty, generals, ministers and prime ministers, politicos, rich men, poor men—everyone, in short, he despised; and often it seemed as if he admired no one at all, except himself. He poured scathing contempt or scorn on everyone else—and hectored their most sacred values.

What protected him, and made his lectures, essays, and plays so tremendously popular, was the man's sparkling wit, shameless egotism, hilarious lampoons, and sheer, whopping *chutzpa*.

He did not marry until quite late, always poked fun at marriage ("Virtue is the trade unionism of the married"), and boasted endlessly and outrageously: "The fickleness of the women I love is only equaled by the infernal constancy of the women who love me." He carried on lush, romantic correspondence with several actresses, but proposed not even an affair with any. He was afraid of sex, I think—or a fussy, old-maidish prude. (But the letters were published, and made priceless publicity.)

A well-known actress/dancer (possibly Isadora Duncan) wrote to him to suggest they have an "engenic" child together, out of wedlock: "Can you imagine a child with my body and your brains?!"

Shaw promptly replied: "But suppose the unfortunate child has my body and your brains?"

The often penetrating, often reckless bent of his intelligence is best illustrated by a sampling of his half-satirical, half-earnest shafts of deadly, serious/satirical witticisms:

★

Dancing is a perpendicular expression of a horizontal desire.

★

It is dangerous to be sincere unless you are also stupid.

★

He who can, does; he who cannot, teaches.

★

Marriage is popular because it combines the maximum of temptation with the maximum of opportunity.

★

Never strike a child in cold blood—it neither can nor should be forgiven.

★

You see things; and say "Why?" But I dream things that never were; and I say "Why not?" [This was appropriated, without credit, by Robert F. Kennedy.]

★

My way of joking is to tell the truth. It is the funniest thing in the world.

★

The most sincere love of all is the love of food.

★

An exchange in *Man and Superman:*
"I am a brigand: I live by robbing the rich."
"I am a gentleman: I live by robbing the poor."

★

And in that last exchange lies Shaw's fatal error: He wrote about politics and economics with exuberant gusto; yet (as he says of a character in one of his plays) "He knows nothing, but thinks he knows everything."

For the sad fact is that this highly intelligent, articulate, emancipated intelligence was a confirmed and naive Marxist, an indefatigable pamphleteer who flayed right and left in the vulnerable cause of leftism—or liberalism or labor or revolution. His *The Intelligent Woman's Guide to Socialism* is a reckless and quite superficial work; I do not think it would pass a course in elementary economics. It rests on every cliché a propagandist can muster in the service of an extremely complex, difficult subject—about which, only in very recent times (except for George Orwell), have we learned the awful, dreadful, hateful truth. In the final analysis, G.B.S. was fooled by Marxist illusions and socialist naïveté. He was hoodwinked by decent men spouting economic nonsense and awful errors. Shaw, the supreme skeptic, was the victim of noble, starry-eyed misconceptions.

In this area, compare him to the hardheaded, thoroughly knowledgeable, sloganproof H. L. Mencken. Both men were journalists, not professors; wits, not analysts; lusty critics of the social order—its obvious imperfections, inequities, and injustices. But Shaw grasped at lofty, juvenile, chimerical panaceas—and they turned out to be fatal. Mencken remained hardheaded, realistic—and, as history proved, right.

Shaw's political radicalism has already been forgotten—brushed under the rug, so to speak; but his humor and superlative wit continue to roll down the many aisles in which his argumentative plays are performed. He remains a conjurer of epigrams that tantalize the mind and tickle the ribs.

I have never been able to decide whether Shaw was pulling all our legs when he wrote in the *Saturday Review*, in 1896, in his review of some play by Shakespeare:

There is no eminent writer, not even Walter Scott, whom I can despise so entirely as I despise Shakespeare—when I measure my mind against his. . . . It would be a relief to me to dig him up and throw stones at him. . . .

In his later years, Mr. Shaw expatiated again and again on exactly how much he was superior to Shakespeare—as a playwright, a psychologist, a writer of dialogue, a contriver of plot, a humorist, a dramatist, and so on.

Make of that what you will. *I* think that in his heart he believed that, and deliberately published his startling views, half disguising yet expressing them—to, as it were, test the waters of public approbation.

I wonder whether in all of literature there is so audacious, perverse, wrongheaded, and ludicrous a revelation of vanity, or tomfoolery, or a touch of paranoia—and genius.

Shlemiel

Shlemiel is often found in English writings during recent decades. It is a priceless word, embracing a mélange of simpletons, luckless souls, misfits, patsies, pip-squeaks, suckers, born losers, Milquetoasts, et al. I know no better way to pinpoint the characterization than by a few recent definitions.

Please note that *shlemiels* are usually regarded with pity, not scorn, for they cannot be blamed for the infirmities of their judgment, the folly of their choices, or the naïveté that governs their hapless course through life.

A *shlemiel* falls on his back and breaks his nose. —YIDDISH SAYING

A *shlemiel* takes a bath and forgets to wash his face.
—YIDDISH SAYING

If it rained soup, a *shlemiel* would have only a fork.
—YIDDISH SAYING

A *shlemiel* rushes to throw a drowning man a rope—both ends.
—YIDDISH SAYING

A shlemiel has accidents that start out to happen to someone else.

—YIDDISH SAYING

* * *

A *shlemiel* doesn't know how to find a notch in a saw.

—YIDDISH SAYING

A *shlemiel* wonders if a flea has a navel.

—JEWISH SAYING

Signs

Sign in Israeli barracks:
PRIVATES WILL REFRAIN FROM GIVING ADVICE TO OFFICERS

A cashier's desk:
THERE IS NO SUCH THING AS PETTY CASH

In restaurant window:
EAT HERE AND YOU'LL NEVER EAT ANYPLACE ELSE AGAIN

On back of ten-wheel truck:
WATCH MY REAR—NOT HERS

Sign in Rome:
SPECIALIST IN WOMEN AND OTHER DISEASES

In students' dormitory in Sweden:
ITALIANS ARE NOT ALLOWED TO SING AFTER MIDNIGHT. GERMANS
ARE NOT PERMITTED TO GET UP BEFORE 5:00 A.M.

Sign on newlyweds' car:
FROM HERE TO MATERNITY

Sign in Tokyo (in English):
> COMING SOON
> HOTEL AND OFFICES
> BIGGEST ERECTION IN TOKYO!

Sign on car bumper:
> BAN BUMPER STICKERS

First prize:
> Sign pinned to dress of pregnant woman at masquerade ball:
> I SHOULD HAVE DANCED ALL NIGHT

In dress shop:
> SPORTY SUNDRESSES FOR CONVERTIBLES. GREAT WITH TOPS DOWN

At Arizona roadside:
> IF YOU DRIVE LIKE HELL, YOU'RE SURE TO GET THERE

Sign on hotel elevator door in Bucharest:
> LIFT IS BEING FIXED. UNTIL THEN, WE REGRET YOU ARE UNBEARABLE

Sign in elevator in Belgrade hotel:
> TO MOVE THE CABIN, PUSH BUTTON OF WISHING FLOOR. IF INTO THE CABIN SHOULD ENTER MORE PERSONS, EACH ONE SHOULD PRESS NUMBER OF WISHING FLOOR. DRIVING IS THEN GOING ALPHABETICALLY BY NATURAL ORDER.
> (Thanks to Donald Carroll)

Sign on lingerie shop:
> GAY NIGHTIES

Sign in Dade County realtor window:
> GET LOTS WHILE YOUNG

Sign on door to hospital ward
> VISITORS
> HUSBANDS, ONLY ONE PER BED

Sign chalked on post-no-bills wall:
> DOWN WITH GRAFFITI!

Sign over dormitory bathtub:
DON'T FORGET YOUR RING!

In Kowloon tailor shop:
CUSTOMERS GIVING ORDERS
WILL BE SWIFTLY EXECUTED

Sign in girdle department of western store:
UNLIKE THE GOVERNMENT, WE GIVE AID TO OVERDEVELOPED AREAS

Sign on chicken incubator:
CHEEPERS BY THE DOZEN

Sign over bed in friends' guest room:
BE IT EVER SO HUMBLE
THERE'S NO PLACE LIKE HOME

Sign on mathematics professor's house:
AFTER MATH

On menu:
TODAY'S SPECIAL
Barely soup

Sign on housepainter's truck:
LOVE THY NEIGHBOR—PAINT THY HOUSE

Sign in lingerie-shop window:
WE FIX FLATS

Sign over entrance to morgue:
REMAINS TO BE SEEN

Sign in pharmacy window:
ON EVERY PRESCRIPTION, WE DISPENSE WITH CARE

On newly seeded lawn:
DON'T RUIN THE GAY YOUNG BLADES

Sign in a hotel elevator in Madrid:
BUTTON RETAINING PRESSED POSITION SHOWS RECEIVED COMMAND FOR VISITING STATION.

Dance Hall marquee:

> GOOD CLEAN DANCING
> EVERY NIGHT
> EXCEPT SUNDAY

Sign outside church:

THIS IS A C H - - C H (What is missing?)

On door of photography store, after a fire:

GOOD NIGHT, SWEET PRINTS

Traffic sign in eastern village:

SLOW, NO HOSPITAL

Sign in go-go bar:

4 GORGEOUS DANCE GIRLS
3 COSTUMES

Sign in antiques shop:

IF YOU DON'T KNOW WHAT YOU WANT, WE HAVE IT

In old phonograph-record store:

THE CHANTS OF A LIFETIME

At school crossing:

GIVE OUR KIDS A BRAKE!

At bottom of steep incline in Colorado:

RESUME BREATHING

On city bus:

TAKE TWICE A DAY—TO RELIEVE CONGESTION

Sign in undertaker's parlor:

EVENTUALLY YOURS

Road sign:

DRIVE CAREFULLY. DON'T INSIST ON YOUR RITES.

At reducing salon:

WHY NOT BE THE MASTER OF YOUR FAT?

On awning manufacturer's factory:
JUST A SHADE BETTER

On Sunnyvale Sanitarium:
NOBODY LEAVES HERE MAD

Over author's study:
WRITER'S CRAMP

On doctor's house:
BEDSIDE MANOR

On retired admiral's house:
ALL ABODE

Sign in Austrian hotel:
IN CASE OF FIRE
PLEASE DO UTMOST TO
ALARM THE PORTER

Silence

I grew up among wise men and learned that nothing is better than silence. —*SAYINGS OF THE FATHERS*

Eloquent silence often is better than eloquent speech.
—ANONYMOUS

You may regret your silence once, but you will regret your words often. —ADAPTED FROM IBN GABIROL

Silence is the only good substitute for intelligence.   —ANONYMOUS

You have not converted a man because you have silenced him.
—CHRISTOPHER MORLEY

I am better able to retract what I did not say than what I did.
—IBN GABIROL

An inability to stay quiet is one of the most conspicuous failings of mankind.   —WALTER BAGEHOT

Silence: The mother of truth.   —BENJAMIN DISRAELI

*The man who does not understand your silence
will probably not understand your words.*
                                          —ELBERT HUBBARD

                         *   *   *

He knew the precise psychological moment when to say nothing.
                                          —OSCAR WILDE

To sin by silence when they should protest makes cowards of men.
                                          —ABRAHAM LINCOLN

If you keep your mouth shut you will never put your foot in it.
                                          —AUSTIN O'MALLEY

Silence is the most perfect expression of scorn.
                                          —GEORGE BERNARD SHAW

Silence is the unbearable repartee.   —G. K. CHESTERTON

That man's silence is wonderful to listen to.
                                          —THOMAS HARDY

Silence is not always golden. Sometimes it's just plain yellow.
                                          —ANONYMOUS

Men fear silence as they fear solitude, because both give them a glimpse of the terror of life's nothingness.   —ANDRÉ MAUROIS

There is something fascinating about silence. One gets such wholesale returns of conjecture out of such a trifling investment of fact.

—MARK TWAIN

It ain't a bad plan to keep still occasionally even when you know what you're talking about.   —FRANK McKINNEY ("KIN") HUBBARD

Words can sting like anything,
But silence breaks the heart.   —PHYLLIS McGINLEY

Sin

It is much easier to repent of sins that we have committed than to repent of those we intend to commit.

—JOSH BILLINGS

A Litvak is so clever that he repents *before* he sins.

—JEWISH SAYING

The only time a son should disobey his father is when [if] the father orders him to commit a sin.   —TALMUD

If you're going to do something wrong, at least enjoy it.

—YIDDISH SAYING

A little sin is big when a big man commits it.
—ABRAHAM IBN EZRA

*   *   *

Sin is sweet in the beginning but bitter in the end.   —TALMUD

If not for fear, sinning would be sweet.   —JEWISH SAYING

Sins repeated seem permitted.   —ANONYMOUS

Men are not punished for their sins, but by them.
—FRANK McKINNEY ("KIN") HUBBARD

Hate the sin and love the sinner. —MOHANDAS K. GANDHI

If Jupiter hurled his thunderbolt as often as men sinned, he would soon be out of thunderbolts. —OVID

Only the sinner has a right to preach.
—CHRISTOPHER MORLEY

* * *

The Anglo-Saxon conscience does not prevent the Anglo-Saxon from sinning; it merely prevents him from enjoying his sin.
—SALVADOR DE MADARIAGA

To speak of unforgivable sin is to impugn divine power.
—THOMAS AQUINAS

Sin is geographical.
—BERTRAND RUSSELL

* * *

Faith heightens guilt, it does not prevent sin. —CARDINAL NEWMAN

Skeptics

Nothing fortifies skepticism more than that there are some who are not skeptics. —BLAISE PASCAL

If a man really has strong faith, he can indulge in the luxury of skepticism. —FRIEDRICH WILHELM NIETZSCHE

Few men speak humbly of humility, chastely of chastity, skeptically of skepticism.	—Pascal

Skill

All things require skill except an appetite.	—George Herbert

Slander

Slander: To lie, or tell the truth, about someone.	—Ambrose Bierce

Even if all of a slander is not believed, half of it is.	—Midrash

Scandal is gossip made tedious by morality.	—Oscar Wilde

Slander is worse than weapons, for weapons hurt from near, slander from afar.	—Talmud

Your ears belong to yourself; your tongue is heard by others.	—Folk saying

Slavery

Whenever I hear anyone arguing for slavery, I feel a strong impulse to see it tried on him personally.

—Abraham Lincoln

*   *   *

It is dangerous to free people who prefer to be slaves.

　　　　　　　　　　　　　　—MACHIAVELLI

Slavery is an institution for converting men into monkeys.

　　　　　　　　　　　　—RALPH WALDO EMERSON

If slavery is not wrong, nothing is wrong.　　—ABRAHAM LINCOLN

A slave should never be addressed as "slave," for the very name is contemptible.　　　　　　　　　　　　　　—TALMUD

Those who set out nobly to be their brother's keeper sometimes end up by becoming his jailer. Every emancipation has in it the seeds of a new slavery, and every truth easily becomes a lie.　—I. F. STONE

Socialism

Socialism is like a dream. Sooner or later you wake up to reality.

　　　　　　　　　　　　—WINSTON CHURCHILL

To the ordinary workingman . . . socialism does not mean much more than better wages and shorter hours and nobody bossing you about.

　　　　　　　　　　　　—GEORGE ORWELL

Those who promised us paradise on earth never produced anything but a Hell.　　　　　　　　　　　　—KARL POPPER

"Liberal socialism" . . . is purely theoretical; practical socialism is totalitarian everywhere.　　　　　　　　—F. A. HAYEK

If the workers and peasants do not wish to accept socialism, our reply will be: Why waste words when we can apply force?　—V. I. LENIN

> The inherent vice of capitalism is the unequal sharing of bless-
> ings; the inherent virtue of socialism is the equal sharing of
> miseries.   —WINSTON CHURCHILL
>
> Socialists think profits are a vice; I consider losses the real vice.
>   —WINSTON CHURCHILL

Socialism is a vast machine for churning out piles of goods marked
"Take it or leave it."   —ARTHUR SELDON

From each according to his abilities, to each according to his needs.
                       —KARL MARX (BUT LOUIS BLANC BEFORE HIM)

*Authoritarian socialism has failed almost ev-
erywhere, but you will not find a single Marxist
who will say it has failed because it was wrong
or impractical. He will say it has failed because nobody went far enough with it.*
                              —JEAN-FRANÇOIS REVEL

                     *   *   *

The true socialist is happiest when organizing, controlling, marshaling
people who have been relieved of their liberties—for their own good,
of course. . . . The socialist is essentially a sergeant-major with, of
course, a heart of gold.   —ARTHUR SELDON

Socialism is simply the degenerate capitalism of bankrupt capitalists.
Its one genuine object is to get more money for its professors.
                                               —H. L. MENCKEN

Trade unionism is killing socialism in this country [Britain], and it is
time socialists did something about it.   —PAUL JOHNSON

Sociology

*Society cannot exist unless a controlling power
upon will and appetite be placed somewhere;
and the less of it there is within, the more of it
there must be without. It is ordained in the external constitution of things that men of intem-
perate minds cannot be free. Their passions
forge their fetters.*

—EDMUND BURKE

*   *   *

Mankind are greater gainers by suffering each other to live as seems
good to themselves, than by compelling each to live as seems good to
the rest.   —JOHN STUART MILL

Jargon is the opiate of the sociologists.   —LEO ROSTEN

Sociology is the science with the greatest number of methods and the
least results.   —RAYMOND POINCARÉ

Students of social science must fear popular approval.
                                              —ALFRED MARSHALL

*The most urgent task of the social sciences
ought to be studies concerning the unintended
consequences of intended human action.*

—KARL POPPER

*   *   *

People are always sincere. They change sincerities, that's all.
                                              —TRISTAN BERNARD

Soul

Man's "soul"? Where is it located?   —SIGMUND FREUD

I've never met a really healthy person who worried much about his health, or a really good person who worried much about his soul.
                                        —J.B.S. HALDANE

The soul! That unhappy word has been the refuge of empty minds ever since the world began.   —NORMAN DOUGLAS

The immortal soul can have a spiritual birth and spiritual maturity; bodily age is no prejudice to its life. It can attain a perfect age when the body is young, and be born again when the body is old.
                                        —THOMAS AQUINAS

The soul of man is infinite in what it covets.   —BEN JONSON

I wish there was windows to my soul, so that you could see some of my feelings.   —ARTEMUS WARD

O Lord, if there is a Lord, save my soul, if I have a soul.
                                        —JOSEPH ERNEST RENAN

Catholic teaching has a twofold basis; it rests, on the one hand, upon the asceticism which we already find in St. Paul, on the other, upon the view that it is good to bring into the world as many souls as possible, since every soul is capable of salvation. For some reason which I do not understand, the fact that souls are equally capable of damnation is not taken into account, and yet it seems quite as relevant.   —BERTRAND RUSSELL

Flowers are the sweetest things that God ever made and forgot to put a soul into.   —HENRY WARD BEECHER

No medicines heal sick souls.   —ANONYMOUS

The soul is the Lord's candle.   —OLD TESTAMENT

When a soul is sent down from Heaven, it contains both male and female elements; the male part enters the male child, the female enters the female; and if they are worthy, God reunites them in marriage.   —ZOHAR

Sour Notes

I can forgive Alfred Nobel for having invented dynamite, but only a fiend in human form could have invented the Nobel Prize.
                          —GEORGE BERNARD SHAW

The chief obstacle to the progress of the human race is the human race.   —DON MARQUIS

Nothing is more annoying than to be obscurely hanged.

                          —VOLTAIRE

          *   *   *

The Holy Roman Empire was neither holy, Roman, nor an empire.
                          —VOLTAIRE

If I were running the world I would have it rain only between 2 and 5 A.M.—anyone who was out then ought to get wet.
                          —WILLIAM LYON PHELPS

Something unpleasant is coming when men are anxious to tell the truth.   —BENJAMIN DISRAELI

A conference is a gathering of important people who singly can do nothing, but together can decide that nothing can be done.
—FRED ALLEN

Meetings are indispensable when you don't want to do anything.
—JOHN KENNETH GALBRAITH

Oxford University: A sanctuary in which exploded systems and obsolete prejudices find shelter and protection after they have been hunted out of every corner of the world.   —ADAM SMITH

There are many who dare not kill themselves for fear of what the neighbors will say.   —CYRIL CONNOLLY

From the poetry of Lord Byron they drew a system of ethics . . . a system in which the two greatest commandments were to hate your neighbor and to love your neighbor's wife.
—THOMAS BABINGTON MACAULAY

*   *   *

If it's good, they'll stop making it.   —HERBERT BLOCK

He who laughs has not yet heard the bad news.
—BERTOLD BRECHT

I have a simple philosophy: Fill what's empty. Empty what's full. Scratch where it itches.   —ALICE ROOSEVELT LONGWORTH

Acquaintance: A person whom we know well enough to borrow from, but not well enough to lend to.   —AMBROSE BIERCE

One of the first things schoolchildren in Texas learn is how to compose a simple declarative sentence without the word "shit" in it.
                                        —ANONYMOUS

* * *

Love me a little less, but longer.   —FOLK SAYING

So many hymns—and so few noodles.   —JEWISH SAYING

The only thing you get free in this life is garbage.   —ANONYMOUS

It is difficult to see why lace should be so expensive; it is mostly holes.
                                        —MARY WILSON LITTLE

I'm convinced there's a small room in the attic for the Foreign Office where future diplomats are taught to stammer.   —PETER USTINOV

A fishing rod is a stick with a hook at one end and a fool at the other.
                                        —SAMUEL JOHNSON

Paying alimony is like feeding hay to a dead horse.
                                        —GROUCHO MARX

* * *

With soap, baptism is a good thing.   —ROBERT GREEN INGERSOLL

As a nation we are dedicated to keeping physically fit—and parking as close to the stadium as possible.
                                        —BILL VAUGHAN

* * *

"Every man has his price." This is not true. But for every man there exists a bait that he cannot resist swallowing. To win over certain people to something, it is only necessary to give it a gloss of love of humanity, nobility, gentleness, self-sacrifice—and there is nothing you cannot get them to swallow. To their souls, these are the icing, the tidbit; the other kinds of soul have others.

—FRIEDRICH WILHELM NIETZSCHE

Spoonerisms

I remember your name perfectly, but I just can't think of your face.
—REVEREND WILLIAM ARCHIBALD SPOONER, SOMETIMES ATTRIBUTED TO ALEXANDER WOOLLCOTT AND FOLLOWED BY "AND PLEASE DON'T TELL ME."

* * *

"Good evening, ladies and gentlemen of the audio radiance."

She conks to stupor.

Roonlight & Moses.

Your cook is goosed.

Time wounds all heels.

It is kisstomery to cuss the bride now.

Usher: "May I sew you to your sheet?"

Churchgoer: "Excuse me, ma'am, but is that pie occupewed?"

"And now—the president of the United States, Hoobert Heever."

"You have been listening to a message by our honorable minister of wealth and hellfire."

"It is a privilege to present to you now the distinguished virgin of Governor's Island."

Radio M.C., introducing Walter Pidgeon: "Mr. Privilege, this is indeed a pigeon."

"Why not drop in on your nearest A and Poo Feed Store?"

"This news roundup has come to you through the wild-word facilities of Appociated Sess."

Texan: "That blowhard? He's the biggest lamp dyer in Texas!"

Singer in London: "I have dedicated the next song to our queer old dean."

"We take you now to Rome, where we will hear the Christmas greeting from His Holiness, Pipe Poess the Fifth."

Sports

Trying to sneak a pitch past him is like trying to sneak the sunrise past a rooster. —FRED ALLEN

Professional football is getting very rough. You have to wear shoulder pads, a face mask, and a hard helmet—and that's just to sit in the stands. —ANONYMOUS

Fishing is a delusion entirely surrounded by liars in old clothes. —DON MARQUIS

My father gave me a bat for Christmas. The first time I tried to play with it, it flew away. —RODNEY DANGERFIELD

Sports is the toy department of human life.
—HOWARD COSELL

*   *   *

If I had my way, any man guilty of golf would be ineligible for any office of trust in the United States. —H. L. MENCKEN

That team was so bad . . . if anyone on that team got a hit, he used to stop at first base and ask for directions. —ANONYMOUS

Sports do not build character. They reveal it.
—HEYWOOD HALE BROUN

We had such lousy hitters on our team that a foul ball was considered a rally. —ANONYMOUS

Statistics

The death rate is the same everywhere—100 percent—if you wait long enough. —LEO ROSTEN

When you are told something is an "average" you still don't know very much about it unless you can find out which kind of average it is: mean, median, or mode. —DARRELL HUFF

Figures won't lie, but liars will figure. —ANONYMOUS

Nothing is so fallacious as facts, except figures.
—GEORGE CANNING

There are three kinds of lies: lies, damned lies, and statistics.
—BENJAMIN DISRAELI/MARK TWAIN

How do you get a random sample? If you go into the streets, you bias your sample against stay-at-homes. Go from door to door—and you miss most of the employed people. Switch to evening interviews—and you neglect moviegoers and night-clubbers. The operation of a poll comes down to a battle against "bias"—and that battle is never won.

—ADAPTED FROM DARRELL HUFF,
HOW TO LIE WITH STATISTICS

If you want to know what people read, it's no use asking them. You can learn more by going to their houses and saying you want to buy old magazines.

—DARRELL HUFF

He uses statistics as a drunken man uses lampposts—for support rather than for illumination.

—ANDREW LANG

What people tell pollsters about brushing their teeth only reveals what people *say* about brushing their teeth.

—DARRELL HUFF

If there is a 50 percent chance of success, that means a 75 percent chance of failure.

—ANONYMOUS

Statisticians are men who know that if you put a man's head in a sauna and his feet in a deep freeze, he will feel pretty good—on the average.

—ANONYMOUS

＊　　＊　　＊

Statistics are mendacious truths.

—LIONEL STRACHEY

Smoking is one of the leading causes of statistics.

—FLETCHER KNEBEL

Statistically, a horrible hand (in poker or gin rummy or bridge) is exactly as rare and remarkable as a perfect hand.

—LEO ROSTEN (AFTER WARREN WEAVER)

❂ Casey Stengel ❂

The most deft confuser of English in our time was surely Mr. Casey Stengel, legendary manager of the New York Yankees baseball club. Whether Mr. Stengel committed his coruscating faux pas intentionally, to emphasize his unique identity as Supreme Mangler of English, or whether he truly tortured our syntax—letting participles dangle, inventing metaphors unknown to the most ardent *mavens* of offbeat English, mixed singular subjects with plural verbs (or vice versa), gave equal billing to transitive and intransitive verbs, created syntactical sea monsters, or just let his tongue drift with his totally free free associations—no one seems to know for sure.

I have decided that Mr. Stengel simply spoke his mind the way he thought, enjoying every moment of it and refusing to waste the precious juicing of life on purifying diction or untangling oxymorons, or chivvying the subjunctive mood.

The best way to make my point is to quote, more or less verbatim, from one stretch of Mr. Stengel's testimony, delivered to a committee of the U.S. Senate (on antitrust and monopoly), in July 1958. The official record, like the newspaper reports, were full of proper capital letters and commas, and other proper signals of meaning; but if you had *heard* Mr. Stengel (say, on radio or TV), here is what your ears would have imbibed in a patois dubbed "Stengelese" years ago by dazed but delighted members of the press:

> *Mr. Stengel:* Well, I started in the minors with Kansas City and played as low as Class D ball, which that was at Shelbyville, in Kentucky, and also Class C ball and also Class A ball and I advanced in baseball as a ballplayer, but I had many years that I was not so successful, as playing ball is a game of skill—and then I was no doubt discharged in which I had to go back to the minors as a manager and after being in the minor leagues as a manager I became a major-league manager in several cities and was—well—discharged, which we call "discharged" because there is no question I had to leave on orders from the owners. . . .

> *Senator Kefauver:* One further question. . . . How many players do the Yankees control, Mr. Stengel?

> *Mr. Stengel:* I am going to go on the road as we are a traveling ball club and since you know the cost of transportation now— we travel sometimes with three Pullman coaches, the New

York Yankees, and remember I am just a salaried man and do not own stock in the company. I found out that in traveling with the team on the road and all, that it is the best, and we have broken records in Washington this year, we have broken them in every city but New York and we have lost two clubs that have gone out of the city of New York. Of course we have had some bad weather, I would say that they are mad at us in Chicago, we fill the parks. They have come out to see good material. I will say they are mad at us in Kansas City, because we broke their attendance record.

Now on the road we only make possibly twenty-seven cents a ticket, all expenses counted. But I am not positive of these figures, as I am not an official.

If you go back fifteen years—or if I owned stock in the club—I would give them to you.

Senator Kefauver: Mr. Stengel, I am not sure that I made my question clear. [Laughter.]

Mr. Stengel: Well that is all right, I'm not sure I am going to answer yours poifictly either. [Laughter.]

Senator Kefauver: I was asking you, sir, why baseball's owners want this bill passed.

Mr. Stengel: I would say: I would not know. But I would say the reason why they would want it passed is to keep baseball going as the highest-paid ball sport that has gone into baseball and from the baseball angle, I am not going to speak of any other sport.

I am not in here to argue about other sports, I am in the baseball business. It has been run cleaner than any baseball business that was ever put out in the past hundred years at the present time. . . .

Senator Kefauver: One further question, and then I will pass to the other senators. How many players do the Yankees control, Mr. Stengel?

Mr. Stengel: Well, I will tell you: I hire the players and if they make good with me I keep them without there being any criticism from my ownership. I do not know how many players they own as I am not a scout so I cannot run a ball club during the daytime and be busy at night and up the next day and find out how many players that the Yankees own.

After the grammatical dust settled, the next witness, Mickey Mantle, a most stellar star for Mr. Stengel, was asked a question by Senator Kefauver, who had apparently learned nothing from his demented confrontation with Mr. Stengel: "How," asked the senator, "would you answer the question I asked Mr. Stengel—which I now repeat to you—about the owners. . . ."

Clean-cut, All-American Mickey Mantle promptly said, "I agree with every word Casey gave you."

I can best summarize my own interior speculations about Mr. Stengel's anarchic use of English by reminding you that once, in a press conference before a decisive World Series game, Stengel was asked by a horde of reporters if he would quit baseball if his Yankees lost the Series to the Pittsburgh Pirates.

Casey wrinkled his leathery brow and answered, "Well, I have given that thought a lot of thinking lately, too, and last night, well— I finally made up my mind!"

"Which way?"

Casey doffed his hat formally. "I made up my mind both ways," said Casey.

That ought to lay to rest any doubts you may have clung to up to this very moment about Casey Stengel and H. W. Fowler.

There is one personal encounter I had with Mr. Stengel that may more vividly give you the flavor of his wholly original pattern of speech. Years ago (I was eleven) the Pittsburgh Pirates, on which Mr. Stengel then buoyantly played center field (occasionally beginning a game by lifting his cap—to set free a baby pigeon or other small bird he had concealed there, taking elaborate mock bows from the bleachers for his achievement) were in town. Casey met a group of young admirers just outside the visiting team's entrance to their dressing room in Wrigley Field.

I happened to be closest to my hero. In answer to a question from some other True Believer, Casey ad-libbed, in one swift, long, uninterrupted speech, "Well, that's an interesting question because no matter which way you look at it, you get stymied or even worse, if you catch my drift. Like that skinny fellow who plays for the Cubs, there, with which team we are locking horns shortly. The fella on third they have is a whiz at robbin' you of a line drive to left, and their shortstop is from a town you never heard of, like Pokamatooso, but it was so small it like had a base on every streetcorner, which that will sharpen any resident's eyesight or footwork—it beats being brought up on sidewalks anytime—which I figger gives us the advantage in that special department, slice it any angle you try, if ya get the drift of my remarks—not that there ain't a dozen old-timers won't tell you the same thing." He reached out, rubbed my hair, winked very, very conspicuously—as if to say, "It's all a rib, son!" Or "Do you think they'll fall for that melarkey?" or even "How do you like *them* tomatoes?"—and vanished into the tunnel.

He was, by the way, a very good ballplayer, and a superb manager, as full of surprises, resourcefulness, cleverly thought-out plays, and a knowledge of baseball that was nothing short of cosmic. No one ever beat Ole Case in the think tank, that's for sure. Yogi Berra learned about catching—and all about the intricacies of language, too—from his manager, Casey Stengel.

Student Rebellion

The people who parade and holler "All power to the people" want all power to be handed over to the people who holler "All power to the people."
                                                            —LEO ROSTEN

Student rebellions are "psychodramas masquerading as revolution."
                                                            —DAVID L. GUTMAN

The chiefs of this youth movement were mentally unbalanced neurotics. Many of them were affected by a morbid sexuality; they were either profligate or homosexual. . . . Their names are long since forgotten; the only trace they left were some books and poems preaching sexual perversity. . . .
                                            —LUDWIG VON MISES [GERMANY, PRE-WWI]

I cannot be impartial as between the fire brigade and the fire.
                                                            —WINSTON CHURCHILL

Must each generation learn for itself that virtue does not solve equations? That ideology is blind? That when altruists turn militant they become tyrants?
                                                            —LEO ROSTEN

The first part of the Yippie program, you know, is kill your parents.
                                                —JERRY RUBIN

The actions of some students were violent and criminal, and those of some others were dangerous, reckless, and irresponsible. The indiscriminate firing of rifles into a crowd of students and the deaths that followed were unnecessary, unwarranted, and inexcusable.
                    —THE PRESIDENT'S COMMISSION ON CAMPUS UNREST,
                                                OCTOBER 1970

Students would be much better off if they could take a stand against taking a stand.   —DAVID RIESMAN

It has always been the task of the new generation to provoke changes.
                                                —LUDWIG VON MISES

Is your faculty, by and large, any more uninspired, boring, and dull than, say, your classmates?   —LEO ROSTEN

Study

Some men study so much, they don't have time to know. —TALMUD

There is no satiety in study.   —ERASMUS

The chief thing is not to study but to do.
                                          —*SAYINGS OF THE FATHERS*

Stupidity

It is better to keep your mouth shut and appear stupid than to open it and remove all doubt.   —MARK TWAIN

Against stupidity, God Himself is helpless. —JEWISH SAYING

Genius has limitations; stupidity is boundless. —ANONYMOUS

He's a fool that makes his doctor his heir. —BENJAMIN FRANKLIN

To err is human; to remain in error is stupid. —ANONYMOUS

Man: The inventory of stupidity. —RÉMY DE GOURMONT

Rascality has limits; stupidity has not. —NAPOLEON BONAPARTE

The greatest of all sins is stupidity. —OSCAR WILDE

Success

Failure has no friends. —JOHN F. KENNEDY

Every man has a right to be conceited until he is successful.
—BENJAMIN DISRAELI

All you need in this life is ignorance and confidence, and then success
is sure. —MARK TWAIN

Success is getting what you want, and happiness is wanting what you
get. —DAVE GARDNER

The secret of success is this: There is no secret of success.
—ELBERT HUBBARD

It is twice as newsworthy that a charlatan can become a success. His
charlatanry makes him even more of a personality.
—DANIEL J. BOORSTIN

It is not enough to succeed; others must fail.   —GORE VIDAL

The common idea that success spoils people by making them vain, egotistic, and self-complacent is erroneous; on the contrary, it makes them, for the most part, humble, tolerant, and kind. Failure makes people cruel and bitter.

—W. SOMERSET MAUGHAM

* * *

The toughest thing about success is that you've got to keep on being a success.   —IRVING BERLIN

Moderation is a fatal thing. Nothing succeeds like excess.

—OSCAR WILDE

* * *

There's always something about your success that displeases even your best friends.   —MARK TWAIN

The door to success has two signs: PUSH and PULL.

—YIDDISH SAYING

It takes twenty years to make an overnight success.

—ATTRIBUTED TO EDDIE CANTOR

Success is only a matter of luck. Ask any failure.   —ANONYMOUS

Suffering

We can understand neither the suffering of the good nor the prosperity of the wicked.

—ADAPTED FROM *SAYINGS OF THE FATHERS*

There is no more miserable being than one in whom nothing is habitual but indecision. —WILLIAM JAMES

One day's happiness makes us forget suffering, and one day's suffering makes us forget all our past happiness.

—OLD TESTAMENT, ADAPTED

Hold no man responsible for what he says in his grief. —TALMUD

Not to have felt pain is not to have been human. —JEWISH SAYING

Suicide

No man is educated who never dallied with the thought of suicide.

—WILLIAM JAMES

Superstition

Men . . , enriched by your sweat and misery . . . make you superstitious, not that you might fear God but that you might fear them.

—VOLTAIRE

In the mind of the masses superstition is no less deeply rooted than fear. . . . —BARUCH SPINOZA

The superstition of science scoffs at the superstition of faith.

—JAMES A. FROUDE

New truths begin as heresies and end as superstitions.

—THOMAS H. HUXLEY

Superstition is rooted in a much deeper and more sensitive layer of the psyche than skepticism.   —GOETHE

Sympathy

If you can't help out with a little money, at least give a sympathetic groan.   —YIDDISH SAYING

I have no need of your goddamned sympathy. I only wish to be entertained by some of your grosser reminiscences.

—ALEXANDER WOOLLCOTT

Sympathy doesn't provide food, but it makes hunger more endurable.

—ANONYMOUS

People in distress never think that you feel enough.

—SAMUEL JOHNSON

Talk

The reason that talk is as cheap as it is is that supply greatly exceeds demand. —ANONYMOUS

If you talk too much, you'll say what you didn't intend to.
—ADAPTED FROM OLD TESTAMENT

No one is exempt from talking nonsense; the misfortune is to do it solemnly. —MONTAIGNE

The opposite of talking isn't listening. The opposite of talking is waiting. —FRAN LEBOWITZ

Taxation

The one thing that hurts more than paying an income tax is not having to pay an income tax. —THOMAS ROBERT DEWAR

At the beginning of the empire, the tax rates were low and the revenues were high. At the end of the empire, the tax rates were high and the revenues were low.   —Ibn Khaldun (1332–1400)

The art of taxation consists in so plucking the goose as to obtain the largest amount of feathers with the least amount of hissing.
                                                   —Jean-Baptiste Colbert

Tears

Tears are no proof of cowardice.   —Laurence Sterne

Tears are the silent language of grief.   —Voltaire

Even when the gates of Heaven are closed to prayer, they are open to tears.   —Talmud

Tears: *A copious discharge of hydrated chlorine of sodium from the eyes.*
                                   —Ambrose Bierce

＊ ＊ ＊

The stars in Heaven weep with him who weeps at night. —Talmud

We often shed tears that deceive ourselves after deceiving others.
                                   —François de la Rochefoucauld

Ink dries fast; tears do not.   —Jewish saying

What soap is for the body, tears are for the soul.
—ANONYMOUS

*   *   *

The most effective water power in the world—woman's tears.
—WILSON MIZNER

What good is a golden urn that is full of tears?   —ANONYMOUS

Telegrams

A newspaper sent this telegram to Cary Grant, on his birthday:
HOW OLD CARY GRANT?

The imperturbable star replied:
OLD CARY GRANT FINE! HOW YOU?

Television

The radio listener saw nothing; he had to use his imagination. . . .
With the high cost of living and the many problems facing him in the
modern world, all the poor man had left was his imagination. Television has taken that away from him.   —FRED ALLEN

Television is the first truly democratic culture—the first culture avail-
able to everybody and entirely governed by what the people want.
The most terrifying thing is what the people do want.
—CLIVE BARNES

TV—chewing gum for the eyes.   —FRANK LLOYD WRIGHT

Television is for appearing on—not for looking at. —NOËL COWARD

Television: A medium. So called because it is neither rare nor well done.   —ERNIE KOVACS

Television: The literature of the illiterate, the culture of the lowbrow, the wealth of the poor, the privilege of the underprivileged, the exclusive club of the excluded masses.
                    —LEE LOEVINGER (FORMER COMMISSIONER OF THE
                              FEDERAL COMMUNICATIONS COMMISSION)

Imitation is the sincerest form of television.   —FRED ALLEN

TV: A medium of entertainment which permits millions of people to listen to the same joke at the same time and yet remain lonesome.   —T. S. ELIOT

Why should people pay good money to go out and see bad films when they can stay home and see bad television for nothing?
                                                      —SAMUEL GOLDWYN

Television is a device that permits people who haven't anything to do to watch people who can't do anything.   —FRED ALLEN

Television: The device that brings into your living room characters you would never allow in your living room.
                                           —RED SKELTON/DAVID FROST

The human race is faced with a cruel choice: work or daytime television.   —ANONYMOUS

Television has proved that people will look at anything rather than at each other.   —ANN LANDERS

People will say a spot announcement does not give the audience a chance to get to know the candidate. Sometimes that is a good thing for the candidate.

—RICHARD NIXON

* * *

Television in our country . . . is, even more than movies, the American dream made visible. —IRWIN SHAW

I must say I find television very educational. The minute somebody turns it on, I go to the library and read a good book.

—GROUCHO MARX

Temptation

If the Evil Impulse says: "Sin—God will forgive you," don't heed it.

—TALMUD

The most effective defense against temptation is this: Shut your eyes.

—IBN GABIROL

There are several protections against temptation, but the surest is cowardice. —MARK TWAIN

There are terrible temptations which it requires strength and courage to yield to. —OSCAR WILDE

I can resist everything except temptation. —OSCAR WILDE

Abstainer: A weak person who yields to the temptation of denying himself a pleasure. —AMBROSE BIERCE

> Why resist temptation? There will always be more.
> —DON HEROLD
>
> There is not any memory with less satisfaction in it than the memory of some temptation we resisted.
> —JAMES BRANCH CABELL

Let us be grateful to our parents: Had they not been tempted, we would not be here. —TALMUD

Temptation laughs at the fool who takes it seriously.
—THE CHOFETZ CHAIM

In a maiden, temptation sleeps; in a wife, it's wide awake.
—ANONYMOUS

Theft

It's hard to rob a thief. —ANONYMOUS

Many a man is saved from being a thief by finding everything locked up. —EDGAR W. HOWE

What is property? Theft. —PIERRE-JOSEPH PROUDHON

Thought/Thinking

Thinking is strenuous art—few practice it; and then only at rare times. —DAVID BEN-GURION

Thought is a universe of freedom. —ANONYMOUS

Most people would die sooner than think; in fact, they do so.
—BERTRAND RUSSELL

Thinking is more precious than all five senses.
—NACHMAN OF BRATSLAV

Great men are they who see that spiritual is stronger than any material force—that thoughts rule the world.
—RALPH WALDO EMERSON

Thinking is harder work than hard work. —LEO ROSTEN

Minds are like parachutes: They only function when open.
—THOMAS ROBERT DEWAR

A great many people think they are thinking when they are merely rearranging their prejudices.

—WILLIAM JAMES

*   *   *

The school should always have as its aim that the young man leave it as a harmonious personality, not as a specialist. This in my opinion is true in a certain sense even for technical schools. . . . The development of general ability for independent thinking and judgment should always be placed foremost, not the acquisition of special knowledge.
—ALBERT EINSTEIN

There is nothing so unthinkable as thought, unless it be the absence of thought. —SAMUEL BUTLER

Control over thought is a long, painful, and laborious process. But I am convinced that no time, no labor, and no pain is too much for the glorious result to be reached. —MOHANDAS K. GANDHI

It is astonishing what an effort it seems to be for many people to put their brains definitely and systematically to work.

—THOMAS ALVA EDISON

There is no effort, to my mind . . . that is so taxing to the individual as to think, to analyze fundamentally.　　—LOUIS D. BRANDEIS

I pay attention only to what people do or say.
I never pay attention to what they think.
　　　　　—NAPOLEON BONAPARTE

*　　*　　*

Thinking is the hardest work there is, which is the probable reason why so few engage in it.　　—HENRY FORD

The working of great institutions is mainly the result of a vast mass of routine, petty malice, self-interest, carelessness, and sheer mistake. Only a residual fraction is thought.　　—GEORGE SANTAYANA

Thought is better than words, because it guides them.

—THE MEZERITZER RABBI

Tradition

Tradition does not mean that the living are dead, but that the dead are living.　　—G. K. CHESTERTON

Transgression

A silk thread begins as the weakest of things, the mucus of a worm; yet how strong it becomes when entwined many times! . . . So it is with transgressions; they grow strong with repetition.

—BAHYA IBN PAQUDA

The reason the way of the transgressor is hard is because it's so crowded.   —FRANK McKINNEY ("KIN") HUBBARD

The heart and the eyes are like spies for the body: The eye sees, the heart covets, and the body commits the transgression.   —RASHI

Troubles

Though the world is full of trouble, each man feels only his own.
                                        —ANONYMOUS

The chief cause of problems is solutions.   —ERIC SEVAREID

Little troubles are really not so bad—for someone else.
                                    —SHOLEM ALEICHEM

Troubles are drawn to wetness—to tears and to brandy.
                                        —ANONYMOUS

Bygone troubles are a pleasure to discuss.   —JEWISH SAYING

Truth/Truths

Truth is beautiful—without doubt; but so are lies.
                                —RALPH WALDO EMERSON

Truth has a halo.   —SAMUEL HA-NAGID

There is nothing more likely to drive a man mad than . . . an obstinate, constitutional preference of the true to the agreeable.
                                    —WILLIAM HAZLITT

For thirteen years, I taught my tongue not to tell a lie; and for the next thirteen, I taught it to tell the truth.

—THE KORETZER RABBI

If one tells the truth, one is sure, sooner or later, to be found out.

—OSCAR WILDE/BERNARD SHAW

Whoever undertakes to set himself up as a judge in the field of truth and knowledge is shipwrecked by the laughter of the gods.

—ALBERT EINSTEIN

Men occasionally stumble over the truth, but most of them pick themselves up and hurry off as if nothing had happened.

—WINSTON CHURCHILL

A thing is not necessarily true because badly uttered, nor false because spoken magnificently.   —ST. AUGUSTINE

If you are out to describe the truth, leave elegance to the tailor.

—ALBERT EINSTEIN

*   *   *

I care about truth not for truth's sake but for my own.

—SAMUEL BUTLER

When you add to the truth, you subtract from it.   —TALMUD

For here we are not afraid to follow truth wherever it may lead, not to tolerate error so long as reason is free to combat it.

—THOMAS JEFFERSON

Truth is for the minority.   —BALTHASAR GRACIAN

Truth is neither alive nor dead; it just aggravates itself all the time.
—MARK TWAIN

We never fully grasp the import of any true statement until we have a clear notion of what the opposite untrue statement would be.
—WILLIAM JAMES

Truth is everlasting, but our ideas of truth are not. Theology is but our ideas of truth classified and arranged.
—HENRY WARD BEECHER

If we begin with certainties, we shall end in doubts; but if we begin with doubts, and are patient in them, we shall end in certainties.
—FRANCIS BACON

One often makes a remark and only later sees how true it is.
—LUDWIG WITTGENSTEIN

No other purpose should be attached to truth than that you should know what is true.
—MAIMONIDES

What is true is what I can't help believing.
—OLIVER WENDELL HOLMES, JR.

It is the customary fate of new truths to begin as heresies and to end as superstitions.
—THOMAS H. HUXLEY

The least initial deviation from the truth is multiplied later a thousandfold.
—ARISTOTLE

Man is least himself when he talks in his own person. But give him a mask and he will tell the truth.
—OSCAR WILDE

It is a piece of idle sentimentality that truth, merely as truth, has any inherent power . . . of prevailing against the dungeon and the stake.
—JOHN STUART MILL

Truth is said to be stranger than fiction; it is to most folks.
—JOSH BILLINGS

Truth is stranger than fiction because life doesn't give a damn about being plausible.   —LEO ROSTEN

What now is proved was once only imagined.   —WILLIAM BLAKE

When you read a biography remember that the truth is never fit for publication.   —GEORGE BERNARD SHAW

Most writers regard the truth as their most valuable possession, and therefore are most economical in its use.   —MARK TWAIN

Convictions are more dangerous foes of truth than lies.
—FRIEDRICH WILHELM NIETZSCHE

When you tell the truth you don't have to remember what you said.
—MARK TWAIN

It is unfortunate, considering that enthusiasm moves the world, that so few enthusiasts can be trusted to speak the truth.
—ARTHUR BALFOUR

I am conquered by truth.   —ERASMUS

Of *course*, "Truth is stranger than fiction." Fiction is obliged to stick to possibilities. Truth isn't.   —MARK TWAIN

The pure and simple truth is rarely pure and never simple.
—OSCAR WILDE

Reality has actually very little to do with truth; there is no necessary connection between the two. Truth may be as unreal as fiction.
—EDITH HAMILTON

A truth does not become greater by repetition.   —MAIMONIDES

A half-truth is a whole lie.   —JEWISH SAYING

A thing is not necessarily true because a man dies for it.
                                        —OSCAR WILDE

The truth never dies—but it lives a wretched life. —JEWISH SAYING

Men like the opinions to which they have become accustomed . . . and this prevents them from finding truth, for they cling to the opinions of habit.   —MAIMONIDES

One can live in this world on soothsaying, but not on truthsaying.
                              —GEORG CHRISTOPH LICHTENBERG

The true use of speech is not so much to express our wants as to conceal them.   —OLIVER GOLDSMITH

Tyrants/Tyranny

There are few minds to which tyranny is not delightful.
                                      —SAMUEL JOHNSON

Dictators always look good until the last minutes.
                                      —THOMAS MASARYK

"The czars were autocratic, they were stupid, they may not have recognized human rights, but they were not totalitarian. There were many areas of human rights they stayed out of." Even under the czar, he said, a dissident could find work because there was more than one employer.   —CHRISTOPHER S. WREN

I captured some of the people who tried to assassinate me. I ate them before they ate me.   —IDI AMIN

When men have yielded without serious resistance to the tyranny of new dictators, it is because they have lacked property. They dared not resist because resistance meant destitution.

—WALTER LIPPMANN

Tyrants never perish from tyranny, but always from folly—when their fantasies have built up a palace for which the earth has no foundation.
—WALTER SAVAGE LANDOR

*   *   *

It is laudable in a prince to keep his faith and be an honest man, not a trickster. But experience shows that the princes who have done great things are the ones who have taken little account of their promises and who have known how to addle the brains of man with craft. Since men are wicked and do not keep their promise to you, you likewise do not need to keep yours to them.   —MACHIAVELLI

My parliament is the army.   —GAMAL ABDEL NASSER

Each man, too, is a tyrant in tendency, because he would impose his idea on others.   —RALPH WALDO EMERSON

Fascism is capitalism plus murder.   —UPTON SINCLAIR

All despotism, under whatever name they masquerade, are efforts to freeze history, to stop change, to solidify the human spirit.
—CHARLES BEARD

*   *   *

Severities should be dealt out all at once, that by their suddenness they may give less offense; benefits should be handed out drop by drop, that they may be relished the more.   —MACHIAVELLI

Unemployment

There are but few men who have character enough to lead a life of idleness.   —JOSH BILLINGS

A man can die if he has nothing to do.
                                    —*ABOT DE RABBI NATHAN*

The trouble with unemployment is that the minute you wake up in the morning you're on the job.   —ANONYMOUS

Unions

However immoral some of the methods used by the trade unions are felt to be, their basic aim—improving the lot of working people—is still felt to be work of almost religious significance.
                                    —PEREGRINE WORSTHORNE

With all their faults, trade unions have done more for humanity than any other organization of men that ever existed. They have done more for decency, for honesty, for education, for the betterment of the race, for the developing character of man, than any other association of men.   —CLARENCE DARROW

British trade unionism has become a formula for national misery.
—PAUL JOHNSON

Universe

Just as your hand, held before the eye, can hide the tallest mountain, so this small earthly life keeps us from seeing the vast radiance that fills the core of the universe.   —NACHMAN OF BRATSLAV

Earth: A moon of the sun.   —LEONARDO DA VINCI

This most beautiful system [the cosmos] could only proceed from the dominion of an intelligent and powerful Being.   —ISAAC NEWTON

There is . . . a certain respect and a general duty of humanity not only to beasts that have life and sense, but even to trees and plants.
—MONTAIGNE

World: But a small parenthesis in eternity.   —THOMAS BROWNE

We . . . live on an insignificant planet of a humdrum star lost in a galaxy tucked away in some forgotten corner of a universe in which there are far more galaxies than people.
—CARL SAGAN

*   *   *

For time itself is contained in the universe, and therefore when we speak about creation we should not inquire at what time it happened.
—THOMAS AQUINAS

Vanity

Never underestimate a man who overestimates himself.

—FRANKLIN D. ROOSEVELT
(ON GENERAL DOUGLAS MACARTHUR)

* * *

A man who is not a fool can rid himself of every folly but vanity.
—JEAN-JACQUES ROUSSEAU

The vanity of being known to be trusted with a secret is generally one of the chief motives to disclose it.　　—SAMUEL JOHNSON

Aristocracy has three successive ages: the age of superiorities, that of privileges, and that of vanities. Having passed out of the first, it degenerates in the second, and dies away in the third.
—CHATEAUBRIAND

493

Virtue would not go far if vanity did not keep it company.
　　　　　　—FRANÇOIS DE LA ROCHEFOUCAULD

*　　*　　*

Self-love is often rather arrogant than blind; it does not hide our faults from ourselves, but persuades us that they escape the notice of others.
　　　　　　—SAMUEL JOHNSON

Vice

Vice is such a hideous creature that the more you see of it, the better you like it.　　　　—FINLEY PETER DUNNE ("MR. DOOLEY")

Folks who have no vices have very few virtues.
　　　　　　—ABRAHAM LINCOLN

To a philosophic eye the vices of the clergy are far less dangerous than their virtues.　　　　　　—EDWARD GIBBON

When our vices leave us, we flatter ourselves that we are leaving them.　　　　—FRANÇOIS DE LA ROCHEFOUCAULD

Those who hate vice, hate mankind.
　　　　　　—PLINY THE YOUNGER

*　　*　　*

His was the sort of career that made the Recording Angel think seriously about taking up shorthand.　　　—NICOLAS BENTLEY

Violence

Violence is the last refuge of the incompetent.   —ISAAC ASIMOV

Nonviolence is the first article of my faith. It is also the last article of my creed.   —MOHANDAS K. GANDHI

The enemies of freedom do not argue, they shout and they shoot.
     —WILLIAM RALPH INGE

Virtue

Virtue is insufficient temptation.   —GEORGE BERNARD SHAW

Be good and you will be lonesome.   —MARK TWAIN

Virtue is more to be feared than vice, because its excesses are not subject to the restraints of conscience.
     —ALBERT JAY NOCK

* * *

He first revealed clearly by word and by deed that he who is virtuous is happy. Alas, not one of us can equal him.
     —ARISTOTLE (OF PLATO)

There is an imperialism in virtue that compels us to acquiesce to those who exploit it. For each of us is a slave to guilt, and acts out lifelong expiation—however disguised, however symbolic.   —LEO ROSTEN

The resistance of a woman is not always a proof of her virtue, but more frequently of her experience.   —NINON DE LENCLOS

I do not know if she was virtuous, but she was ugly, and with a woman that is half the battle.   —HEINRICH HEINE

Few men have virtue to withstand the highest bidder.
—GEORGE WASHINGTON

Virtue has never been as respectable as money.   —MARK TWAIN

Virtue craves a steep and thorny path.   —MONTAIGNE

There is no man so good, who, were he to submit all his thoughts and actions to the laws, would not deserve hanging ten times in his life.
—MONTAIGNE

On the whole, human beings want to be good, but not too good and not quite all the time.   —GEORGE ORWELL

What is virtue but the trade unionism of the married?
—GEORGE BERNARD SHAW

*   *   *

Virtue is admired—and shivers with cold.   —JUVENAL

Happiness is secured through virtue; it is a good attained by man's own will.   —THOMAS AQUINAS

It's easier to find faults in others than virtues in oneself.
—ANONYMOUS

That good deed is most meritorious of which no one knows.
—ADAPTED FROM MAIMONIDES

Nothing is more unpleasant than a virtuous person with a mean mind.
—WALTER BAGEHOT

* * *

No one knows what he is doing so long as he is acting rightly; but of what is wrong one is always conscious. —GOETHE

All fear springs from love. Ordered love is included in every virtue, disordered love in every vice. —THOMAS AQUINAS

Many an attack of depression is nothing but the expression of regret at having to be virtuous. —WILHELM STEKHEL

Voting

Voting is simply a way of determining which side is the stronger without putting it to the test of fighting. —H. L. MENCKEN

W

War/Peace

All wars are popular for the first thirty days.
—ARTHUR SCHLESINGER, JR.

*War is a series of catastrophes that result in a
victory.*
—GEORGES CLEMENCEAU

*　*　*

Military glory, that attractive rainbow that rides in showers of blood,
that serpent's eye that charms to destroy.　—ABRAHAM LINCOLN

How good bad music and bad reasons sound when we march against
an enemy.　—FRIEDRICH WILHELM NIETZSCHE

War makes rattling good history; but peace is poor reading.
—THOMAS HARDY

The gift of rhetoric has been responsible for more bloodshed on this earth than all the guns and explosives that were invented.

—Stanley Baldwin

The quickest way of ending a war is to lose it.   —George Orwell

My first wish is to see this plague of mankind—war—banished from the earth. —George Washington

War is the unfolding of miscalculations.   —Barbara Tuchman

I wouldn't tell the people anything until the war is over, and then I'd tell them who won. —Anonymous

I hate war only as a soldier who has lived it can, only as one who has seen its brutality, its futility, its stupidity.

—Dwight D. Eisenhower

The art of war is simple enough. Find out where your enemy is. Get at him as soon as you can. Strike at him as hard as you can, and keep moving on.

—Ulysses S. Grant

*   *   *

I am tired and sick of war. Its glory is all moonshine. Only those who have never fired a shot nor heard the shrieks and groans of the wounded cry aloud for blood, more vengeance, more desolation. War is Hell. —William Tecumseh Sherman

It is well that war is so terrible, or we should grow too fond of it.

—Robert E. Lee

The professional military mind is by necessity an inferior and unimaginative mind; no man of high intellectual quality would willingly imprison his gifts in such a calling. —H. G. Wells

In peace, sons bury their fathers; in war, fathers bury their sons.

—HERODOTUS

When I warned [the French] that Britain would fight on alone . . . their general told their prime minister: "In three weeks England will have her neck wrung like a chicken." Some chicken. Some neck!

—WINSTON CHURCHILL

In all of Nature, which fights for life because it loves life, there is nothing like human war.   —DONALD CULROSS PEATTIE

It is an unfortunate fact that we can only secure peace by preparing for war.   —JOHN F. KENNEDY

Is not life miserable enough, comes not death soon enough, without resort to the hideous enginery of war?

—HORACE GREELEY

The way to win an atomic war is to make certain it never starts.

—OMAR BRADLEY

Wellington is a bad general, the English are bad soldiers; we will settle the matter by lunchtime.   —NAPOLEON (JUNE 18, 1815)

In war there is no second prize for the runner-up.

—OMAR BRADLEY

We make war that we may live in peace.   —ARISTOTLE

Rules of war: The rules, solemnly observed by sovereign nations, that make it illegal to hit below the toes.   —LEO ROSTEN

War is delightful for those who have had no experience with it.

—ERASMUS

War is too important to be left to the generals.
—GEORGES CLEMENCEAU

To delight in war is a merit in the soldier, a dangerous quality in the captain, and a positive crime in the statesman.
—GEORGE SANTAYANA

Mankind must put an end to war, or war will put an end to mankind.
—JOHN F. KENNEDY

I launched the phrase [about World War I] "the war to end war"—and that was not the least of my crimes.   —H. G. WELLS

We lost sight of one of the cardinal maxims of guerrilla war: the guerrilla wins if he does not lose, the conventional army loses if it does not win.   —HENRY KISSINGER

In war there is no substitute for victory.
—DOUGLAS MACARTHUR

✳ ✳ ✳

It is possible, even probable, that hopelessness among a people can be a far more potent cause of war than greed. War—in such case—is a symptom, not a disease.   —DWIGHT D. EISENHOWER

The reward of the general is not a bigger tent, but command.
—OLIVER WENDELL HOLMES, JR.

Only when arms are sufficient beyond doubt can we be certain without doubt that they will never be employed.   —JOHN F. KENNEDY

War, which used to be cruel and magnificent, is now cruel and squalid.
—WINSTON CHURCHILL

I know I am among civilized men because they are fighting so savagely.   —VOLTAIRE

Nothing in war ever goes right except by accident.

—WINSTON CHURCHILL

A war leaves the country with three armies: an army of cripples, an army of mourners, and an army of thieves.   —GERMAN PROVERB

The War Office kept three sets of figures: one to mislead the public, one to mislead the cabinet, and one to mislead themselves.

—H. H. ASQUITH

The only alternative to coexistence is codestruction.

—JAWAHARLAL NEHRU

You can't win through negotiations what you can't win on the battlefield.   —HENRY KISSINGER

History is littered with wars which everybody knew would never happen.   —J. ENOCH POWELL

We are in the midst of a cold war.   —BERNARD BARUCH

Nothing except a battle lost can be half so melancholy as a battle won.

—DUKE OF WELLINGTON

Nothing should be left to an invaded people except their eyes for weeping.   —OTTO VON BISMARCK (À LA MACHIAVELLI)

♥ Mae West ♥

My first job as a screenwriter, in 1938(!), sent me to the studio of Major Pictures, a spin-off from Paramount. My office was in the writers' building, next to a bungalow that was rarely occupied.

One morning, Allen Rivkin, a dear friend, was in my office, shooting the breeze with his customary irreverence. Suddenly we heard a tremendous rattle of trap drums, the earsplitting crash of cymbals, and the cavernous boom-boom of a foot pedal striking a huge bass drum.

"What in the world—!" I cried.

"Calm down, kid. That's Mae West. That's how she relaxes."

I looked out of my window. Not forty feet away was the usually deserted bungalow. Miss West, I learned, was about to start shooting a picture on our lot.

That afternoon I caught a glimpse of this queen of risqué wise-cracks. (In an earlier movie she had asked a leading man, "Is that a gun in your pocket, or are you just glad to see me?") She was tiny, voluptuous, twirling a seductive parasol and, in her parody of a Gay Nineties strut by a lady of exceptionally easy virtue, was sashaying from her bungalow to a limousine, parked ahead, its door held open by a very handsome chauffeur in flamboyant livery and highly shined knee-high boots.

And trailing Miss West was a file of musclemen, three pairs of them, six in all, in marching formation. Each "courtier" was young, good-looking in a vapid way, and most conspicuous for the muscles *bulging* beneath his coatsleeves. An entourage of studs (as everyone said they were) always preceded or followed Miss West whenever she appeared in public. Her twitting of moral decorum was unmatched among the stars of stage or screen.

The "campy" march in and out of the bungalow continued for all the weeks Miss West was shooting. Occasionally, if I ran into the sexy procession, I would exchange a pleasant "Good morning" or "Hi, Miss West" with the lady. Occasionally I overheard a snatch of naughty conversation between the blond bombshell and her platoon of "escorts."

I persuaded the director of the film to let me visit the set, to linger in the background, and watch her tease the camera, her leading man or men, the army of grips, gofers, cameramen, lighting technicians, et al. who ply their trade behind or around every camera in Hollywood.

Her breezy manner, her caustic cracks, her sheer verbal licentiousness all added up, in my mind, to a rebellious, taunting, never speechless woman.

"Do you think she is simply amoral?" a friend once asked me.

"Oh, yes," I replied. "But she is also simply immoral."

That remark would not have offended her.

Her bawdy, "Come up 'n' see me sometime" salutation, and her raunchy wisecracks, appeared in her Broadway plays and burlesque and Hollywood dialogue. She caricatured the courtesan—and with gusto. She was the archetype of the savvy gold digger: wanton and shamelessly cynical. She affected *enormous* feathered hats and fans, a juicily padded hourglass figure, a devastatingly invitational leer, a Gay Nineties walk that was a sexy sashay without peer, and a manner that mocked her role. She was the quintessence of narcissism redeemed by a wicked sense of parody.

Miss West was given to tossing off sardonic wisecracks:

♥

I like only two kinds of men: domestic and imported.

♥

She may be good for nothing, but she's not bad for nothing.

♥

I always say, keep a diary—and someday it will keep you.

♥

He who hesitates is a damn fool.

♥

Don't fight over me, boys, there's plenty to go around.

♥

Peel me a grape, Beulah.

♥

To err is human, but it feels divine.

♥

When I'm good, I'm very, very good, but when I'm bad, I'm better.

♥

He's the kind of man a woman would have to marry to get rid of.

♥

You're never too old to get younger.

♥

Her wisecracks, many of which she invented (or freely embroidered from the texts of those who wrote her plays and movies), can hardly be omitted from this unorthodox chrestomathy.

♥

Wisdom

Who is wise? He that learns from everyone.
Who is powerful? He that governs his passions.
Who is rich? He that is content.
Who is that? Nobody. —BENJAMIN FRANKLIN

*The farther he went West, the more convinced
he felt that the wise men came from the East.*
—SYDNEY SMITH

* * *

They told me that the fish . . . were cold-blooded and felt no pain. But
they were not fish who told me. —HEYWOOD BROUN

Wisdom comes by disillusionment. —GEORGE SANTAYANA

When a wise man is angry, he is no longer wise. —TALMUD

The wise only possess ideas; the greater part of mankind are possessed by them. —SAMUEL TAYLOR COLERIDGE

The height of wisdom is to take things as they are . . . to endure what
we cannot evade. [We must learn] how to rule our behavior and understanding, how to live and die well. —MONTAIGNE

The wise man hears one word—and understands two.
—JEWISH SAYING

The beginning of wisdom is to desire it. —IBN GABIROL

Wisdom is God's raiment. —THE MEZERITZER RABBI

A wise man's question contains half the answer.
—JEWISH PROVERB

Without wisdom there is no piety; without piety there is no wisdom.
                    —*Sayings of the Fathers*

A man should have no purpose in learning except this: to learn wisdom
itself.   —Maimonides

> *I am in constant fear lest I may become too*
> *wise to remain pious.*
>   —the Koretser rabbi

                    *   *   *

Without experience there is little wisdom.   —Apocrypha

Wisdom is a hoard from which nothing is lost.   —Ibn Gabirol

What is wisdom but the capacity to confront intolerable ideas with
equanimity?   —Leo Rosten

There is this difference between happiness and wisdom: He that
thinks himself the happiest man, really is so; but he that thinks himself
the wisest is generally the greatest fool.   —C. C. Colton

> *A wise man lowers a ladder before he jumps*
> *into a pit.*
>   —Folk saying

                    *   *   *

More than any other time in history, mankind faces a crossroads. One
path leads to despair and utter hopelessness. The other, to total extinction. Let us pray we have the wisdom to choose correctly.
                    —Woody Allen

Wisecrack

I'd like to say we're glad you're here. I'd like to say it.
—HENNY YOUNGMAN (THE MCS' DEAN AT HIS BEST)

Business was so bad in a club I worked last week that one night the orchestra was playing "Tea for One." —HENNY YOUNGMAN

No, Groucho is not my real name. I'm breaking it in for a friend.
—GROUCHO MARX

Living in California adds ten years to a man's life. And those extra ten years I'd like to spend in New York. —HARRY RUBY

Our club is having a membership drive—to drive him out of the club.
—ATTRIBUTED TO GEORGE JESSEL

There's no more crime in New York—there's nothing left to steal.
—HENNY YOUNGMAN

Wit

The hardest thing is writing a recommendation for someone you know.
—FRANK McKINNEY ("KIN") HUBBARD

A gentleman never heard the story before. —NOËL COWARD

Nothing puzzles me more than time and space, and yet nothing puzzles me less, for I never think about them. —CHARLES LAMB

*The only way of catching a train I ever discov-
ered is to miss the train before.*
                                    —G. K. CHESTERTON

                    *   *   *

It's very easy to find something you were not looking for.
                                    —LEO ROSTEN

His judgment is so poor that he runs a risk every time he uses it.
                              —EDGAR WATSON ("ED") HOWE

I want there to be one man who will regret my death.
            —HEINRICH HEINE (BEQUEATHING HIS ENTIRE ESTATE TO
HIS WIFE—ON THE CONDITION THAT SHE GET MARRIED AGAIN)

*Wit is the sudden marriage of ideas which be-
fore their marriage were not perceived to have
any relation.*
                                    —MARK TWAIN

                    *   *   *

Nothing is made in vain, but the fly came near it.   —MARK TWAIN

The best way to keep children home is to make the home atmosphere
pleasant—and let the air out of the tires.   —DOROTHY PARKER

I have made this rather long letter because I haven't the time to make
it shorter.   —BLAISE PASCAL

Bing [Crosby] doesn't pay an income tax anymore. He just asks the
government what they need.   —BOB HOPE

I just got wonderful news from my real-estate agent in Florida: They
found land on my property.   —MILTON BERLE

Cooking is a minor art. I can't imagine a hilarious soufflé, or a deeply moving stew. —KENNETH TYNAN

I regard golf as an expensive way of playing marbles.
—G. K. CHESTERTON

There's a divinity that ends our shapes.
—L. R.

*   *   *

Fifteen years ago one could have bought the Federal Steel Company for twenty million dollars. And I let it go.   —STEPHEN LEACOCK

Kapital will not pay for the cigars I smoked writing it.
—KARL MARX

Worth seeing? Yes; but not worth going to see.
—SAMUEL JOHNSON

Melancholy men of all others are most witty.   —ARISTOTLE

He can compress the most words into the smallest ideas of any men I ever met.   —ABRAHAM LINCOLN

If I called the wrong number, why did you answer the phone?
—JAMES THURBER

*   *   *

To stop smoking is the easiest thing I ever did. I ought to know; I've done it a thousand times.   —MARK TWAIN

There isn't much to be seen in a little town, but what you hear makes up for it.   —FRANK MCKINNEY ("KIN") HUBBARD

A woman will buy anything she thinks a store is losing money on.
　　　　　　　　　　—Frank McKinney ("Kin") Hubbard

You can pretend to be serious, but you can't pretend to be witty.
　　　　　　　　　　—Sacha Guitry

＊　　＊　　＊

If he does really think that there is no distinction between virtue and vice, why, Sir, when he leaves our house, let us count our spoons.　　　　　　　　　　—Samuel Johnson

The louder he talked of his honor, the faster we counted our spoons.　　　　　　　　　　—Ralph Waldo Emerson

---

A bank is a place where they lend you an umbrella in fair weather and ask for it back again when it begins to rain.
　　　　　　　　　　—Robert Frost/Mark Twain

I happen to know quite a bit about the South. Spent twenty years there one night.　　　　　　　　　　—Dick Gregory

I get my exercise acting as a pallbearer to my friends who exercise.
　　　　　　　　　　—Chauncey Depew/Robert M. Hutchins

I bet you have no more friends than an alarm clock.
　　　　　　　　　　—Henny Youngman

Everybody talks about the weather but nobody does anything about it.　　　　　　　　　　—Charles Dudley Warner (*before* Mark Twain)

*There's something about a closet that makes a
skeleton terribly restless.*

—JOHN BARRYMORE

*   *   *

If I'm not in bed by eleven at night, I go home.

—HENNY YOUNGMAN

The cost of living has gone up another dollar a quart.

—W. C. FIELDS

She got her good looks from her father—he's a plastic surgeon.

—GROUCHO MARX

A hen is only an egg's way of making another egg.

—SAMUEL BUTLER

I suppose you could never prove to the mind of the most ingenious
mollusk that such a creature as a whale was possible.

—RALPH WALDO EMERSON

Perfection has one grave defect: It is apt to be dull.

—W. SOMERSET MAUGHAM

Impropriety is the soul of wit.

—W. SOMERSET MAUGHAM

*   *   *

My agent gets 10 percent of everything I get, except my blinding
headaches.   —FRED ALLEN

The Arabs never miss an opportunity to miss an opportunity.

—ABBA EBAN

Early to bed and early to rise take most of the zing out of living.

—LEO ROSTEN

If you don't know where you're going, any road will take you there.
—DANIEL BELL

A hair in the head is worth two in the brush.   —OLIVER HERFORD

I came into my hotel room one night and found a strange blond in my bed. I would stand for none of that nonsense. I gave her exactly twenty-four hours to get out.   —GROUCHO MARX

Nothing in the world is so exhilarating as to be shot at without result.
—WINSTON CHURCHILL

*   *   *

Do you know what it means to come home at night to a woman who'll give you a little love, a little affection, a little tenderness? . . . It means you're in the wrong house, that's what it means.
—HENNY YOUNGMAN

Secondhand diamonds are better than none.   —MARK TWAIN

By working faithfully eight hours a day, you may eventually get to be a boss and work twelve hours a day.   —ROBERT FROST

Is it progress if a cannibal uses a fork?
—STANISLAW J. LEC

*   *   *

Those who lie on the rails of history must expect to have their legs chopped off.
—*RUDE PRAVO* (AFTER THE CZECH REVOLUTION OF 1989)

I think this is the most extraordinary collection of talent, of human knowledge, that has ever been gathered together at the White

House—with the possible exception of when Thomas Jefferson dined here alone.
    —JOHN F. KENNEDY (AT DINNER FOR NOBEL PRIZE WINNERS)

Wit has truth in it; wisecracking is simply cal-isthenics with words.
                                    —DOROTHY PARKER

* * *

People will buy anything that's one to a customer.
                                            —SINCLAIR LEWIS

If "horse sense" is such a valuable attribute, how come it did so little for the horse?   —LEO ROSTEN

You are never so easily fooled as when you are trying to fool someone else.   —FRANÇOIS DE LA ROCHEFOUCAULD

Consistency is the last refuge of the unimag-inative.
                                    —OSCAR WILDE

* * *

A holding company is a thing where you hand an accomplice the goods while the policeman searches you.   —WILL ROGERS

I was going to thrash them within an inch of their lives, but I didn't have a tape measure.   —GROUCHO MARX

Schizophrenia beats dining alone.
                           —ATTRIBUTED TO OSCAR LEVANT

Last year wasn't all that bad. We led the league in flu shots.
            —BILL FITCH (COACH OF THE CLEVELAND CAVALIERS
                                    BASKETBALL TEAM)

Animals talk to each other; I never knew but one man who could understand them—I knew he could because he told me so himself.
—MARK TWAIN

Wit consists in knowing the resemblance of things that differ, and the difference of things that are alike.
—MADAME DE STAËL

*   *   *

I was once thrown out of a mental hospital for depressing the other patients.   —OSCAR LEVANT

An adage is sober, an aphorism arresting, but an epigram must tickle the ribs.   —LEO ROSTEN

Wit sometimes enables us to act rudely with impunity.
—FRANÇOIS DE LA ROCHEFOUCAULD

Vulgarity is simply the conduct of others.   —OSCAR WILDE

Fear of losing is what makes competitors so great. Show me a . . . gracious loser and I'll show you a perennial loser.   —O. J. SIMPSON

It always takes longer to get back.   —LEO ROSTEN

She's been in more laps than a napkin.   —MAE WEST

No girl was ever ruined by a book.   —"JIMMY" WALKER

The more he talked of his honor, the faster we counted our spoons.
—RALPH WALDO EMERSON/SAMUEL TAYLOR COLERIDGE

I do not care to belong to a club that accepts people like me as members.   —GROUCHO MARX (ON RESIGNING FROM THE FRIARS CLUB)

Horse sense is what a horse has that keeps him from betting on people. —W. C. FIELDS

When I came back to Dublin I was court-martialed in my absence and sentenced to death in my absence, so I said they could shoot me in my absence.

—BRENDAN BEHAN

* * *

Dirt is not dirt, but only matter in the wrong place.
—LORD PALMERSTON

My folks didn't come over on the *Mayflower*, but they were there to meet the boat. —WILL ROGERS

There's one thing about baldness: It's neat. —DON HEROLD

How much would you charge to haunt a house?
—ARTHUR ("BUGS") BAER

I am one person who can truthfully say, "I got my job through the *New York Times*." —JOHN F. KENNEDY

I heard him speak disrespectfully of the equator. —SYDNEY SMITH

Many men can make an epic who cannot make an epigram.
—G. K. CHESTERTON

If you get there before it's over, you are on time.
—"JIMMY" WALKER

What contemptible scoundrel stole the cork from my lunch?
—W. C. FIELDS

It has always been my rule never to smoke when asleep and never to refrain when awake. —MARK TWAIN

How can they tell?
—DOROTHY PARKER (ON HEARING OF THE DEATH OF CALVIN COOLIDGE)

Flying saucers are just an optical conclusion. —LEO ROSTEN

The first Rotarian was the first man to call John the Baptist Jack.
—H. L. MENCKEN

You never know what you can do without until you try.
—FRANKLIN PIERCE ADAMS

Santa Claus has the right idea: Visit people once a year.
—VICTOR BORGE

Shake, shake the catsup bottle;
None comes out—and then a lot'll. —RICHARD ARMOUR

Writing to you is like corresponding with an aching void.
—GROUCHO MARX

It's purty hard to be efficient without being obnoxious.
—FRANK McKINNEY ("KIN") HUBBARD

It was so hot here that I found there was nothing for it but to take off my flesh and sit in my bones. —SYDNEY SMITH

There never is enough time—unless you're serving it.
—MALCOLM FORBES

If it weren't for the last minute, nothing would get done.
—ANONYMOUS

I was the first woman to burn my bra—it took the fire department four days to put it out! —DOLLY PARTON

Where there's a will, there's a lawsuit. —ADDISON MIZNER

When Mark Twain registered in a hotel in Canada, he placed his signature below this one, that read:

Sir Edmund Lee and valet
Mark Twain and valise.

When I state that my lectures were followed almost immediately by the Union of South Africa, the Banana Riots in Trinidad, and the Turco-Italian War, I think the reader can form some opinion of their importance. —STEPHEN LEACOCK

Wives

I never call my wife "wife"; I call her "home"—for it is she who makes my home. —ADAPTED FROM TALMUD

When you see what some girls marry, you realize how much they must hate to work for a living. —HELEN ROWLAND

Try praising your wife, even if it does frighten her at first.
—BILLY SUNDAY

An obedient wife commands her man. —MAORI SAYING

One man's folly is another man's wife. —HELEN ROWLAND

My wife is the sweetest, most tolerant, most beautiful woman in the world. This is a paid political announcement. —HENNY YOUNGMAN

My wife was too beautiful for words, but not for arguments.
—JOHN BARRYMORE

Wives save men from sin. —TALMUD

My wife is probably the world's worst cook. She has a certain knack of preparing food that's inedible. She cooks from a cookbook called *Condemned by Duncan Hines.* —HENNY YOUNGMAN

Women

Woman was God's second mistake.
—FRIEDRICH WILHELM NIETZSCHE

She who hesitates is won. —OSCAR WILDE

Here's to woman! Would that we could fall into her arms without falling into her hands.
—AMBROSE BIERCE

* * *

Woman is unrivaled as a wet nurse. —MARK TWAIN

I like a woman with a head on her shoulders. I hate necks.
—STEVE MARTIN

If women didn't exist, all the money in the world would have no meaning. —ARISTOTLE ONASSIS

Women are "sphinxes without secrets." —OSCAR WILDE

Women: The best other sex men have.
—WILSON MIZNER/DON HEROLD

Some women'll stay in a man's memory if they once walk down a street. —RUDYARD KIPLING

A woman prefers poverty with love to riches without love.
—ADAPTED FROM MISHNAH

Women? You suffer before you get them, while you have them, and after you lose them. —SHOLEM ALEICHEM

It is not true that woman was made from man's rib; she was really made from his funny bone.

—JAMES BARRIE

＊　＊　＊

I hate women because they always know where things are.
—JAMES THURBER

If you want to know how old a woman is, ask her sister-in-law.
—EDGAR WATSON ("ED") HOWE

The worst feature of a new baby is its mother's singing.
—FRANK McKINNEY ("KIN") HUBBARD

A woman can be evaluated by her cooking, her dressing—and her husband. —SHOLEM ALEICHEM

When women kiss, it always reminds one of prizefighters shaking hands. —H. L. MENCKEN

Women's Liberation is just a lot of foolishness. It's the men who are discriminated against— they can't bear children. And no one's likely to do anything about that.

—GOLDA MEIR

＊　＊　＊

A woman is only a woman, but a good cigar is a smoke.

—RUDYARD KIPLING

There are few virtuous women who do not tire of their role.

—FRANÇOIS DE LA ROCHEFOUCAULD

To me the expression "Ms." really means misery.

—PHYLLIS SCHLAFLY

Anyone who says he can see through women is missing a lot.

—GROUCHO MARX

The years a woman subtracts from her age are not lost; they are simply added to the ages of her friends.

—DIANE DE POITIER

Time and tide wait for no man, but time always stands still for a woman of thirty.

—ROBERT FROST

A woman's tears are a form of bribery.   —THE SHATZOVER RABBI

Women have a wonderful sense of right and wrong, but little sense of right and left.   —DON HEROLD

Women would rather be right than reasonable.   —OGDEN NASH

Have you ever noticed that many jewels make women either incredibly fat or incredibly thin?   —JAMES MATTHEW BARRIE

A lady is a woman who makes a man behave like a gentleman.

—RUSSELL LYNES

If you wish women to love you, be original; I know a man who used to wear felt boots summer and winter, and women fell in love with him.   —ANTON CHEKHOV

It goes far toward reconciling me to being a woman when I reflect that I am thus in no danger of marrying one.

—LADY MARY WORTLEY MONTAGU

A woman with a past has no future. —OSCAR WILDE

She may be good for nothing, but she's never bad for nothing.

—MAE WEST

* * *

There are two kinds of women: those who want power in the world, and those who want power in bed.

—JACQUELINE KENNEDY ONASSIS

At any age the ladies are delightful, delectable, and, most important, deductible. —GOODMAN ACE

I don't know of anything better than a woman if you want to spend money where it'll show. —FRANK McKINNEY ("KIN") HUBBARD

Her capacity for family affection is extraordinary: When her third husband died, her hair turned quite gold from grief.

—OSCAR WILDE

What passes for woman's intuition is often nothing more than man's transparency.

—GEORGE JEAN NATHAN

* * *

A full bosom is actually a millstone around a woman's neck. . . . [Breasts] are not parts of a person but lures slung around her neck, to be kneaded and twisted like magic putty, or mumbled and mouthed like lolly ices. —GERMAINE GREER

A capacity for self-pity is one of the last things that any woman surrenders. —IRVIN S. COBB

A woman's mind is cleaner than a man's: She changes it more often. —OLIVER HERFORD

The happiest women, like the happiest nations, have no history. —GEORGE ELIOT

One should never trust a woman who tells her real age; a woman who would tell one that would tell one anything. —OSCAR WILDE

The Gorgons looked like women, but more horrible.

—A CHILD

*   *   *

Very ugly or very beautiful women should be flattered on their understanding, mediocre ones on their beauty. —LORD CHESTERFIELD

The mass of women today lead lives of noisy desperation. —PETER PRESCOTT

She [his wife] is an excellent creature, but she never can remember which came first, the Greeks or the Romans. —BENJAMIN DISRAELI

Youth had been a habit of hers for so long that she could not part with it. —RUDYARD KIPLING

In her first passion, woman loves her lover; in all the others, all she loves is love. —LORD BYRON

The great question that has never been answered, and that I have not yet been able to answer despite my thirty years of research into the feminine soul, is: What does a woman want?

—SIGMUND FREUD

(answer: "Shoes.")

No woman can call herself free until she can choose consciously whether she will or will not be a mother.   —MARGARET SANGER

I kissed my first woman and smoked my first cigarette on the same day; I have never had time for tobacco since.

—ARTURO TOSCANINI

A lady of a "certain age" means certainly aged.   —BYRON

The way to fight a woman is with your hat. Grab it and run.

—JOHN BARRYMORE

There are no ugly women; there are only women who do not know how to look pretty.   —JEAN DE LA BRUYÈRE

When a woman says, "I don't wish to mention any names," it ain't necessary.   —FRANK MCKINNEY ("KIN") HUBBARD

From birth to age eighteen, a girl needs good parents; from eighteen to thirty-five, she needs good looks; from thirty-five to fifty-five, she needs a good personality; and from fifty-five on, she needs cash.

—SOPHIE TUCKER

A woman will always sacrifice herself if you give her the opportunity. It's her favorite form of self-indulgence.

—W. SOMERSET MAUGHAM

A woman will flirt with anybody in the world as long as other people are looking on.   —OSCAR WILDE

Men are more interesting than women, but women are more fascinating.   —JAMES THURBER

When a woman really loves a man, he can make her do anything she wants to.   —ANONYMOUS

Thirty-five is a very attractive age; London society is full of women who have of their own free choice remained thirty-five for years.
                   —OSCAR WILDE

In order to avoid being called a flirt, she always yielded easily.
                   —CHARLES-MAURICE DE TALLEYRAND

No woman is better than two.   —ANONYMOUS

Wordplay

I have Bright's Disease, and he has mine.   —S. J. PERELMAN

He writes the worst English that I have ever encountered. It reminds me of a string of wet sponges; it reminds me of tattered washing on the line; it reminds me of stale bean soup, of college yells, of dogs barking through endless nights. It is so bad that a sort of grandeur creeps into it. It drags itself out of the dark abysm of pish, and crawls insanely up the topmost pinnacle of posh. It is rumble and bumble. It is flap and doodle. It is balder and dash.
                   —H. L. MENCKEN (ON PRESIDENT WARREN G. HARDING)

When ideas fail, words come in very handy.   —GOETHE

This is the sort of English up with which I will not put.
—WINSTON CHURCHILL (OBJECTING TO A PROOFREADER'S EFFORT
TO AVOID ENDING A SENTENCE WITH A PREPOSITION)

No more powerful, alluring words have ever been invented by the human race than these four: "Once upon a time . . ."
— ANONYMOUS

Gentlemen, you have just been listening to that Chinese sage, On Too Long.   —WILL ROGERS

Include me out.   —SAMUEL GOLDWYN

Even the youngest among us is not infallible.
—BENJAMIN JOWETT/BENJAMIN DISRAELI/
OSCAR WILDE/LORD CHESTERFIELD

George Washington's Farewell Address was Mount Vernon.
—LEO ROSTEN

Widow's weeds: The easiest to kill. You have only to say, "Wilt thou?" and they wilt.   —HENRY FIELDING

Since lawyers are disbarred and ministers unfrocked, perhaps sailors are debunked . . . funeral directors rehearsed . . . infielders debased . . . dieters expounded . . . electricians refused . . . club workers dismembered . . . tailors depressed.

— ANONYMOUS

*   *   *

It is worse than a crime; it is a blunder.
—CHARLES-MAURICE DE TALLEYRAND

Wordplay: Time wounds all heels.   —ANN LANDERS

Careful of what you write. The Mafia may come along and spray garlic on your lawn.   —JOE GARAGIOLA (WARNING SPORTSWRITERS)

The swaggering underemphasis of New England.
                                        —HEYWOOD BROUN

The prevalence of "y'know" is one of the most far-reaching and depressing developments of our time.   —EDWIN NEWMAN

If you can't give me your word of honor, will you give me your promise?   —SAMUEL GOLDWYN

Mischief in English:

Kingdoms are ruled by kings: Why are there no queendoms?

Grocers do not groce.

An alarm clock goes off by going on.

Vegetarians eat vegetables. What do humanitarians eat?

We wear a pair of pants but never a pair of shirts.

How can news be old?

How can ugly be pretty?

Why does "hold up" mean to support—or hinder?

Why does "left" mean to remain—or to depart?

Why does "commencement" mean conclusion—or beginning?

There is no ham in hamburger.

Guinea pigs are not pigs, nor do they come from Guinea.

A boxing ring is square.

Quicksand works very slowly.

We drive on a parkway, but park in a driveway.

Hot as hell equals cold as hell.

A *hot* cup of coffee is not necessarily a cup of *hot* coffee.

Harmless is the opposite of harmful, but shameless and shameful are the same.

"Hair on his head" means much more than "hairs on his head."

Words

Those who truly shape our destiny . . . are those who use words with clarity, grandeur, and passion: Socrates, Jesus, Luther, Lincoln, Churchill. —LEO ROSTEN

Words are the root of all evil. —JAPANESE PROVERB

Words were man's first, immeasurable feat of magic. They liberated us from ignorance and our barbarous past. —LEO ROSTEN

The most moving moments of our lives find us all without words. —MARCEL MARCEAU

The righteous need no tombstones; their words are their monuments. —TALMUD

Words should be weighed, not counted. —JEWISH SAYING

You can forget a blow, but not a word. —MY MOTHER

Be brief; for it is with words as with sunbeams, the more they are condensed the deeper they burn. —ROBERT SOUTHEY

We live by words: LOVE, TRUTH, GOD. We fight for words: FREEDOM, COUNTRY, FAME. We die for words: LIBERTY, GLORY, HONOR.

Words: They sing. They hurt. They teach. They sanctify.

If a picture is worth a thousand words, please paint me the Gettysburg Address.

—LEO ROSTEN

Work

Work is a form of nervousness.   —DON HEROLD

Any man can do any amount of work, provided it isn't the work he's supposed to be doing.   —ROBERT BENCHLEY

My father taught me to work; he did not teach me to love it.
—ABRAHAM LINCOLN

To earn a living can be as hard as to part the Red Sea.   —TALMUD

I go on working for the same reason that a hen goes on laying eggs.
—H. L. MENCKEN

Not to teach your son to work is like teaching him to steal.
—TALMUD

One of the symptoms of an approaching nervous breakdown is the belief that one's work is terribly important. —BERTRAND RUSSELL

Worry

The reason why worry kills more people than work is that more people worry than work. —ROBERT FROST

God gave me such a good brain that in one minute I can worry more than others do in a year. —SHOLEM ALEICHEM

Writers

You must not suppose, because I am a man of letters, that I never tried to earn an honest living. —GEORGE BERNARD SHAW

There are three rules for writing a novel. Unfortunately, no one knows what they are. —W. SOMERSET MAUGHAM

To write well, express yourself like the common people, but think like a wise man. —ARISTOTLE

Ralph Waldo Emerson called Montaigne the most honest of all writers: "Cut these words and they would bleed."

Unprovided with original learning, unformed in the habits of thinking, unskilled in the arts of composition, I resolved to write a book.
—EDWARD GIBBON

* * *

There are no dull subjects. There are only dull writers.
—H. L. MENCKEN

The only reason for being a professional writer is that you can't help it. —LEO ROSTEN

No man but a blockhead ever wrote except for money.
—SAMUEL JOHNSON

I was sorry to have my name mentioned as one of the great authors, because they have a sad habit of dying off. Chaucer is dead. Spencer is dead, so is Milton, so is Shakespeare, and I am not feeling very well myself. —MARK TWAIN

A writer is working when he's staring out of the window.
—BURTON RASCOE

The principle of procrastinated rape is said to be the ruling one in all the great best-sellers.
—V. S. PRITCHETT

* * *

Writers: Schmucks with Underwoods. —JACK WARNER

In composing, as a general rule, run your pen through every other word you have written; you have no idea what vigor it will give your style. —SYDNEY SMITH

If you steal from one author, it's plagiarism; if you steal from many, it's research. —WILSON MIZNER

Writing is easy. All you do is stare at a blank sheet of paper until drops of blood form on your forehead. —GENE FOWLER

How can you write if you can't cry? —RING LARDNER

When my sonnet was rejected, I exclaimed: "Damn the age; I will write for antiquity." —CHARLES LAMB

Writing is not hard. Just get paper and pencil, sit down, and write it as it occurs to you. The writing is easy—it's the occurring that's hard.
—STEPHEN LEACOCK

Writing isn't hard; no harder than ditch-digging.

> —PATRICK DENNIS

* * *

[Literary] prizes are for the birds. They fill the head of one author with vanity and thirty others with misery.   —LOUIS AUCHINCLOSS

A writer is rarely so well inspired as when he talks about himself.
> —ANATOLE FRANCE

If a writer has to rob his mother he will not hesitate; the *Ode on a Grecian Urn* is worth any number of old ladies.
> —WILLIAM FAULKNER

Marry money.   —MAX SHULMAN (ADVICE TO ASPIRING AUTHORS)

One should not be too severe on English novels; they are the only relaxation of the intellectually unemployed.

> —OSCAR WILDE

* * *

When in doubt, have two guys come through the door with guns.
> —RAYMOND CHANDLER

Your manuscript is both good and original; but the part that is good is not original, and the part that is original is not good.
> —SAMUEL JOHNSON

People do not deserve to have good writing, they are so pleased with the bad.   —RALPH WALDO EMERSON

E. Zola is determined to show that if he has not got genius, he can at least be dull.   —OSCAR WILDE

Authors are easy enough to get on with—if you are fond of children.
—MICHAEL JOSEPH

A writer is congenitally unable to tell the truth,
and that is why we call what he writes fiction.
—WILLIAM FAULKNER

*   *   *

If you want to get rich from writing, write the sort of thing that's read by persons who move their lips when they're reading.
—DON MARQUIS

He writes dialogues by cutting monologues in two.
—ARTHUR ("BUGS") BAER

He was an author whose works were so little
known as to be almost confidential.
—STANLEY WALKER

*   *   *

Income-tax returns are the most imaginative fiction being written to-day.
—HERMAN WOUK

I never desire to converse with a man who has written more than he has read.
—SAMUEL JOHNSON

A great many people now reading and writing would be better employed keeping rabbits.
—EDITH SITWELL

I am always at a loss to know how much to believe of my own stories.
—WASHINGTON IRVING

Only a mediocre writer is always at his best.
—W. SOMERSET MAUGHAM

Writers are, in a sense, the unofficial oracles of society. They shape the dreams of men; they sing for the mute and dare for the timid. They are, as someone said, the "divine skeptics." But in Hollywood they say, "We only make movies."   —LEO ROSTEN

He writes so well he makes me feel like putting my quill back in my goose.   —FRED ALLEN

Y

Youth

[Youth] have exalted notions, because they have not yet been humbled by life or learned its necessary limitations. . . . They would always rather do noble deeds than useful ones; their lives are regulated more by moral feeling than by reasoning. . . . All their mistakes are in the direction of doing things excessively and vehemently. . . . They love too much, hate too much; they think they know everything; this, in fact, is why they overdo everything.   —ARISTOTLE

Hyperboles are the peculiar property of young men; they betray a vehement nature.   —ARISTOTLE

Today's younger generation is no worse than my own. We were just as ignorant and repulsive as they are, but nobody listened to us.
                    —AL CAPP

*   *   *

It is the malady of our age that the young are so busy teaching us that they have no time left to learn.   —ERIC HOFFER

Don't laugh at a youth for his affectations; he is only trying on one face after another to find his own.
                    —LOGAN PEARSALL SMITH/ERIK ERIKSON

No young man believes he will ever die.   —WILLIAM HAZLITT

Disco dancing is really dancing for people who hate dancing, since the beat is so monotonous. . . . There is no syncopation, just the steady thump of a giant moron knocking in an endless nail.
                    —CLIVE JAMES

Youth had been a habit of hers for so long that she could not part with it.   —RUDYARD KIPLING

What youth is afraid of is that in old age the strength for protest will be gone, but the terror of life will remain.
                    —HARRY REASONER

                    *   *   *

The generation gap is just another way of saying that the younger generation makes overt what is covert in the older generation; the child expresses openly what the parent represses.
                    —ERIK ERIKSON

Youth measures in only one direction . . . from things as they are to an ideal of what things ought to be, while the old measure things as they are against the past the old remember.   —ARCHIBALD COX

The hardest job kids face today is learning good manners without seeing any.   —FRED ASTAIRE

Our major obligation is not to mistake slogans for solutions.
                                        —EDWARD R. MURROW

The old believe everything, the middle-aged suspect everything, the
young know everything.   —OSCAR WILDE

It is unbecoming for young men to utter maxims.   —ARISTOTLE

I can live with the robber barons, but how do you live with
these pathological radicals?   —DANIEL PATRICK MOYNIHAN

It is easy enough to praise men for the courage of their convictions. I wish I could teach the sad young of this mealy generation the courage of their confusions.   —JOHN CIARDI

There's nothing wrong with teenagers that reasoning with them won't
aggravate.   —ANONYMOUS

What music is more enchanting than the voices of young people when
you can't hear what they say?   —LOGAN PEARSALL SMITH

Youth is a disease from which we all recover.
                                        —DOROTHY FULDHEIM

I am not young enough to know everything.
        —JAMES BARRIE/OSCAR WILDE/BENJAMIN DISRAELI

Youth is such a wonderful thing. What a crime to waste it on
children.   —GEORGE BERNARD SHAW/OSCAR WILDE

Throughout man's history, no group has done more harm, shed more
blood, caused more tragedy than those who, sincerely ignorant, added

passion to their certitudes. That is what I fear most about sincere youth.   —LEO ROSTEN

The secret of staying young is to live honestly, eat slowly, and lie about your age.   —LUCILLE BALL

Until you're prepared to kill your parents, you're not really prepared to change the country, because our parents are our first oppressors.   —JERRY RUBIN

Only the young die good.   —OLIVER HERFORD

When you've got a problem with swine, you call in the pigs [police].   —S. I. HAYAKAWA

Youth is always too serious, and just now it is too serious about frivolity.   —G. K. CHESTERTON

> *I suppose it's difficult for the young to realize that one may be old without being a fool.*
>   —W. SOMERSET MAUGHAM

*   *   *

Historians may note with surprise that the sons and daughters of an affluent middle class flaunt the fake work shirts and torn knees and dirty, spotted Levi's of proletarians, floater cowboys, and outright derelicts.   —LEO ROSTEN

He was ignorant of the commonest accomplishments of youth. He could not even lie.   —MARK TWAIN

The idealism of youth usually rests upon guilt and ignorance.   —LEO ROSTEN

That physicist is so young—yet has contributed so little.   —WOLFGANG PAULI

It is the mistake of youth to think imagination a substitute for experience; it is the mistake of age to think experience a substitute for intelligence. —LYMAN BRYSON

My favorite of all the sharp, glimmering play of words may well surprise you:

Two women emerge from a gynecologist's clinic: "Well, I see you're pregnant, too!"

"Thank God," said the second woman.

"Are you hoping for a boy or a girl?"

Not a split second passed before the answer:

"Certainly."